THE
HOME WORKSHOP
PLANNER

A guide to planning, setting up, equipping, and using your own home workshop

WOOD® BOOKS

Des Moines, Iowa

WOOD® BOOKS

is an imprint
of Meredith® Books

President, Book Group: Joseph J. Ward
Vice President, Editorial Director: Elizabeth P. Rice
Executive Editor: Connie Schrader
Art Director: Ernest Shelton
Project Manager: Benjamin W. Allen
Production Manager: Randall Yontz

Produced by North Coast Productions,
650 Mount Curve Blvd., St. Paul, MN 55116
Gene Schnaser, Editor
Jeanne Fredensborg, Managing Editor

Russ Barnard, Technical Consultant

Book design by Barbara Bowen
Illustrations by Brian Jensen and Marlyn Rodi

Cover photo: Mark Duginske and Gregory Foye

Meredith Corporation Corporate Officers:
Chairman of the Executive Committee: E. T. Meredith III
Chairman of the Board, President and Chief Executive
Officer: Jack D. Rehm
Group Presidents: Joseph J. Ward, Books; William T.
Kerr, Magazines; Philip A. Jones, Broadcasting; Allen L.
Sabbag, Real Estate
Vice Presidents: Leo R. Armatis, Corporate Relations;
Thomas G. Fisher, General Counsel and Secretary;
Larry D. Hartsook, Finance; Michael A. Sell, Treasurer;
Kathleen J. Zehr, Controller and Assistant Secretary

The editors of Meredith® Books are dedicated to
giving you the information and ideas you need to
enjoy woodworking to its fullest. We guarantee your
satisfaction with this book for as long as you own it.
We welcome your comments and suggestions.
Please address your correspondence to:
Meredith Books, 1716 Locust Street, RW-240,
Des Moines, IA 50309-3023.

Special thanks to the many people, companies, and
organizations who helped directly or indirectly to
make this book possible, including Jim Fassel of CJV
Associates, Sil Argentin and Terry Treacy of S-B Power
Tool Co. (Skil), Roger Benedict and Ed Veome of Sears,
Eugene Sliga of Delta, Michael Mangan of MKM
Communications, and Jay Holtzman of Donnelly &
Duncan. Also a very special thanks to those whose
practical ideas and thoughts are found throughout this
book, including Russ Barnard, Robert Tupper, Howard
Silken, Norm Abram, Hugh Foster, Patrick Spielman,
Jacob Schulzinger, Garretson Wade Chinn, Hugh
Williamson, Marlyn Rodi, Don Taylor, Vince
Koebensky, Roger Wade, Mark Duginske, Ted
McDonough, Paul Maire, Kim Rasmussen, Robert
Snider, and all of the other workshop enthusiasts who
contributed their time and talents to this book (see
credits, page 192).

Note to the Reader: The information, plans, and
instructions in this book have come from a variety
of sources. Every effort has been made to ensure the
accuracy of data presented. However, due to differing
conditions, tools, and individual skills, Meredith Books
and the author assume no responsibility for any injuries
suffered, damages, or losses incurred during or as a
result of following this information. Before beginning
any project, review the plans and procedures carefully
and, if any doubts or questions remain, consult local
experts or authorities. Read and observe all of the
safety precautions provided by any tool or equipment
manufacturer, and follow all accepted safety procedures.

PREFACE
THE MAGIC OF A HOME WORKSHOP

If there is one thing we've learned in assembling this book, it is that people who have set up a home shop are among the happier in the world. And despite what you may been led to believe, they are regular folks; they come in all sizes, shapes, and ages, but are unique in one respect: They put an extremely high value on the creative process and on using their hands and tools to create something useful out of basic raw materials.

The workplaces where their creativity unfolds vary as much as the personalities of their owners. Some have small shops with just a few basic tools; others have magnificent, spacious shops complete with just about every tool imaginable. Some have shops designed to tackle a wide variety of projects, while others have small, specialized production shops designed to make a specific project on a repetitive basis.

Most will tell you that setting up a home workshop is often a life-long pursuit, a slow but steady accumulation of knowlege and tools over many years. That is the ideal way to do it. However, if you've always wanted to set up a shop of your own and never had time to get one together before, it is never too late to start. This book is designed to help you get started from scratch, or to expand and refine the home workplace you already have.

It's worth it. First, there are financial rewards to be gained from a home shop. If you don't believe this, you haven't reviewed the price tags at craft shops or furniture stores lately. However, even more important, the biggest reward of setting up a workshop can be psychological; it can become your special refuge from a high-pressure job where it is hard to tell if anything is getting done except by looking at numbers on paper.

As noted in the book, *On The Road With Charles Kuralt*, most people in this country aren't making anything on their jobs anymore. If you take a minute and count on your fingers the people you know whose livelihood involves physically making something, you may not need more than one hand. As our society becomes more high-tech, and more oriented toward shuffling information or providing services, fewer of us are able to physically see the results of our work. A home shop, however, can help provide some of this instant feedback missing on our jobs. In your shop you can let the project determine the pace and enjoy an instant feeling of accomplishment, even if it is just watching a board taking a new shape on a bandsaw.

A home workshop can be a cheap psychiatrist, especially if we can let go of our usual grim purposefulness and just enjoy what we are doing. The most joy comes when you get so wrapped up in a project that a whole evening slips away before you know it. When this happens, you enter a state of mind where you and your project become one; you become oblivious to almost everything else except the project at hand. It is this kind of magic that makes a home workshop more than what it seems to be.

The feeling is hard to describe, but Nick Lindsay, carpenter-poet interviewed by Studs Terkel for the book *Working*, comes close:

"Suppose you're driving an eight-penny galvanized finishing nail. Your whole universe is rolled onto the head of that nail. Each lick is sufficient to justify your life. You say, 'Okay, I'm not trying to get this nail out of the way so I can get on to something important. There's nothing more important. It's right there.' And it goes—pow! It's not getting that nail in that's in your mind. It's hitting it—hitting it square, hitting it straight. Getting it now. That one lick."

To generate mind-soothing benefits, a home shop does not have to be a sterile laboratory where nothing gets done. However, too often we all carry questionable work habits we learned in school and on the job into our home workplaces. Many times these can get in the way and keep us from experiencing the magic every shop has to offer. Setting lofty goals, giving ourselves unforgiving deadlines, and putting efficiency first are surefire ways to evaporate shop magic.

Many of the workplaces enjoyed most by their owners are often far from picture-perfect layouts. In fact, many are a little small, a little messy, and a little homemade. The key is that they are used and enjoyed. That's the beauty of having a workplace of your own; you can start with what you have and build from there. All along the way that shop can help you to eclipse your problems and worries. And if you realize that this is one of the great benefits of a home workshop, then every project you work on, no matter how small or insignificant, will be worthwhile just for the peace of mind it produces.

Gene Schnaser,
Editor

CONTENTS

PLANNING

SETTING UP

THE CRAFTSMAN WORKSHOP 101

THE PROFESSIONAL WORKSHOP 115

PLANNING QUICK FINDER

EQUIPPING

USING

SECTION I
PLANNING THE HOME WORKSHOP

A PLACE OF YOUR OWN

Setting up an efficient shop can be one of life's more pleasant challenges. On one hand it can be many times as involved as planning a bathroom, or even a conventional kitchen. The reason is that the best arrangement for you depends on many more factors, such as the space you have available, where it is located, the tools you have already, the tools you plan to buy, your interests now, what your projects will be in the future, and how much you can invest as time passes.

But, on the other hand, setting up and improving a workshop has some convenient advantages over other types of home remodeling challenges. It generally lacks the sense of urgency involved when kitchens or bathrooms are torn up, disrupting daily life. And it allows much more flexibility. With a shop, you can arrange it one way and, if it doesn't work quite right, you can change it around tomorrow, next month, next year, or basically whenever the time or the spirit moves you.

How you set up your workshop may actually be influenced by that first power tool you bought 10 years ago, those used kitchen cabinets left over after a major kitchen remodeling, or the good deals on either tools or materials that you happen to run across. No matter how you have started to set up your workshop, there are many ways that you can make better use of the space you have available, make your tools and materials more convenient to use, and—above all—make the time that you spend on your projects more enjoyable.

One great advantage over planning bathrooms or kitchens is that your workshop doesn't have to look like or function like anyone else's. Flexibility is on your side. The final criterion is that if it works for you, and if that's the way you want it, that is all that counts. It's your shop. Consider what others have done, but mostly consider yourself. A home workshop is a personal affair

Designing a workshop from scratch offers definite advantages, says TV's favorite carpenter Norm Abram. But a shop can be set up wherever you can find the space, and can be refined over time to make it your own personal sanctuary.

and, unlike a production shop that is set up to manufacture a product, your shop should be your own personal sanctuary.

How you set up your shop does not have to be exactly what efficiency experts would advise, does not have to be equipped with a full fleet of the newest tools, and it does not have to be as perfectly tidy as the shop room you remember from high school. Make a place of your own. Use your own ideas and change, alter, and adapt other concepts that fit your own ideas on what your shop should be.

A good example of catering to your own preferences is how Norm Abram set up the New Yankee Workshop, one of the most famous workshops in America, located in the outskirts of Boston, Massachusetts. Throughout his years as a contractor, and continuing after he became the voice of carpenter wisdom on TV's *This Old House*, Norm had always hoped to someday set up a dream workshop, one with all the tools and space needed to take on the most challenging of projects.

With the planned launching of the *New Yankee Workshop* series, Norm's dream came true. He designed the workshop from the ground up, and even did most of the construction himself, including the workshop's handcrafted door. Talk to him about how it all worked out, and you might be surprised at what Norm likes most about the shop: its high ceiling.

"So many homeowners have their workshops in a basement or garage," he explains, "and their ceilings are typically very low. In the New Yankee Workshop, we have the luxury of a very high cathedral ceiling. There is actually sixteen feet between the floor and the steel I-beam that supports the rafters. The I-beam runs right under the ridge, spanning the entire thirty-six-foot length of the shop. There aren't any posts to break up open space, so I never have a problem moving things

In designing the most famous workshop in America, Norm Abram experimented with various systems of storing portable tools, hardware, and materials to keep project work from bogging down. He advises to guard against taking shortcuts during the final steps of projects, such as in sanding and finishing.

around or bumping into obstructions. And there's always plenty of natural light during the day, because of the skylights in the roof and the bank of windows built into the south wall."

The shop's ample overhead clearance and 936 sq. ft. of floor area, however, still present a space challenge when a television program must be taped. "When we're

"Because it is the workhorse of the shop, I gave the tablesaw a good, central position …"

shooting, I might have enough room to move around, but that is not always true for our camera crew. To gain space quickly, I have mobile bases under the larger shop tools, including the jointer, shaper, and bandsaw. You can buy mobile bases for different tools, or make your own, with heavy-duty, locking casters. Either way, this kind of mobility is a great asset in any small shop, where you often need to move one tool out of the way to be able to use another."

Norm admits that being able to design a workshop from scratch gave him a tremendous advantage; his only restriction was that the shop be connected to an existing garage. "I actually determined the workbench and machine locations as I designed the space," he says. "First and foremost was where to put the tablesaw. Because it is the workhorse of the shop, I gave it a good, central position. For power, I ran electrical conduit before pouring the concrete slab so I would have a floor outlet right where the saw would set."

Norm's tablesaw is not a cheap one, and he didn't stop with what came from the factory. By adding extension tables and an auxiliary fence, he increased both the saw's capacity and accuracy. "With the saw's extended table surface," he says, "it is a lot easier and safer to rip or crosscut large pieces, especially plywood panels."

Another challenge in laying out the New Yankee Workshop was to make sure there wasn't a shortage of benchtop space. There is a large workbench against the west-facing gable wall, with a pair of wide, long shelves above it. The shelves are home to books, screws, drill bits, and hardware, while the lower part of the bench stores a full complement of portable power tools.

The largest expanse of bench space stretches 16′ along the south wall, and incorporates workstations for the power miter saw (also called a chop saw or motorized miter box) and the radial-arm saw. When the sawdust begins to fly here, it signals the beginning of a new creation. "I first like to lay out a selection of boards and choose the best ones to make certain pieces," Norm says. "Then I usually cut pieces to rough size on the radial-arm saw or chop saw. This procedure lets me group the pieces according to the section or subassembly where they will be used. It's an important first step because it eliminates the aggravation of discovering, in the middle of a project, that I'm missing a crucial piece."

To maximize convenience and safety in the shop, Norm planned an abundance of electrical outlets. Unlike the wall outlets in a home, which are typically close to the floor, most of his shop outlets are high on the wall, several inches above workbench height. This makes it easy to plug in portable power tools. Just above the main workbench, Norm uses a retractable, coil-type extension cord that comes down from the ceiling. "I really like the overhead cord," he says. "It lets me move easily around the bench while using a portable power tool, without tripping over any conventional-type extension cord. You can find the coiled cord at most hardware stores, and mail-order tool suppliers also stock them."

Probably the most unique feature designed into the New Yankee Workshop is the heating system. The shop has a hydronic radiant floor system, heated by a solution of water and antifreeze that circulates through tubing embedded in the concrete slab. Perimeter and underslab insulation helps retain the heat transferred to the slab from the heating solution. "The idea has been used in Europe with great success," Norm says. "I like it in the shop because the heat is even, and because there are no ducts, baseboards, or radiators to collect dust or get in the way."

The illustration on the following pages give a detailed look at how Norm set up his dream shop, and the illustrations on page 49 show the basic details of the hydronic heating system he used.

A home workshop becomes a miniature hardware store, lumberyard, and tool room put together. How well it works can be improved by making alterations as it is tested over time. Norm made certain his dream shop had plenty of head room, power outlets, mobile tool bases, and a separate finishing area.

THE NEW YANKEE WORKSHOP LAYOUT

This artist's rendering shows the layout and components of *The New Yankee Workshop*, the setting for Norm Abram's PBS series of the same name. Norm considers this workshop, with just a few future modifications, to be his dream shop, a fantasy come true that had gestated for years in the thinking stage. The television series, produced by Morash Associates and WGBH Boston, began its first season in 1989.

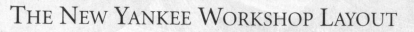

EQUIPMENT KEY

1. Shaper	9. Drill Press
2. Belt Sander	10. Workbench
3. Overarm Router	11. Bandsaw
4. Power Miter Saw	12. Tablesaw
5. Router Table	13. Jointer
6. Thickness Planer	14. Lumber Storage
7. Air Compressor	15. Roller Support
8. Radial-arm Saw	16. Wood Lathe

20 Ideas
For Any Workshop

The section, Tool-Buying Strategies, starting on page 17, gives you an overview of tool-buying approaches to use in equipping your shop. Pursuing A Dream Workshop, beginning on page 35, offers ideas on where to house the tools, accessories, and supplies you accumulate. In the meantime, here is a sampling of general ideas that are worth considering in setting up any workshop.

1 Check Working Surfaces. Being short on work surfaces can often be an unnoticed source of project frustration. Think for a moment: Would more work surfaces increase your pleasure while using your shop? Would building another workbench or assembly table make things easier? Work surfaces don't have to be fancy. For example, you can convert a salvaged metal table to a portable workbench by adding casters. That way you can pull it to where it is needed, or push it out of the way when you need more room. Many shop owners have put sturdy used kitchen tables into service, positioning them around the shop as they are needed. Commercial folding workbenches, like the Black & Decker Workmate, can also be a solution that offers portability as well as clamping power. Even sawhorses and a sheet of plywood can provide valuable temporary workspace.

2 Consider Working Heights. If your workbench, auxiliary benches, or tables, saws, and other equipment are all of different heights, consider bringing as many as possible to a standard height. Generally workbenches are about 4″ below waist level, but the height of power tools can vary. If you build a portable workbench to match the height of your tablesaw, then that bench can be used for extra support when sawing oversize materials. Another example: If you simply have your power miter saw setting on top of your workbench, you will lack any support for long boards when they are cut.

Outfitting a shop can be accomplished using a combination of planning, scrounging, and improvising. Besides using other sources, visit the shops set up by others; each one will reveal at least one good idea.

Consider dropping the saw into the bench, so the bench sides are in line with the miter saw table. Or else, with the saw remaining above the bench, build supports on both sides of the miter saw.

3 Make Tools Accessible. It can be one thing to find a spot to keep a tool, quite another to find and retrieve it. Ways to beat the problem include using small rolling carts and special tool carriers, sometimes called tool boards or tool totes, that are vertically oriented versions of the carpenter's tool box. If, for example, your shop vacuum must be stored in an out-of-the-way place, cut out a space under one of your benches so that it can be readily accessible when needed, but out of the traffic. Consider putting less-used equipment, such as a small oxy-acetylene welding set, on a shop-built cart that you can also roll out of the way or under a bench. Such things as a chainsaw and its related gear can be kept in a shop-built carrier with a carrying handle.

4 Make Sure You Can See. Don't be caught in the dark; you have to see what you are doing for projects to be enjoyable and well executed. Poor lighting is a common shop problem only because many shop owners don't stop to think of how more light could change the personality of their workspace. If lighting in your shop is marginal, first consider ways to bring in more natural light by cutting more windows or by installing skylights. Also consider rearranging your shop to take advantage of any existing natural light; should your workbench be moved over next to a window instead of where it is now? Use hanging fluorescent fixtures, shaded incandescent lamps, even small portable task lights to your best advantage. Maybe you want to line the perimeter of your shop with fluorescent lights, or perhaps newer halogen lamps and fixtures are just what your shop needs. Most critical is the lighting over your work areas. A good way to monitor light levels is to place a small object like a pencil on end and check for shadows.

5 Organize Special-Task Tools. Tool boards or even plastic buckets can help you organize tools and also make them portable. Tool boards can be sections of pegboard fitted with 2x4 stock at the bottom and with a cutout handle at top that you can slide into a space under a workbench side by side with other tool boards. You can put related tools on separate boards, for example, one for metalworking tools, one for measuring tools, one for upholstery tools, etc. Each can be pulled out and set across the front of your workbench one at a time as needed. Tool boards can be made in a variety of styles and can, for example, be made in right- and left-hand versions so they can be fastened together back to back to make a balanced tool carrier you can take wherever you need it.

6 Make Tools Portable. Unlike a kitchen, where all major appliances are built in, you can adapt major workshop tools with casters to keep everything portable and flexible. Consider how being able to move tools around might solve space problems in your shop, then equip certain tools with casters. They will cost you some money, but they can pay off big dividends in flexibility. (If you don't want to attach caster wheels directly to the tool's base, you can make a platform of plywood and 2x stock and put casters underneath.) Wheeled tools are easy to rearrange, plus they can be moved over near the workshop door for special operations, such as ripping long lumber, or to take advantage of daylight or good weather. Even a master workbench, for example, can be outfitted with two swivel casters under one end and two straight casters at the other end so that it can be moved around the shop as needed.

7 Deal With Cord Problems. A modern workshop depends on electrical power, and sometimes plenty of it. Stumbling over cords, using extensions to get to hard-to-reach outlets, and dealing with tangled cords present dangerous situations, slow efficiency, and boost frustration levels. If you are setting up a shop from scratch, make certain you don't get stingy about installing receptacles, especially near the workbench. Have at least one outlet every 3'. Also consider installing outlets in several areas of the shop's ceiling. Ceiling outlets can let you group power tools in the center of a small workshop. The idea is to minimize the use of extension cords. Cord reels, multiple outlets, and continuous outlet strips can also help you beat cord problems.

8 Plan For Material Storage. Space for project materials is crucial, so devote some thinking to how and where lumber and other supplies will be stored. The solution may be stationary racks, or perhaps a portable rack on casters, divided into sections for stock of varying lengths and widths. What you use will depend on the layout of your shop and what you need to store. You can, for example, assemble overhead racks using water pipe materials to hang 18" or so down from the ceiling.

Such racks can use floor flanges screwed to ceiling joists and ¾" pipe sections screwed to tees and elbows. Remember that not all lumber racks need be rectangular. Perhaps the best rack for your shop may be one that is 6' high and 1' wide, set behind a workbench.

9 Consider Creative Customizing. If a modification to your shop increases its efficiency, don't hesitate to make it. If you need "portholes" in your garage shop to feed lumber to power tools, cut them out and install hinged trapdoors. If you don't have room for lumber anyplace inside your shop, consider a "bump-out" on one side or end, or overhead storage racks or boxes attached to the ceiling near the perimeter. Garage workshop additions can range from adding a lean-to for a workbench to doubling the width or length of the garage. Doubling the length of a garage, for example, can let you use the old part for shop space while allowing cars to be parked behind in the new addition.

10 Borrow Forgotten, Unused Space. When shop space is scarce, every square inch can count big. Look for unused space in unconventional places. Some shop owners purposely leave the space between the ceiling joists uncovered so that space can be used for storage. Look for ways to better use space. In a basement, for example, perhaps the space under a staircase is now going to waste or could be put to better use. Other places to search for space include between open studs, behind doors, under stationary benches, as well as in under-utilized rooms and closets nearby.

11 Use Organizing Weapons. With a full complement of hooks, brackets, and accessories, pegboard can be one of a shop organizer's best weapons for gaining space. Some shop owners have all shop walls covered with pegboard. You can also make up pegboard sections that hang off the wall like pages in a book (see Storing Tools Book-Style, page 96). The idea is like the swinging panel displays at lumberyards and home centers. You can use the swinging pegboards for both tools and materials. When using pegboard, there are several ways to improve its function with special no-fall hooks and by using hot-melt glue. For hanging tools, short sections of ¼" or ⅜" dowels can be pounded into pegboard of corresponding sizes.

12 Avoid Hiding Small Parts. Workshops are more efficient if the hundreds of small parts needed are visible, accessible, and organized. Small-parts cabinets are one answer. But try to stick with clear plastic drawers. Then mount those cabinets at eye level, if possible, so you don't have to shuffle through all the drawers to find what you need. Another idea is to build banks of drawers in a workbench, and make cutouts directly above them in the bench. Then you can remove the cutout and bring the drawer with the materials you need to the top position for easy access while working.

13 Don't Overlook Recyclables. What can make setting up a shop more fun and more economical than conventional home spaces is the opportunity to put castoffs and discards back to work. Unless you have an unlimited budget and an understanding spouse, recycling "found" fixtures can help you get shop gear organized. An old portable dishwasher, for example, can not only provide storage shelves but also, with the heating element plugged in, can give you a place to warm materials. Properly modified, other worn-out appliances such as refrigerators can likewise make excellent storage. Wood cabinets can often be found at bargain prices at garage sales. Metal kitchen cabinets, such as those popular in the Fifties, can provide great storage for materials like glue, paint, nails, and small tools. Also consider adapting economical homeware items, such as plastic bins stacked in a slide-in rack, and other kitchen organizers for use in your shop. Even items like plastic milk cases can provide convenient, floor-to-ceiling "cubby-hole" storage.

14 Consider Multi-Use Tools. If you are short on space, investigate multi-function tools of the type sold by Shopsmith. One such tool can let you do multiple operations, and can take the place of a shop full of big power tools: tablesaw, drill press, horizontal boring machine, lathe, and disc sander. If such a tool is out of your price range, look at the smaller benchtop tools like tablesaws, bandsaws, and jointers. You can store these scaled-down versions under the bench and pull them out as needed. Another option is to make your own combination tools. For example, you might be able to rig up a disc sander and a couple of belt sanders to run off a jackshaft powered by a single motor.

15 Make Small Tools Work Harder. Accessory manufacturers are coming to the rescue of shop owners short on space. In fact, one power drill outfitted with accessories can give you light drill-press capability and provide power for light bandsaws, sanders, bit sharpeners, wood lathes, and other basic tool operations. Compact work centers let you clamp portable tools onto one table for light-duty work in small spaces. Handy work centers available commercially can turn your drill into a drill press, your circular saw into a tablesaw, and your router into a shaper—all on a compact bench complete with a woodworking vise, bench dogs, and a power switch. Router accessories likewise give you full-shop capabilities in minimal space.

16 Don't Chintz On Small Tools. Small hand tools, like pliers, screwdrivers, and open-end wrenches, have a habit of either disappearing or being in the wrong place at the right time. A solution is to buy a few more of each to cut run-around time when preparing to do small projects around the home. Consider accumulating three sets of small hand tools and keep one in the kitchen, one in the garage, and one in your shop. The

time you will save running around will more than pay for the extra cost of the tools.

17 Set Up For Thinking. Up to half the work you do in a shop can be thinking and planning, so provide yourself with the space and equipment for this important stage. Outfit your shop with plenty of paper, drawing tools, tape, and other planning aids. Two essentials are a desk lamp and a comfortable stool. Take time to provide yourself other creature comforts, such as standing mats for concrete floors, a good desk surface with a T-square, and a clock. If you have kids who like to be in the shop with you, set up a place for them so they will be out of the way of power tools, yet feel included. You might want to install a large window in the wall of a basement shop so you can get on with projects and still keep an eye on the kids.

18 Consider A Part-Time Shop. If you live in cramped quarters, don't give up on shop projects. If you live in an apartment, for example, you can devise a portable work surface you can use on the kitchen counter. Basically just two plywood sections nailed together, it can also cover seldom-used "wet bars," and can also be outfitted as elaborately as you want with tool holders, even a small vise. Another option is outdoors, especially in southern climates. A workbench sheltered by a canvas-covered framework can work.

19 Avoid Pack-Ratting. Hardest of all, make it a habit not to collect junk in your shop area. No matter if your shop is large or small, a pack-rat habit can lead to reduced efficiency and wasted space. If your space is cramped, get in the habit of making decisions on what you really need to keep and what you really need to throw away. At the very least, regularly sort like-size lumber into piles. But don't make the piles too big; chances are good you won't use what you can't see. If necessary, store materials like big sheets of plywood in other places. Long lumber can be kept in the garage, for example, and cut to approximate length before being brought down to a basement workshop.

20 Control Shop Pollution. Sawdust, wood chips, and foul air drag down shop precision and are unhealthy as well. A shop vac is a must. Because it makes cleanup easier, you are likely to do it more often. Wet/dry vacs and larger dust collectors can be hooked up directly to tools, or to a permanent central vacuum line with individual shutoffs at each tool. Smaller portable tools like belt sanders can often be accessorized with dust bags. You can make up special sanding tables, special finishing areas within your shop with ventilation fans, or use shop fans to exhaust fumes from the workplace. In some cases you can add special sawdust "exhaust pipes" from such tools as a miter saw, to direct sawdust into a collection box, or rig up special collection boxes for wood chips for planers and jointers.

TOOL-BUYING STRATEGIES

As you pursue setting up your own home workshop, it will pay you to start thinking about developing an overall tool-buying strategy. Try to format a general approach that will guide you as you add tools to your shop, but not one that is so rigid that you miss tool-buying opportunities or go for years without a tool because you are saving up for "the best."

The best tool-buying approach for you will likely evolve with time and experience. The tools you should buy, their quality and approximate price, will change depending on your stage of experience, what your budget is, and what your goals are. You can buy tools on an individual project need basis. Or, you can plan tool buying in stages by the kind of shop capability you would like to maintain. A Tool-Buying Evolution, beginning on page 18, will give you some general examples of an individual approach to accumulating tools from scratch. For suggestions on buying tools using the shop capability approach, see the Shop Tool Planning Menu beginning on page 26.

Buying portable or stationary power tools is not the same as investing in gold, diamonds, stocks, or bonds. Once they have been used, tools depreciate immediately. But unlike a car, which becomes less valuable with each year and each mile, tools have a one-step depreciation. The first time you use them, they go from new to used at that moment. From then on, assuming you keep them in good shape, they can be sold for a price hovering around half the price the same tools sell for new.

This will be true no matter how long you have the tools. Due to inflation, a good tool you bought 20 years ago can bring you back as much as you paid for it originally and perhaps even a little more. To a stockbroker, this would be a bad investment. However, if you used that tool for the past 20 years, it has paid for itself time and again.

The projects you eventually concentrate on may have a dramatic impact on your tool buying line-up. With some specialties, such as bandsaw work, a single tool becomes the workhorse of the shop.

Some tools, however, may not be a good investment if they have very limited use and are expensive. If you are interested in pursuing woodworking, you soon will discover the multi-use tools available, like the Shopsmith, which can be used to saw, turn, drill, and sand wood. If you plan to buy one of these machines, it should be an early decision. Likewise, the same is true of a saw like the radial-arm saw. If you invest about $400 in a good radial-arm saw, for about another $100 you can convert that saw with accessories to let you do operations that would take equipment worth thousands.

But what about price versus quality in tools? How much you spend will determine the features, power, and service life you get. Not everyone needs industrial-quality tools across the board; the real challenge when buying tools is to get as much tool quality as you can for the money you are spending. The sections later in this book provide much more detailed suggestions on buying hand tools, portable power tools, and major stationary shop tools. Basically, good tool-buying strategy starts with determining what your needs are. If you are going to put an addition on your house or build a garage, for example, then buy those tools that will adequately help you do the job. And figure in the cost of the tools as part of your expense of making the improvements.

Experienced woodworkers seem to agree that cheaper tools will work okay if your budget is limited and you're just starting to set up a shop or are planning only light-duty projects. A cheap circular saw can last for years if it's used only occasionally, but the same saw in the hands of a professional remodeler might burn up in a few days. The key is your level of expectation. If you buy tools off the bargain table and expect them to do heavy, professional work day after day, there is little

(continued on page 20)

A Tool-Buying Evolution

1 Beginner

At this point you may be young, of moderate income, married, and just moved into an apartment or small rented house where you can claim a corner for your shop. So far you haven't done much with your hands, but you enjoyed industrial art classes in school and are sure you want to take a stab at using power tools. A good set of basic tools for you will include a portable circular saw, a sabersaw, a power drill, a router, a bench grinder, orbital and finishing sanders, and a hand miter box. These tools, and a starter assortment of accessories and supplies, will get you off to a good start. In general, you do not need to buy the best at this point; tools in the better homeowner category will work, but if you can afford tools in the light-duty industry range, so much the better. (Note that the sabersaw is sometimes also called a jigsaw, scrollsaw, or bayonet saw.) Consider a router rated at ¾ to 1 hp, and make sure you can remove the router from its base.

3 Advanced Amateur

Now you are making progress and the tools you've acquired are really starting to pay off. You are redoing a kitchen, or perhaps making bunk beds for the kids, a few built-ins here and there, and a new Parsons table for the living room. You are now ready for your first stationary tools, in addition to the tools you already have bought. Over time, you slowly add a stationary tablesaw, a scrollsaw, a benchtop bandsaw, a floor-model drill press, a belt/disc sander, a jointer, some air tools, and a cordless drill/driver. Before you haul home a tablesaw, look at the radial-arm saws, as well as combination machines. When buying a major shop saw, buy it where you can go back and get instructions. If the dealer runs a school, try to attend. If nothing else, be sure to study the operator's manual and search out books available on using your type of saw. Since this is a big investment, don't blow it. Don't be fooled by prices. No matter how inexpensive the saw is, it is not worth anything if it is not rigid or does not hold its accuracy. Get a good one. If you decide on a radial-arm saw, be sure the arm is cast iron and the roller-head bearings ride in milled grooves in the arm. Check to see that every metal-to-metal wear point has take-up, and every locator pin falls into iron or steel instead of soft aluminum.

2 AMATEUR

With some projects under your belt, you find you like working with power tools and enjoy what you can do with them. You may own your home and find it's time to finish off the basement, build a screen porch, make a shed for the backyard, or build planters or even smaller pieces of furniture. These are projects you can do yourself and you enjoy saving the cost of hiring someone to do them. To the tools you have acquired already, you add a benchtop tablesaw, a power miter saw, a scrolling sabersaw, a benchtop drill press, a belt sander, a shop vacuum, and a low-end air compressor. With appropriate accessories and supplies, you now have what could be called a good all-around basic workshop.

4 INTERMEDIATE

You now could be called an advanced woodworker, edging into the craftsman category. Besides the projects you have tackled over the years, you are making furniture, doors, inlays, turnings, and frames. Your work is beginning to be as good as, or better than, that of professionals. To the tools you have already purchased, you add a stationary radial-arm saw and bandsaw, as well as a thickness planer, a router/shaper, and a lathe. To get started on working with metal, you add an arc welder, a rotary grinder, and a ½″ power drill to take the burden off your original ⅜″ drill. You are now at a point where, if you replace any of your portable tools, the new tools are in the medium- or heavy-duty industrial range. Consider a 14″ drill press with four speeds, 4″ to 6″ of quill travel, and a tilt table. Buy a 10″ bandsaw, unless you can afford a 14″, one with two wheels and ball bearing guide. Look for a wood lathe with 10″ over the gap, outboard turning, and 36″ between centers. You'll find the lathe won't be a high payback investment since you will rarely turn enough items for the tool to pay for itself. It is, however, a fun tool to own.

5 PROFESSIONAL

You are now what most would call a professional, even though you might make your living at an office job. At this point, new tools will depend on what you develop as specialties. If, however, you are aiming to develop a workshop with all-around capabilities, you will concentrate on filling holes in your woodworking tool lineup, and expanding your metalworking ammunition. In the area of woodworking, you could add a random-orbit sander, a surface sander, and a biscuit joiner (also called a plate joiner). For working metal, you could add one or two welders, a metal bandsaw, a grinder equipped with wire wheels, and possibly a hammer drill. There are, of course, other fine tools that you can spend your money on, and the following pages give some suggestions and alternatives. And, if you've progressed this far, you will have no trouble thinking of accessories and supplies to buy to help you boost your project capabilities.

question that you will be disappointed.

More often woodworkers with many projects or years under their belt will advise buying the best tools you can afford, with one major caution: Go slow on tool buying if you're just starting, either in remodeling or in woodworking. It is not uncommon for beginners, excited about becoming a woodworker, to buy $1,500 worth of equipment, only to find out later that they don't have enough time or don't enjoy it enough to pursue many projects. If you are just beginning, consider buying tools at the middle of the price scale—a $50 drill instead of a $120 drill, for example. If you find you are getting a lot of use out of that tool, and you need more power or features, then you can buy the more expensive tool later. You'll have the confidence that it will be used and that its extra features will be worthwhile to you.

Sometimes you have to look hard to see the differences between what are called homeowner-quality tools and what are called industrial-quality tools. Both will accomplish what they were designed to do, but the features designed into an industrial-quality tool will allow it to perform better under constant punishment over a longer period of time. Until recently it was hard to find industrial tools in most lumberyards, hardware stores, or home centers, even if the label indicated that the tool was "industrially rated." This term usually meant only a better grade of "homeowner" or "consumer" tool. You had to go to a tool supply store to purchase a true industrial-quality tool. Today, industrial-quality tools are increasingly available, but you still may want to visit a tool supply store for more selection.

How much a power tool costs can depend on how the tool is built, its amperage, rpm, horsepower, and torque, as well as the manufacturer's reputation. As price goes up, you can expect longer and better cords, heavier-duty switches, and housings of supertough nylon instead of lower-grade plastics. Inside, you can expect more use of ball bearings, copper windings, brass brush holders, and hardened wrought-steel gears. Overall, you can expect a higher power-to-weight ratio and more special features such as case-hardened drill chucks, variable speed control, and higher-quality accessories.

You may decide to stay away from lower-priced stationary tools, and put out the extra money right away to get a professional-quality tool. The lower-priced benchtop tools won't have the features of more expensive stationary tools, but they still may provide what you need. (See Benchtop or Stationary on page 132.) Should you buy foreign- or domestic-made tools? In many cases you can get superior quality in foreign-made tools. However, occasionally you need to be a sharper tool buyer to make sure the price you are paying is actually fetching the quality you think it is.

Even in a shop where the lathe becomes the focus, other tools are needed to support its work. A tablesaw, photo opposite, would help you to save money by allowing you to make your own blanks.

When you are in the market for new tools, decide what you need, then try to wait for that tool to go on sale. The first part of the year is usually a good time to watch the ads. For used tools, consider the classified ads or garage sales. You can also get some good bargains at auctions, especially on heavy, specialized tools that other bidders aren't that familiar with. But be cautious: people at auctions often get caught up in the bidding so much that they end up paying more for the tools than they should. (For more tips on going the used-tool route, see Buying Used Shop Tools, page 160.)

"Once you use a new tool, its value drops and hovers around 50% of its original price."

If you are buying tools secondhand, consider sticking to the industrial-quality tools. The service life of a low-priced tool can be quite short. Most of its life may already be used up, and you can't tell by looking at it. When a cheap drill or sander dies, there's not much you can do but toss it in the garbage. Repairs can run as much or more than its original price. But repairs may be worthwhile on a higher-priced, industrial-quality tool, and service is more readily available for these tools as well.

The depreciation factor also favors buying more-expensive tools. Once you use a new tool, its value drops and hovers around 50% of its original price. You may be able to resell a higher-quality tool for 60% or more of its cost, but a cheaper tool might sell only for 30% or less of its cost. This is why a good-quality tool can be a decent investment. You use it over the years and, depending upon inflation, you may be able to resell it for a higher percentage of its original price.

Accessories and attachments are critical to tool performance, sometimes more so than the tool itself. You can have problems even with industrial-quality tools if you equip them with cheap blades or bits. If you try to get by with a $10 saw blade instead of a $50 blade, for example, a tablesaw won't perform as well no matter what you paid for it. Consider buying carbide-tipped blades and bits. They are expensive—a set of eight good carbide bits for a router can run $150 or more—but are well worth it if you are serious about doing good work. Anyone concerned about tool performance will keep cutting edges sharp, replace blades and bits when necessary, and store or transport tools with reasonable care.

The best tool to buy depends on how much money you have to spend, what work you plan to do, plus a host of factors including your own buying style. For example, do you tend to buy cheaper products to start out with, then keep trading up? Or do you save your money and go without until you can buy top-of-the-line tools?

Because of the competitiveness in the marketplace, you won't go wrong most of the time if you go by price. Generally manufacturers need to have a reason to charge more for some products than others. If they don't, they couldn't sell enough to make it worthwhile. Many experienced tool buyers will always try to buy the second-to-the-best of the line, but if they find themselves still uncertain, they will go with the more expensive. Most tool experts agree with this general approach. The result of buying a tool that costs $500 instead of one that costs $750 may be that its little defects will grow in your mind every time you use it, and you may eventually wish you hadn't bought it.

When considering tools to buy, don't overlook learning from the experience of others. Word of mouth is still one of the best ways to gather tool-buying advice. It's pretty easy to strike up a conversation about tools almost anywhere someone is working. Talk with other owners about tool performance, but be aware that you are hearing only one opinion, and there are dozens of ways to approach buying tools. Sometimes what owners say can be tainted by pride of ownership, but most often they will give you an honest opinion about how their tools perform, at least in their own mind.

WORKSHOP LAYOUT GUIDELINES

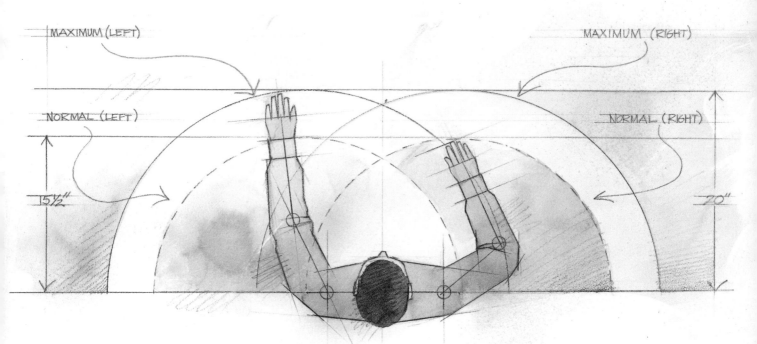

There are few hard and fast rules for setting up the physical dimensions of a workshop or for allowing space for specific tools. However, several general guidelines can be helpful and make your shop more practical, convenient, and comfortable to use.

How much space to allow around tools will depend primarily on two factors: (1) the space available in the workshop, and (2) the largest size boards or sheets that you would like to be able to handle without moving tools. For average woodworking, the longest boards processed generally will be 6′ or 8′ and the largest sheet will be 4x8′. You can allocate shop tool space to accommodate materials of this size, or you can plan to cut materials down to smaller units before being worked on in the shop. Example: If you want your tablesaw to be able to cut full 4x8′ sheets, you will need to allow 4′ to the right of the blade (as you look at the saw), 8′ to the left of the blade, plus 8′ in front of the saw, and 8′ to the rear of the saw. If you need only space enough to process half sheets measuring 4x4′, then you can halve the space required.

The illustrations on page 24 show the space requirements for both full and half sheets, and different maximum-length boards. Here are other ideas to consider when determining how much space to allow for major shop tools:

• Consider in all tool space allocations extra room for yourself, as well as a helper, to stand and maneuver the material on both in-feed and out-feed sides.

• Consider purchasing a panel saw to cut large sheets down to manageable size, instead of setting up equipment to handle them full size.

• Consider allowing at least 1½″ to 2″ from the back of the tool to the wall, but be sure to allow enough space to accommodate the width of any sawdust collection equipment you plan to install, including the ductwork and any attachments to it or to the tool.

• Consider using mobile bases on equipment if space is at a premium. That way you can move a saw or other tool either outside or in line with open doors or windows to process long boards or materials. Afterward the equipment can be wheeled back to its normal position.

• Consider keeping tables and workbenches the same height as, or slightly lower than, major pieces of shop equipment, such as the tablesaw. This way they can also serve as off-feed support for materials being worked.

BENCH SURFACE
31"–39½"

WORK SURFACE HEIGHTS

Below are work surface heights recommended by system design engineers for three types of work done by males and females. Most workbenches would be designed for heavy work, but heights may be altered to serve your preferences, or to serve as outboard support for shop saws.

TYPE OF WORK	MALE	FEMALE
1. Heavy Work	33½–39½"	31–37"
2. Light Assembly Work	39–43"	34½–38½"
3. Precision Work, Elbow Supported	43–47"	40½–44½"

Note: General recommendations commonly given for workbench heights include: 34" high, knuckle high, or hip-pocket high. Engineers suggest that the maximum standing work surface height normally should be below elbow height and should permit a relaxed position of the upper arm.

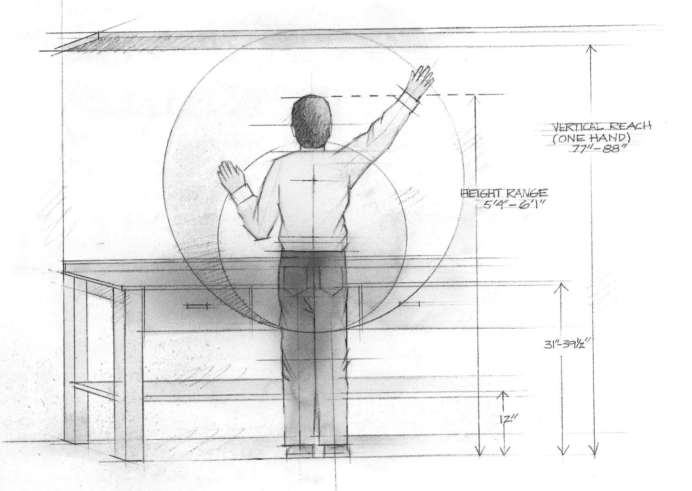

VERTICAL REACH
(ONE HAND)
77"–88"

HEIGHT RANGE
5'4"–6'1"

31"–39½"

12"

SHOP TOOL HEIGHTS

The best heights for shop tools, as well as benches and tables, will depend on your own height, with a general rule being that workbench surfaces should be roughly level with the knuckles (see previous page for tips on adjusting this guideline). For maximum efficiency, the height of a tool's table (or point of operation) above the floor should be approximately as shown* if you stand an average height of 5´9¼˝. These figures can be helpful when you are buying pre-built tool stands for benchtop tools, when you are building your own tool stands, or when you are building benches to accommodate benchtop tools.

*Data adapted from safety requirements for woodworking machinery, American National Standards Institute.

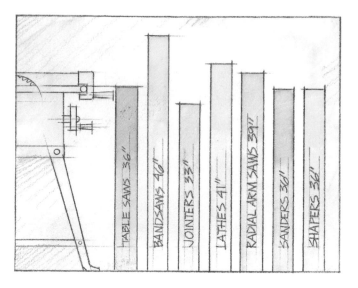

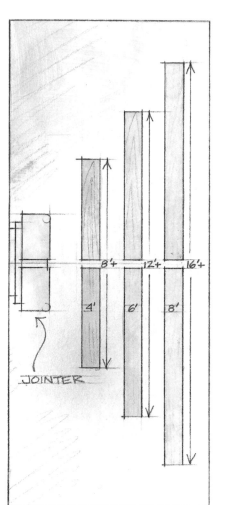

DIMENSIONAL LUMBER. Example space required to process dimensional lumber of various lengths on such equipment as table-, radial-arm, and power miter saws, as well as planers, jointers, and shapers. The figures do not take into account the space required for yourself or a helper to maneuver the lumber.

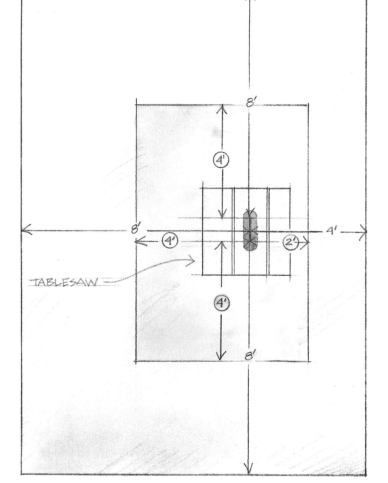

SHEET MATERIAL. Example space required to process full 4x8´ sheets or panels, as well as half sheets. Full sheets would require 12x16´ and half sheets 6x8´. (The circled dimensions are those needed for half sheets on a tablesaw.) Note that to crosscut panels in half, 4´ is needed to the right of the blade for full panels and 2´ for half panels. The dimensions do not account for space needed for yourself or a helper to maneuver the sheets.

DEVISING A TOOL-BUYING PLAN

To help formulate a general plan for accumulating workshop tools by stages, first review the Shop Tool Buying Menu on the following two pages. After determining the level of workshop you would like to have, also skim through the Shop Accessory and Supply Buying Menu on page 28 for ideas on other items you may want to buy. Then find your target workshop in later sections of this book and use the spaces provided to write in your own buying plans.

Be aware that the tool-buying suggestion lists in this book are a general guide, designed to be of most help to most people. Tools that head the buying list for general woodworking include a good major shop saw, a drill press, and a router. Many projects can be built with just these three power tools, along with some hand tools. Priority hand tools to get first include a good plane and a good set of chisels. To use either the plane or chisels successfully, the key is to keep them sharp. You will likely be frustrated with these tools until you learn how to sharpen them. Consider buying a cheap set of chisels on which to practice your sharpening technique. After you've perfected your skill, proceed to buy a more expensive set; you will still find uses for the cheap chisels.

Be aware that it is rare for two shop owners to agree on which tools are the most important in their shops, or in which order the tools should be purchased. For example, below are the type of lists you might get if you asked random woodworkers in what order they would buy the first five tools for their shops if they were starting over. Despite differences of opinion, you would probably find that the tablesaw stands out as being the star of the workshop, and that the bandsaw would also rank quite high. A major reason for differences of opinion is that, after acquiring a major shop saw and equipment to dress up lumber, the tools you will need will depend, to a large degree, on what kind of projects you decide to concentrate on.

You will get a variety of opinions from others on which shop tools to buy first. However, chances are good most will advise the first should be a good shop saw, most likely a tablesaw.

POTENTIAL TOOL PRIORITIES

WOODWORKER A	WOODWORKER B	WOODWORKER C	WOODWORKER D	WOODWORKER E
1. TABLESAW	1. BANDSAW	1. TABLESAW	1. BANDSAW	1. TABLESAW
2. JOINTER	2. JOINTER	2. JOINTER	2. RADIAL-ARM SAW	2. JOINTER
3. PLANER	3. BELT SANDER	3. BANDSAW	3. TABLESAW	3. LATHE
4. BANDSAW	4. ROUTER	4. DRILL PRESS	4. JOINTER	4. BANDSAW
5. SHAPER	5. TABLESAW	5. LATHE	5. DRILL PRESS	5. DRILL PRESS

THE START-UP WORKSHOP (PAGE 63)

STAGE I TOOLS

- Circular saw ($75)
- Sabersaw ($50)
- Power drill, ⅜" ($45)
- Router ($75)
- Bench grinder ($65)
- Sander, pad ($50)
- Sander, palm grip ($60)
- Miter box, manual ($30)

TOTAL: $450

THE HOMEOWNER WORKSHOP (PAGE 75)

STAGE I TOOLS

- Circular saw ($100)
- Sabersaw ($75)
- Power drill, ⅜" ($60)
- Router ($100)
- Bench grinder ($85)
- Sander, pad ($60)
- Sander, palm grip ($75)
- Miter box, manual ($45)

Subtotal: $600

STAGE II TOOLS

- Tablesaw, benchtop ($150)
- Power miter saw ($135)
- Stapler/nailer ($30)
- Scrolling sabersaw ($50)
- Drill press, benchtop ($120)
- Belt sander 3x24" ($80)
- Air compressor ($215)
- Shop vacuum ($60)

Subtotal: $840

TOTAL: $1,440

SHOP TOOL
BUYING MENU

HOW TO USE THE CHART

The chart here summarizes possible approaches to developing a tool-buying strategy for the workshop you would eventually like to own. The chart, which includes 40 tool suggestions, is intended as a planning guide, and the budget prices are based on 1993 dollars. The chart is modular in several ways: (1) Successively complex workshops add additional tool groups and build on tool groups already purchased. For example, the array of Stage I tools purchased for the Start-Up Workshop are also used in each of the more complex workshops. (2) The quality and price of specific tools in each tool group generally increase going from less complex to more complete workshops. For example, the budget for the Stage I tool group starts with $450 for the Start-Up Workshop and increases progressively to a budget of $1,015 for the same tools under the Professional Workshop. (3) Depending on your needs and budget, mix and match tool groups or individual tools under

the example shops for your own plan. For example, if you determine that the Woodworker Workshop is adequate for your needs, you could decide to buy lower-priced Stage I tools from the Start-Up Workshop, but may elect to invest in the higher-priced tools listed under Stage II of the Craftsman Workshop. The tools listed here reappear later, with accessory and supply suggestions, in chapters that elaborate on each of the five example workshops. As the lists are repeated, spaces are provided for you to pencil in your own buying plans. Note that as stationary tools are added that duplicate benchtop tools, the benchtop versions can be sold or used for specialized purposes, as indicated by asterisks:

*Benchtop tablesaw can be used for trimming large parts and cutting small parts during assembly. **Benchtop drill press can be used with sanding drums or for horizontal boring. *** Benchtop bandsaw can be used for small projects. **** First power miter saw can be used for basic cutoff work.

THE WOODWORKER WORKSHOP (PAGE 87)

❏ Circular saw ($125)
❏ Sabersaw ($75)
❏ Power drill, ⅜″ ($75)
❏ Router ($135)
❏ Bench grinder ($100)
❏ Sander, pad ($75)
❏ Sander, palm grip ($85)
❏ Miter box, manual ($60)
Subtotal: $730

❏ Tablesaw, benchtop* ($200)
❏ Power miter saw ($150)
❏ Stapler/nailer ($45)
❏ Scrolling sabersaw ($80)
❏ Drill press, benchtop** ($180)
❏ Belt sander 3x24″ ($90)
❏ Air compressor ($250)
❏ Shop vacuum ($100)
Subtotal: $1,095

STAGE III TOOLS

❏ Tablesaw, stationary ($600)
❏ Scrollsaw ($250)
❏ Bandsaw, benchtop ($140)
❏ Drill press, floor model ($300)
❏ Belt/disc sander, 4″ ($120)
❏ Jointer ($300)
❏ Air tool set ($80)
❏ Drill/driver, cordless ($120)
Subtotal: $1,910

TOTAL: $3,735

THE CRAFTSMAN WORKSHOP (PAGE 101)

❏ Circular saw ($145)
❏ Sabersaw ($90)
❏ Power drill, ⅜″ ($85)
❏ Router ($180)
❏ Bench grinder ($125)
❏ Sander, pad ($80)
❏ Sander, palm grip ($95)
❏ Miter box, manual ($70)
Subtotal: $870

❏ Tablesaw, benchtop* ($225)
❏ Power miter saw ($225)
❏ Stapler/nailer ($45)
❏ Scrolling sabersaw ($100)
❏ Drill press, benchtop** ($220)
❏ Belt sander 3x24″ ($125)
❏ Air compressor ($275)
❏ Shop vacuum ($125)
Subtotal: $1,340

❏ Tablesaw, stationary ($850)
❏ Scrollsaw ($600)
❏ Bandsaw, benchtop*** ($200)
❏ Drill press, floor model ($400)
❏ Belt/disc sander, 4″ ($250)
❏ Jointer ($400)
❏ Air tool set ($100)
❏ Drill/driver, cordless ($140)
Subtotal: $2,940

STAGE IV TOOLS

❏ Radial-arm saw, stationary ($450)
❏ Bandsaw, stationary ($500)
❏ Thickness planer ($450)
❏ Router/shaper ($250)
❏ Wood lathe ($300)
❏ Arc welder ($350)
❏ Grinder, rotary ($140)
❏ Power drill, ½″ ($175)
Subtotal: 2,615

TOTAL: $7,765

THE PROFESSIONAL WORKSHOP (PAGE 115)

❏ Circular saw ($150)
❏ Sabersaw ($100)
❏ Power drill, ⅜″ ($125)
❏ Router ($235)
❏ Bench grinder ($140)
❏ Sander, pad ($90)
❏ Sander, palm grip ($100)
❏ Miter box, manual ($75)
Subtotal: $1,015

❏ Tablesaw, benchtop* ($250)
❏ Power miter saw ($430)
❏ Stapler/nailer ($45)
❏ Scrolling sabersaw ($140)
❏ Drill press, benchtop** ($280)
❏ Belt sander 3x24″ ($180)
❏ Air compressor ($500)
❏ Shop vacuum ($190)
Subtotal: $2,015

❏ Tablesaw, stationary ($1,700)
❏ Scrollsaw ($800)
❏ Bandsaw, benchtop*** ($250)
❏ Drill press, floor model ($600)
❏ Belt/disc sander, 4″ ($375)
❏ Jointer ($700)
❏ Air tool set ($350)
❏ Drill/driver, cordless ($170)
Subtotal: $4,945

❏ Radial-arm saw, stationary ($600)
❏ Bandsaw, stationary ($750)
❏ Thickness planer ($1,000)
❏ Wood shaper ($450)
❏ Wood lathe ($750)
❏ Arc welder ($450)
❏ Grinder, rotary ($180)
❏ Power drill, ½″ ($200)
Subtotal: $4,380

STAGE V TOOLS

❏ Sander, random orbit ($140)
❏ Sander, surface ($1,050)
❏ Power planer ($140)
❏ Compound miter saw**** ($450)
❏ Wire-feed welder ($750)
❏ Sawdust collector ($300)
❏ Reciprocating saw ($150)
❏ Hammer drill ($125)
Subtotal: $3,105

TOTAL: $15,460

SHOP ACCESSORY AND SUPPLY
BUYING MENU

The chart below recaps suggested accessories and supplies for each of the example workshops presented in this book. Check off the equipment you find appropriate for your shop. As with the Shop Tool Buying Menu, mix and match them to your needs. Note that these groups accumulate for the successively complex shops. For example, if you aim for the Woodworker Workshop, consider accessories listed for the Start-Up, the Homeowner, and the Woodworker Workshops. The prices given are intended as a rough guide to help you in your planning; adjust as necessary.

THE START-UP WORKSHOP——Total Budget $725

❏ Eye and ear protection ($25) ❏ Workbench ($50) ❏ Toolbox or bucket ($30) ❏ Machinist's vise ($25) ❏ Sawhorse brackets ($20) ❏ Router bits ($50) ❏ Handsaw, rip ($15) ❏ Handsaw, crosscut ($15) ❏ Hacksaw ($10) ❏ Coping saw ($10) ❏ Screwdriver set ($25) ❏ Pliers set ($20) ❏ Diagonal cutters ($6) ❏ Adjustable wrench, Crescent ($10) ❏ Open-end wrenches, reg. ($30) ❏ Open-end wrenches, metric ($30) ❏ Socket set ($50) ❏ Measuring tape ($10) ❏ Steel square ($8) ❏ Hammer ($15) ❏ Nail sets ($4) ❏ Awl ($4) ❏ Level, 24″ ($25) ❏ Level, torpedo ($10) ❏ Block plane ($10) ❏ C-clamps, four ($25) ❏ Pipe clamps, four ($40) ❏ Multi-meter tester ($20) ❏ Soldering gun ($20) ❏ Putty knife, 1″ ($2) ❏ Broad knife, 6″ ($6) ❏ Utility knife ($5) ❏ Paint scraper ($5) ❏ Extension cord ($10) ❏ Other supplies ($85).

THE HOMEOWNER WORKSHOP——Total Budget $745

❏ Workbench, extra ($50) ❏ Toolboxes or totes, two extra ($40) ❏ Ladder, 5′ step ($30) ❏ Ladder, extension ($75) ❏ Router bits, additional ($75) ❏ Drill bits, additional ($35) ❏ Saw blades, additional ($75) ❏ Extension cords, two extra ($20) ❏ Drop light ($10) ❏ Glass cutter ($5) ❏ Sharpening stones ($25) ❏ Cold chisels ($20) ❏ Deep sockets, ¼″ ($20) ❏ Tin snips ($10) ❏ Caulking gun ($5) ❏ Basin wrench ($10) ❏ Magnifier headset ($15) ❏ Face shield ($15 ❏ Combination square ($10) ❏ Wire brush, hand ($5) ❏ Spring clamps, four ($15) ❏ Tack hammer, magnetic ($5) ❏ Leather punch ($30) ❏ Wire connector set, solderless ($15) ❏ Hot-melt glue gun ($15) ❏ Other supplies ($115).

THE WOODWORKER WORKSHOP——Total Budget $1,400

❏ Toolboxes, additional ($50) ❏ Tool storage cabinet ($140) ❏ Router accessories ($75) ❏ Saw blades, additional ($75) ❏ Wood countersink bits ($30) ❏ Grinder wheels, additional ($35) ❏ Sharpening stone set ($25) ❏ Multi-purpose adjustable vise ($50 ❏ Level, additional ($35) ❏ Bar clamps, additional ($100) ❏ Metal drill bit set ($75) ❏ Mechanic's socket set ($80) ❏ Allen wrench set ($10) ❏ Channel-lock-type pliers set ($10) ❏ File set ($50) ❏ Sledge hammers, two ($50) ❏ Ball peen hammers, two ($30) ❏ Battery charger ($40) ❏ Nail pullers ($50) ❏ Painting accessories, additional ($100) ❏ Respirator ($45) ❏ Electrical tools, additional ($60) ❏ Plumbing tools, additional ($75) ❏ Other supplies($110).

THE CRAFTSMAN WORKSHOP——Total Budget $2,815

❏ Woodworker's bench ($500) ❏ Wood vise ($125) ❏ Wood mallets, two ($35) ❏ Wooden clamps, four ($80) ❏ Bar clamps, four additional ($60) ❏ C-clamps, additional ($20) ❏ Try/miter square ($20) ❏ Dovetail square ($40) ❏ Marking gauge ($25) ❏ Sliding bevel ($15) ❏ Caliper, outside ($30) ❏ Divider ($15) ❏ Steel rule, precision ($10) ❏ Bench level ($75) ❏ Drawing tool kit ($65) ❏ Ripsaw, quality ($40) ❏ Crosscut saw, quality ($40) ❏ Dovetail saw ($20) ❏ Detailing saw, fine-toothed ($15) ❏ Bench plane, short ($150) ❏ Bench plane, medium ($160) ❏ Chisel plane ($120) ❏ Trimming plane ($75) ❏ Spokeshave, convex ($55) ❏ Spokeshave, concave ($55) ❏ Drawknife ($40) ❏ Palm plane ($15) ❏ Brass plane ($30) ❏ Wood-rasp set ($125) ❏ Chisel set ($100) ❏ Carving tool set ($150) ❏ Turning tool set ($150) ❏ Circle cutter ($25) ❏ Forstner bits set ($125) ❏ Screwdriver set ($60) ❏ Other supplies ($150).

THE PROFESSIONAL WORKSHOP——Total Budget $4,258

❏ Professional tool set ($2,400) ❏ Rolling tool cabinet, 15-drawer ($500) ❏ Welding table ($100) ❏ Arbor press ($200) ❏ Machinist's tool chest ($180) ❏ Anvils ($75) ❏ Snap-ring pliers ($8) ❏ Gear pullers, two sizes ($60) ❏ Snap-ring assortment ($20) ❏ O-ring assortment ($15) ❏ Blacksmith hammers and tongs ($100) ❏ Tap and die set ($100) ❏ Wire brushes, extra ($10) ❏ Strap clamp set ($25) ❏ Countersinks, 60°, 82°, 90° ($30) ❏ Carbide metal drill bits ($75) ❏ Center drills, #1, #2, #3 ($30) ❏ Cant-twist clamps ($20) ❏ Grease gun ($20) ❏ Specialized screwdrivers ($40) ❏ Other supplies

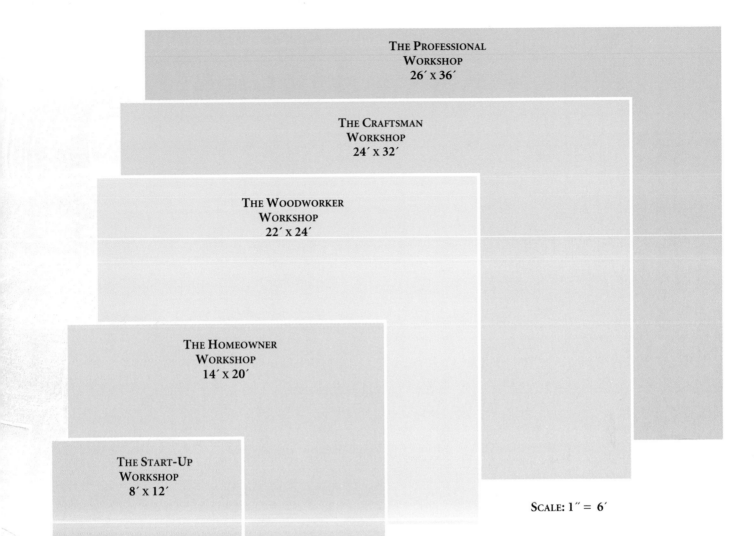

THE PROFESSIONAL
WORKSHOP
26´ x 36´

THE CRAFTSMAN
WORKSHOP
24´ x 32´

THE WOODWORKER
WORKSHOP
22´ x 24´

THE HOMEOWNER
WORKSHOP
14´ x 20´

THE START-UP
WORKSHOP
8´ x 12´

SCALE: 1˝ = 6´

SUGGESTED SPACE ALLOTMENTS

WORKSHOP	TYPE OF SPACE	AREA SUGGESTED	STORAGE COMPONENTS
THE START-UP WORKSHOP	Basement Room or Garage End Wall	8´ x 12´ or 96 sq. ft.	Open Shelving
THE HOMEOWNER WORKSHOP	Basement Room or Single-Car Garage	14´ x 20´ or 280 sq. ft.	Open Shelving, Cabinets
THE WOODWORKER WORKSHOP	Large Basement Room or Two-Car Garage	22´ x 24´ or 528 sq. ft.	Open Shelving, Cabinets, and Under Bench
THE CRAFTSMAN WORKSHOP	Three-Car Garage or Separate Building	24´ x 32´ or 768 sq. ft.	Open Shelving, Cabinets, Under Bench, and Racks
THE PROFESSIONAL WORKSHOP	Separate Building	26´ x 36´ or 936 sq. ft.	Open Shelving, Cabinets, Under Bench, Racks, and Office

WORKSHOP TOOL INVENTORY
POWER TOOLS

Use these pages to keep a running account of your workshop equipment inventory. Space is provided below for power tools (either portable or stationary); use the pages following to list hand tools and accessories. Whenever the list is updated, make double photocopies; place one copy with your tool manuals, and keep the other copy handy with your household records.

Taking time to fill out and maintain a complete listing of your workshop tools in the spaces provided can pay off several ways. First, you will have a complete record of all the tools in your workshop which eventually could value several thousands of dollars. In case of loss, your records could prove invaluable in making a claim. Second, at a glance you will be able to jog your memory as to how long each tool has been in service, the original price, the length of warranty, the model, and serial number. This listing will be handy when, for example, you are going to a tool supply store and need the tool specs to buy parts and accessories, or when you are calling around to locate new parts for repair. Third, by filling out the listings, you will also have a handy record of tool suppliers, including their phone numbers, in your area. Fourth, by keeping this list current, you will be able to watch your shop tool collection grow, and know at a glance the approximate value.

TOOL	MODEL NO.	DATE	DEALER	WARRANTY	COST

Tool	Model No.	Date	Dealer	Warranty	Cost

Tool Repair Service Centers

Service Center	Brand	Address	Phone

WORKSHOP TOOL INVENTORY
HAND TOOLS

TOOL	DESCRIPTION	DATE	DEALER	WARRANTY	COST

WORKSHOP TOOL INVENTORY
ACCESSORIES

TOOL	DESCRIPTION	DATE	DEALER	WARRANTY	COST

PURSUING A DREAM WORKSHOP

Who, among those of us who love tools and what can be done with them, hasn't dreamed about having the time and the money to put together a perfect workshop someday? Instead of having to deal with makeshift arrangements, we could finally pursue our projects in a dignified, organized fashion, and have room enough to handle projects of significance, like building a living room full of furniture, that long-awaited wooden boat, the world's best garden gazebo, or restoring that '47 Ford that is still setting in the grove on some relative's farm.

Refining a home workshop is a worthwhile lifetime pursuit. Even if it is set up to earn its keep, a shop can become your own personal place, where life's worries fade and peace of mind prevails.

The specifics of that dream shop might be hazy to start with. But for certain it would have a good heating and cooling system so you can thumb your nose at the weather, have plenty of light, and best of all have a special workshop office where you can sketch, research, plan, or just relax and survey the tools you have collected over the years as you sip a good cup of coffee.

So how do you begin to pursue your own dream workshop? Though there may be a half-dozen places a shop could be set up, the first step is to decide where you want to put yours: basement, spare room, garage, separate building (see Shop Location Options, page 44). Keep in mind that if you keep most of the workshop's components portable, you can always rearrange them as you gain experience with projects, and also move the entire shop along with you when you decide to sell the old homestead and move across town or across the country.

If you are lucky enough to be planning your workshop from scratch, or are looking for ways to improve the workshop you have already started, it is helpful to do some planning with a pencil.

First, assemble a rough drawing; you can use the layout grid on page 43 or buy a tablet of graph paper with ¼″ squares. Measure the outline of the room, then select an appropriate scale, such as ¼″ equal to 1′. Sketch out a diagram of the shop space, noting existing features such as doors, windows, plumbing lines, heating/cooling vents, electrical lines and receptacles, and lighting fixtures. Start by measuring and drawing in windows and doors, marking distances from outside of trim to outside of trim. Work clockwise around the room, noting any breaks like offsets. Mark which way each door swings, extending a line from the hinge side to denote the swing area.

Because even floor-model tools can be moved around, or kept portable with the use of casters, the goal of sketching out your shop plan is to get started with a basic arrangement. This will help you decide where to locate benches, cabinets, and lumber storage areas, help you picture shopworking patterns, and allow you to pre-plan a dust-collection system. For tool placement, you can photocopy the tool outlines on page 42, cut them out, and move them around on your grid diagram. (The outlines are sized for a ¼″ = 1′ grid; if you are using ½″ = 1′, photocopy them at 200%.) If you want to make your own tool outlines, most tool catalogs will give complete specifications; make a list of the tools planned, noting their height, width, and depth. For benches, cabinets, and the like, you can either sketch them in or make your own cutouts if you know their specific dimensions.

Start by placing main workbenches near available windows to take advantage of natural light. Before positioning major tools, check the guidelines presented on page 24 for tool heights and working areas. The goal, though not always achievable, is to have sufficient workspace around each tool to handle your most common project work. Try to visualize work sequences as you decide where to position specific tools, using what some

(continued on page 38)

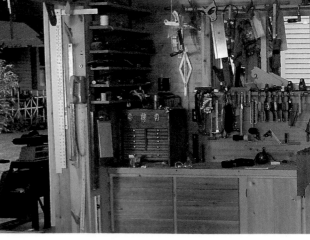

A Clean, Well-Lighted Place. Space, light, and work surfaces are major planning elements of a good workshop. This shop's floor-to-ceiling windows along one wall provide plenty of natural light. Close by is a built-in workbench, photos right, with woodworking vise for handwork or sanding.

SETTING UP FOR PROJECTS. *A major planning consideration is how to arrange and store large and small shop tools. In this shop, major tools form a work triangle, photo above, and three separate benches can be pulled together for large project work. Hand tools, photo below, hang from nails on wood-covered wall, or rest on window ledge.*

designers call the "workstation concept." This line of thinking breaks down projects into subordinate tasks, such as cutting, sanding, and assembly, then grouping all associated accessories and jigs for each of those tasks near designated major stationary shop tools.

The "working triangle" concept used by kitchen designers can be useful in positioning tools, work surfaces, or storage cabinets to minimize steps during project work. The kitchen work triangle distance is figured between sink, range, and refrigerator, and the goal is to keep it under 26′. Keep this in mind, for example, when picturing yourself going from one major tool, to a second tool, and to your assembly bench.

After you have mapped out the top view of your workshop, you may also want to sketch rough elevations for each of the walls to help you decide how high to position benches or cabinets. Note the ceiling height and sketch one wall at a time; doing this can also help you decide where to use pegboard, where to position other shelving, and where to locate electrical receptacles and lighting. (As a helpful reference, note that most kitchen base cabinets are built to be 34½″ high without the countertop. Including a countertop with a 4″ backsplash and 2½″ of additional clearance, this means that 41″ is needed below windows and electrical outlets.)

When measuring your workshop space, also check to determine the squareness and plumb of the walls. A way to do this is to work from a corner and measure and mark 36″along one wall, then measure and mark 48″ along the adjacent wall. The distance between these two points should be 60″. If the measurement is more than 60″, the wall is "out of square, in favor"; if the distance is shorter than 60″, the wall is "out of square, out of favor." Whether the walls are slightly out of square or plumb may not be critical in your workshop. However, if significantly out of whack, you may want to prebuild any benches or cabinets as separate units and install them so any gaps along the wall will be less obvious.

Once you decide where you want to set up your workshop, the first challenge most often will be to clear the area of what is now stored there. That may mean creating storage space not for shop items, but for the materials that are now occupying the chosen shop space. If you decide to clear a space in the basement, you will need to find a home for the stuff of everyday living that now occupies the space, whether it is books, old appliances, craft supplies, paint cans, hobby collections, personal files, used furniture, or other possessions. Often, redistributing home possessions to make room for a workshop requires using multiple approaches.

Before rearranging possessions, first clean out to find what you have. If possible, pick one large clearinghouse space where you can assemble items to sort and select those that should be tossed, recycled, sold at a garage sale, or given to various charities. If you have lived in your home for any amount of time, and have the typical American family's bent for pack-ratting, you may find that the search for storage space will need to extend to every available nook and cranny. This first order of business can be discouraging, but sticking with your plans to sort out and reduce the storage load on available space can pay off handsomely. Suffering through this exercise will not only help create room for your workshop but also with fewer nonessential items using up valuable space, your home will actually feel larger, more organized, and more pleasant to live in.

IMPORTANT: SAFETY FIRST

No workshop or workshop project is worth the risk of personal injury or exposure to unhealthy conditions. Under all circumstances, learn basic safety procedures first and consider the risks of all procedures in the workshop before attempting them. Read and follow all safety precautions in owner manuals, and consider safety the overriding consideration. If any question remains in your mind about any precedure, don't attempt it before consulting with others with more experience. This precaution should include the use of all tools, chemicals, and electrical power in the workshop. Seek proper instruction before using hand and power tools, and observe all safety precautions. For hand tools a good source of safety information is the Hand Tools Institute, 707 Westchester Ave., White Plains, NY 10604.

Certain illustrations in this book may show power tools without guards in place for the purposes of clarity. It is important for you to follow the recommendations of the manufacturer regarding the use of guards, as well as other safety precautions. If you have power tools without owner manuals, obtain copies and read them before using the tools. Never make a cut with cutting tools that will place your hands dangerously close to the turning blade. Stand aside from the piece that is being cut off. Consider investing in foot switches so you can turn off a machine when both hands are busy. Don't attempt any cut that you have doubts about. Make test cuts on large pieces of scrap wood. Keep tables smooth and slick. Keep all power tools and their components in proper adjustment. Keep your eyes on your work at all times, and be sure to wear safety glasses and other safety gear when appropriate.

SHELVING THAT WORKS

3/8" PLYWOOD

DRYWALL SCREWS

1X3

2 X 4

TADO

45"

19"

70"

Shelving is often needed when rearranging possessions to make room for a shop. There are various methods of attaching shelving to stud walls (see Searching Out Shop Space, page 46). However, building individual shelving units that are portable instead of built-in can increase your arrangement options later on.

The type of shelving shown is made of lumberyard 1x3s, 2x4s, and 3/8" plywood sheets. It gains its structural strength through the way its individual components are assembled. Because the 1x3s are attached within dadoes in the 2x4s with drywall screws, and the shelving is fastened to front and back supports, the unit doesn't need extra cross braces, supports, or gussets. The shelving is easy and inexpensive to build, and it will accept whatever you can stack on it without tipping or wavering.

This unit is designed so each shelf will accept three boxes 12¼" high by 12¼" wide by 18¼" deep, allowing its four shelves to store 12 boxes. The total unit measures 45" wide by 19" deep by 70" high, and will require four 8' 2x4s (1½x3½"), approximately 53 running feet of 1x3 boards (¾x2½"), and one 4x8' sheet of 3/8"-thick plywood. The surface finish of the plywood you buy is influenced only by how you want the shelves to look.

To build the shelf unit, first trim the ends of the four 2x4s to the measurement shown, or to your own measurements. Note that the bottom shelf surface is raised off the floor by 3¾" to protect against water damage. Each of the 2x4s is notched to accept 1x3 cross supports. You can make the notches on a tablesaw or radial-arm saw outfitted with a dado blade. Or you can do it with either a portable circular saw or a handsaw. If using a circular or handsaw, clamp the four 2x4s together, outline the areas to be notched, and make parallel cuts in the notch areas to a depth of ¾". Then use a sharp wood chisel to chip out any wood left between the saw kerfs.

With the notches done, install 1x3 cross supports across the first set of two 2x4s, then across the second set of 2x4s, using drywall-type screws with a power drill

or screwdriver. Then attach the side cross supports. If you will be following the measurements shown exactly, first rip the plywood sheet to 42" width, then cut out the shelf 19" wide to get a shelf board measuring 19" by 42". Install each shelf, driving a screw about every 6" into the cross support below. Leave the unit unfinished, or use stain, paint, or polyurethane.

What to put on the shelves? Cardboard boxes, preferably all the same dimensions, with covers, work well. Though expensive, newer storage boxes made by companies like RubberMaid are the ultimate choice. Tip: Before finalizing dimensions of the shelving unit for your own use, first decide what size boxes you will use, then build to fit. Once you have a number of the units built, buy an adequate number of the boxes to store your items. Fill the boxes and note the contents on a 3x5 index card. Make a photocopy of all the index cards, then tape a Ziploc bag containing the content card to the front of each box. Put the photocopy pages in a three-ring binder, and you will have a master index of what you have stored readily available.

SHOP PLAN IDEA STARTERS

The perfect workshop that would satisfy the needs of everyone doesn't exist. Making do, adapting, and improvising are key words in deciding where and how to set up your own home workshop. Consider the total workshop as a major tool in itself, one that has many components that can be arranged one way, tested, then rearranged and refined several times over the years ahead. Remember that your workshop is a means to an end, not an end in itself. The goal is to have a workshop that accommodates your needs as efficiently, safely, and conveniently as possible as you pursue your various projects. Like a car, consider your shop as a vehicle to help you get where you want to go.

Where to start? The floor plans here show a sampling of the diverse arrangements possible, and they are presented to show you that no matter what kind of space you have available, something can be done with it. Review these ideas, then check out the more specific layout arrangements suggested for each of the five prototype workshops in this book. Don't forget, the space that may be available to you can change within just a year or two. With proper planning, however, you will be able to easily move your workshop lock-stock-and-barrel to new spaces as the opportunity arises.

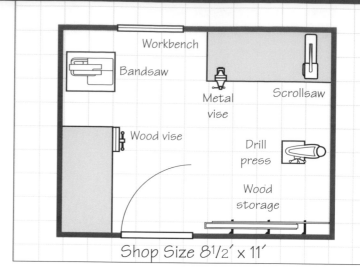

Shop Size 8½′ x 11′

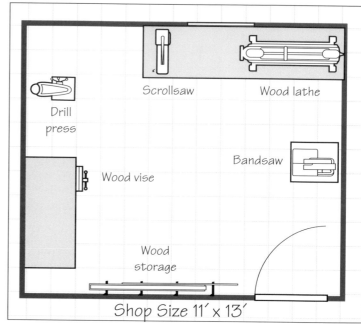

Shop Size 11′ x 13′

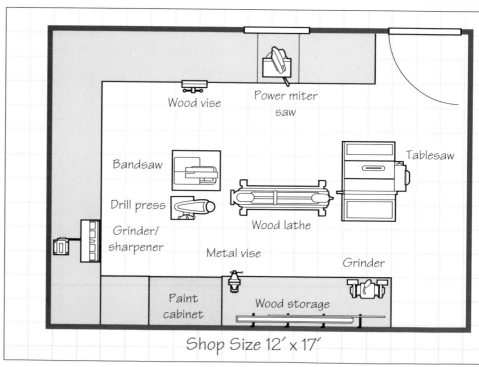

Shop Size 12′ x 17′

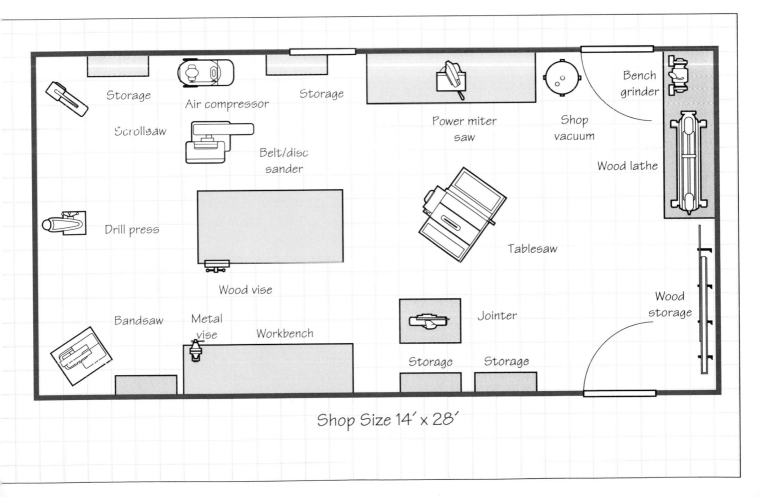

Wood storage

Wood vise

Radial-arm saw

Wood lathe

Metal vise

Tablesaw

Bandsaw

Drill press

Thickness planer

Shop Size 15′ x 21′

Storage

Air compressor

Storage

Power miter saw

Shop vacuum

Bench grinder

Scrollsaw

Belt/disc sander

Wood lathe

Drill press

Tablesaw

Wood vise

Bandsaw

Metal vise

Workbench

Jointer

Wood storage

Storage

Storage

Shop Size 14′ x 28′

MAPPING OUT A WORKSHOP

Planning a workshop often requires a "best information at the time" approach. While it is difficult to foresee the future and know exactly where your interests, budget, and career moves might take you, the best advice is to start now, plan out as much as you can in advance, and keep the plan as flexible as possible.

Photocopies of the shop tool outlines here can be used with copies of the planning grid on the opposite page. The tool outlines are sized to use on a grid where a ¼″ square equals 1′. However, the grid squares may be used to represent other dimensions. Or, the grid can be enlarged or reduced on a copy machine. Remember, however, that the tool outlines must also be enlarged or reduced to correspond to the grid ratio you plan to use. The tool outlines may be copied onto sticky-back paper at a copy shop and then affixed to cardboard to make cut-outs, if you wish, or they may simply be copied onto the grid with carbon paper. You can also tape the cut-outs in position on the grid, then make a photocopy.

After you have decided where to set up your workshop, the first step is to map out the perimeter of the space available onto a photocopy of the grid. Note the scale, then start in one corner and measure in inches to the edge of the trim of windows or doors. For all windows or doors, mark in the width from outside trim to outside trim, then make note of all dimensions for windows and doors below. Note that the total of measurements for Wall 1 must total the same as Wall 3; Wall 2 the same as Wall 4.

Anvil

Arbor press

Floor model bandsaw

Belt sander

Arc welder

Gas welder

Benchtop tablesaw

Benchtop drill press

Benchtop bandsaw

Grinder

Metal vise

Wood vise

Scroll saw

Jointer

Lathe

Floor model tablesaw

Surface sander

Power miter saw

Floor model drill press

Radial-arm saw

Metal bandsaw

Planer

Shaper

Shop vacuum

Spindle sander

Compressor

Belt/disc sander

Wood storage rack

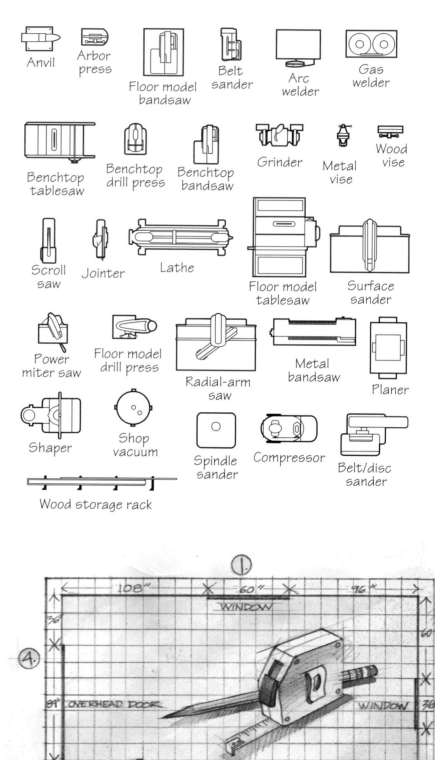

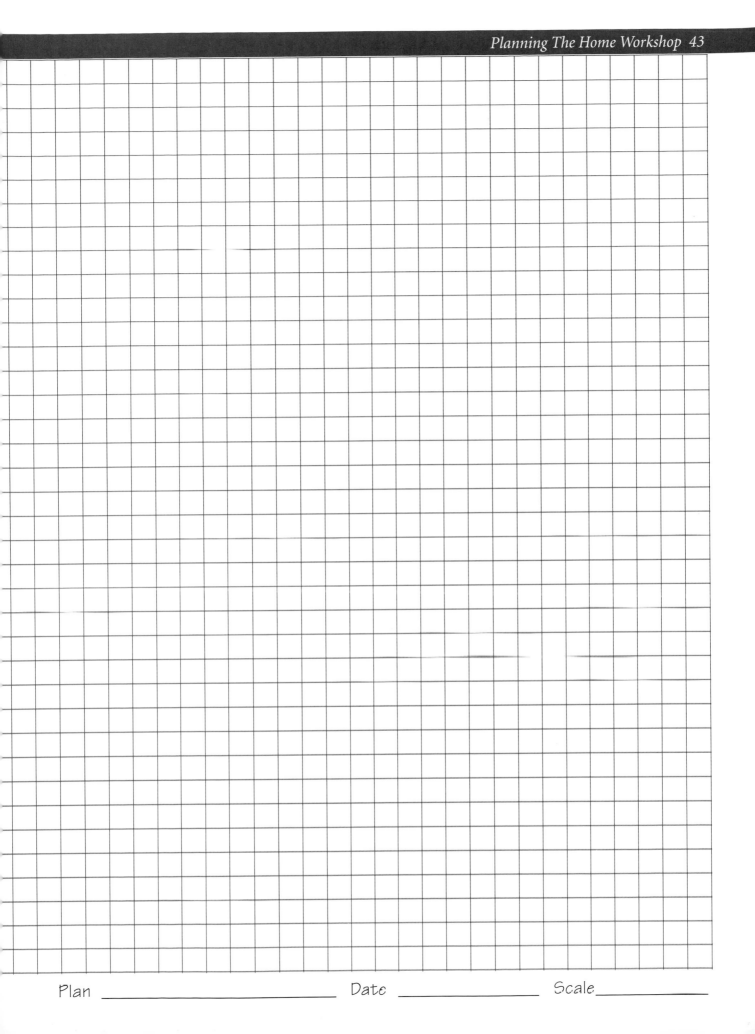

Plan _____ Date _____ Scale_____

SHOP LOCATION OPTIONS

In truth, makeshift workshops can be set up almost anyplace, in any room of the home or other building, or even outside in warmer climates. However, studies show that across this country, roughly about 45% of shop owners have their workshops set up in their garages, about 30% have a workshop in their basements, and about 25% have their workshop in a separate building. Where you set up will be determined by what space is available, what you can spend to prepare the space, and the climate in your area.

GARAGE. An advantage of a garage shop is that the tools are easily accessible in case they need to be moved to a job site. A disadvantage is that in colder climates the garage should be insulated and equipped with some sort of heating system. New two- and three-car garages can easily be tapped for shop use, with the shop set up in the area of one or two bays, or along the side or end. The shop space can be partitioned off so only that part will need heating or cooling. In warmer climates, even one-car garages can be used for shop space, with the vehicle relegated to the driveway. Tools on casters can be rolled outside when needed, and/or cutting can be done in the shop and assembly done outdoors. In colder climates, the garage can often be expanded (see below).

BASEMENT. In its favor, the basement in colder climates offers the true advantage of being warm in winter and cool in summer. Its disadvantages include dampness, lack of light and ventilation, and potential difficulty in moving raw materials (such as lumber) and finished projects in and out. The noise, fumes, and debris of shopwork also can interfere with normal household tranquillity. Though you won't usually have to invest in a special heating/cooling system, you will have to take steps to control humidity and to minimize byproducts of the workshop. Adding insulation, soundproofing, and ventilation, however, can in most cases make the basement shop tolerable to the rest of the home dwellers. A larger dust collector can be installed in a soundproof corner of the basement shop, or it can be installed in an attached garage and piped down to a central duct system in the basement.

SEPARATE BUILDING. A separate building can be a converted separate garage or a building erected specifically for shop use. Larger backyard storage building plans or kits can work for small shops. Or traditional garage plans utilizing truss rafters can be used, with doors, windows, and skylights added or subtracted as needed. Post-frame metal-clad buildings can offer an economi-

cal alternative to conventional construction. If you decide to erect a new shop building, investigate and decide on the heating/cooling system you will use before you start construction. That way you can install ducts, piping, and other components much more easily than building first and deciding on climate control systems later.

Also, before pouring cement slabs, discuss the finish options with other shop owners and/or your contractor; a slightly rough finish offers the advantage of surer footing, but will be somewhat harder to keep swept clean.

OTHER SPACES. Especially if you are planning to specialize in smaller craftwork, or to pursue such specialties as woodturning or scrollsawing, it is possible to utilize smaller spaces, such as an unused porch, attic, or spare room. Also keep in mind that if you live in a milder climate, tools can be stored indoors and rolled out to be used as needed. In worst-case situations, you may have to set your workshop up in a room that also serves another purpose, such as a laundry room. When this is necessary, hinged benches and other space-saving and conversion tactics become invaluable.

If you are setting up a new shop, or want to move your shop out of the basement for more space and light, one way to find space is to add on to your existing garage. One option is to add on to the back end of either a single- or double-car garage, if lot space allows. You can extend it far enough to provide a basic shop area, and still be able to park in the original garage space. In colder climates, you can separate the new part from the old with a wall, or just temporary canvas, so only the new shop area needs to be heated.

Another option, if you have a single-car garage, is to double its width by splitting it in half lengthwise, moving one side over, and then filling in the middle. With at least double the space, you can use the whole thing for your shop, or you can set up shop on one side and still have room for a vehicle. The basic procedure is first to figure out how much to widen the garage, keeping in mind that the roof peak will become higher as a gable-roofed garage is made wider. Then measure out and pour an extension of the original slab. Next, take out the original garage door, then build temporary 2x4 support walls, one on each side of the ridgeboard, about 2′ apart. Once these are in place, you can split the garage using a Sawzall or chainsaw to cut up the front, along each side of the original ridgeboard and down the back.

With this done, the next step is to cut off any anchoring bolts in the original stud wall on the expansion side, and slide the wall over onto the new slab extension. This can be easy using sections of pipe under the walls and temporary support. Next, install new rafter extensions and ridgeboard, then new joists, collar ties, and roof boards to match the originals. Then install a new header over the new door area, new gable studs, new siding to fill in the front and back, and new shingles (either over just the new roof boards or over the entire roof).

EXPANDING A GARAGE

A single-car garage can be expanded to make room for a shop. With one method it is cut in half, then rafter extensions are sistered to original rafters for at least 48″ and nailed to the new ridgeboard. New joists and collar ties are installed while temporary support walls are in place. A 2x4 brace is used between sections at both the front and back of the garage until the header and back wall are installed. One section of the original garage is rolled onto the slab extension on pipe. The back wall may be separated at the rear corner instead of cutting it down the middle. The last step is to remove the temporary support walls. You can reinstall the same door if you need access for only one vehicle, or have a new double door installed by a specialist. The expansion, even if hired done, should run half of what a new garage would cost.

EXTEND THE SLAB

EXTEND OLD RAFTERS

NEW RIDGE BOARD

OLD WALL SLID OVER, NEW HEADER INSTALLED

TEMPORARY SUPPORT WALLS

NEW GARAGE DOOR

SEARCHING OUT SHOP SPACE

If you decide to locate your workshop in the garage, you will need to find a home for usual garage items, such as rakes, shovels, lawn mowers, fertilizer spreaders, snow throwers, and other home maintenance gear. A good answer can be a backyard storage building built with a concrete slab and simple stud frame construction. If you don't have time to build your own, kits are available at local home centers and lumberyards. While this type of yard shed may relieve the demand for space in the garage, you still may need to build new storage shelving units in the basement, attic, or closets. Or you may find, for example, that you can easily install flooring above the ceiling joists to make a small attic for storing items that only rarely need to be retrieved.

When searching out shop space, an option is to consider remodeling an existing building. Older garages or barns can be remodeled if the roof and foundation are in good condition. But before remodeling, compare the cost with installing a newer metal-clad building. For the extra expense, building from scratch can offer many advantages, including up-to-date electrical and plumbing, extra windows and doors, and more space. When building new, try to put the shop building on high ground with good drainage and with floors at least 12″ above the existing grade. Slope the ground gradually away from the building. If possible, face doors away from prevailing winds to minimize wind damage.

It is best to have any heated shop well insulated, including foundation, sidewalls, and ceiling. Try to insulate sidewalls to at least R-13 and the ceiling to at least R-20. Even a warm-weather shop should have at least R-5 insulation in the ceiling or roof to relieve summer heat, and to minimize winter condensation. There are several options for heating a workshop (see Shop Climate Control, page 48), and some specific decisions to make if you are wiring a new or remodeled shop (see Finishing The Workshop, page 50).

Regardless of shop size, designate specific areas of various shop activities, if possible. Benches can be attached to the walls or be freestanding (see illustrations). Though built-in shelves and benches have the disadvantage of not being portable, often built-ins are a practical, inexpensive way to get a shop organized. The specific building method you use may depend on whether the walls are covered or the wall studs are open. The illustrations show methods of attaching supports directly to a wall stud, as well as a method of building shelf supports to be attached to a covered wall.

With one method, plywood gussets are fastened to both sides of the stud, with 2x4 stock used as a spacer. Such a support is attractive, functional, and very strong.

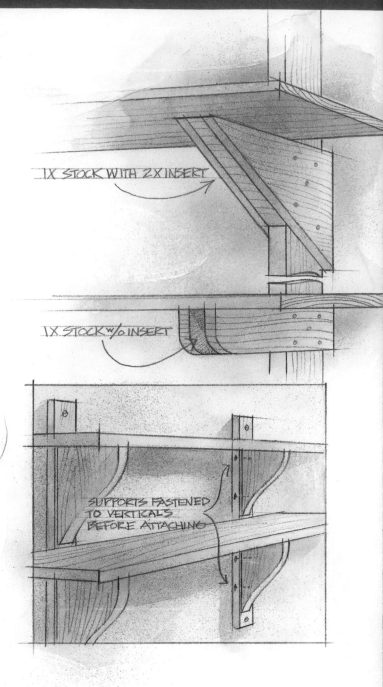

1X STOCK WITH 2X INSERT

1X STOCK W/o INSERT

SUPPORTS FASTENED TO VERTICALS BEFORE ATTACHING

A second method is to build shelf supports directly onto wall studs. This style can be used for shelves that will carry light loads. For covered walls, supports can first be fastened to a wooden standard from behind. Then the entire unit can be attached through the covering into a wall stud.

When fastening the diagonal braces for wall-hung workbenches, it is helpful to predrill nail or screw holes. If benches are freestanding, you can anchor them for more stability. Provide stable bases for tools, but don't fasten them to the floor around work areas; allow for flexibility for large equipment. If your shop will have a welding area, separate it from the woodworking area to reduce fire hazards, and provide space for welders,

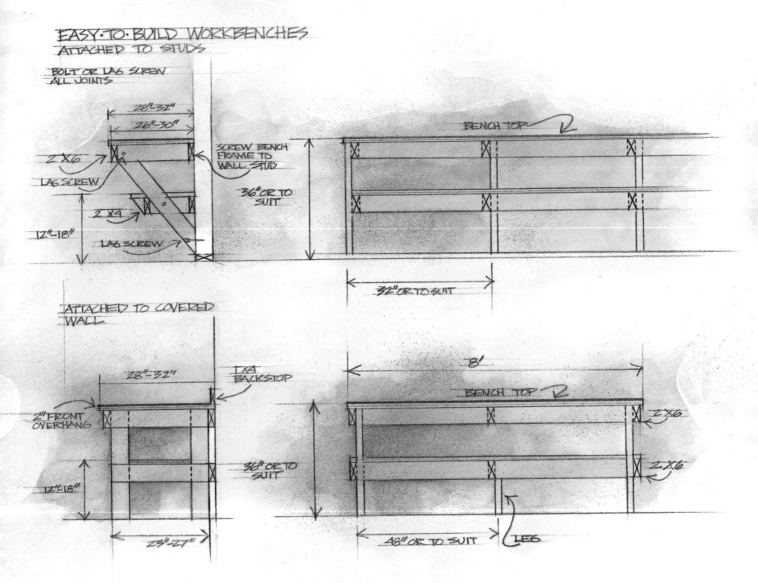

EASY·TO·BUILD WORKBENCHES
ATTACHED TO STUDS

BOLT OR LAG SCREW
ALL JOINTS

28"-32"
26"-30"

2×6

SCREW BENCH
FRAME TO
WALL STUD

LAG SCREW

36" OR TO
SUIT

2×4

12"-18"

LAG SCREW

BENCH TOP

32" OR TO SUIT

ATTACHED TO COVERED
WALL

28"-32"

1×4
BACKSTOP

2" FRONT
OVERHANG

8'

BENCH TOP

2×6

36" OR TO
SUIT

12"-18"

2×6

23"-27"

48" OR TO SUIT

LEG

grinders, anvil, and storage for metal and welding rods. Consider putting the welding area near an outside door. Line the wall in the welding area with fire-retardant materials (see Finishing The Workshop, page 50). If your shop will have a machining area, a good size is 8´ to 24´ long and 8´ to 12´ wide, depending on tool sizes. Consider putting any machining area next to the welding area so that the grinder, anvil, and welding table are available to both. A welding table should be at least 6˝ from the wall. The machining area can include roll-about tool boxes, hoists, and movable tools like bearing presses when they are not in use. They can be moved when the repair area needs to be widened temporarily.

For all shops, it is a good idea to provide convenient

storage for plans, records, and manuals: in a small shop, a section of a workbench, or in a larger shop, an enclosed room in one corner used for an office. Engineers suggest putting any office larger than about 10x12´ in an attached single-story addition, rather than within the shop. Building storage space over an office requires expensive, heavy-duty ceiling framing that cannot be justified in most cases. Although expensive, a restroom improves the working conditions and a convenient cleanup area. In separate shop buildings, at least a sink should be available for cleanup and safety. A frost-free hydrant and drain may be sufficient in smaller shops.

SHOP CLIMATE CONTROL

The biggest factor that keeps many shop owners in northern areas of the country from pursuing more projects is the cold. They do not want a shop in the basement, yet never get around to installing a workable system to heat the shop area in the garage or other building. If this is your case, consider the advantages of making the investment. Instead of being able to use the shop only six months out of the year or less, at the same time other summer activities compete with your shop projects, you will have the option of pursuing projects over the quiet months, and greatly expand your project schedule options.

The first possibility to consider is whether your existing heating/cooling system can be extended to service the shop area, if it is attached to the home. Extending ducts of a forced-air system, or piping for a water heating system, could be the simplest way to go. In many cases heating/cooling systems are oversized and may be able to handle the additional load. Check the Btu capacity of your system, measure out the square footage now being heated or cooled, and check with a heating/air conditioning dealer. If the existing system will not handle the extra load, a second approach is to install an additional conventional forced-air system if the shop is in a garage or separate building. When installing a forced-air system, try to separate it from the workshop area and take precautions to keep dust away from any flames. Cold-air return ducts can be fitted with appropriate filters to keep dust away from the furnace's pilot light and burner.

Another option, regardless of shop location, is simply to install electric baseboard heating, if electricity is reasonably priced, and a room air conditioner if needed. This option will generally increase the operating costs per day of use. However, if the shop is used only occasionally, the extra cost may not be that much. If a forced-air system is not used for cooling, a room-sized air conditioner installed through a window or wall may be enough to make shopwork tolerable. In areas of the Southwest with low relative humidity, some shop owners find that evaporative cooling, using what are called "swamp coolers," can take the sting out of blistering hot days.

Many workshops in rural areas across the country are heated with wood stoves, which vary from the double-barrel stoves that you can build right in your shop with purchased hardware, to conventionally marketed wood stoves, to stoves that are built to desired specs by local metalworkers. Heating with wood does take extra time; however, there is a special satisfaction in being able to work while listening to the fire crackling and being able

to toss in wood scraps as they are produced to both clean up and generate heat. Some types of these stoves can burn coal; others are modified to burn rubber tires, if local ordinances permit, or other available materials such as corncobs. A relatively new option is the "wood pellet" stove, which burns pellets of wood and can be direct vented.

Since the first energy crunch in the Seventies, outside wood furnaces have made their appearance, and offer special advantages. They cut installation expense, save space inside the shop, and keep wood, ashes, smoke, and fire hazards outside your workshop. A typical outside wood furnace might have a heavy-gauge steel combustion chamber mounted inside a double-wall galvanized steel exterior with insulation between the walls, and might be able to produce as much as 400,000 Btu to heat up to 10,000 square feet of space. Some units have a blower mounted on top of the furnace, controlled by a thermostat inside the shop. Burn rate is controlled by manually adjusting a damper on the unit. Such outside furnaces can be installed in as little as two hours, through a window or wall, or can also be connected to existing ductwork.

In colder climates, ceiling-mounted forced-air space heaters work well because they help keep hot air from stagnating near the ceiling. One recommendation is to size shop heating equipment at about 50 Btu per square foot of shop floor area, and to use a minimum of 70,000 Btu/hour if the shop is fan vented at 1,000 cubic feet per minute (cfm). Ceiling-mounted infrared heaters, such as those often used in auto repair shops, may also be a good choice because energy is not wasted heating up air in the shop; only persons and objects struck by infrared rays are heated.

Other options for portable, temporary shop heating include space heaters using kerosene or fuel oil, though these require fresh-air ventilation and have the defect of being smelly. Electric convection heaters, another choice, use a large number of aluminum fins shaped to draw in cold air from the floor and emit a rising stream of warm air without using moving parts. Radiant heaters, on the other hand, use a heavy-duty electric element to generate heat, which is blown into the area by a built-in fan. Available in sizes from about 2,000 on up to 6,000 watts, these can be moved around to different areas, or suspended from the ceiling.

New technology has made an older radiant heating concept a viable choice for some shop owners (see The Hydronic Option, opposite). The system involves attaching a grid of special plastic piping to the rebar of a slab before it is poured. The heart of the system is simply a water heater that pushes fluid through the pipes in the slab. It is also possible to install such a system over existing slabs, or if need be, in the ceiling of a workshop.

With hydronic floor heating, a water heater can be used to heat the workshop area. A special type of polyethylene (PEX) tubing is installed in a serpentined pattern within a slab before it is poured. With appropriate brass fittings and manifolds, the system is connected to a water heater which circulates either warm water or an appropriate glycol solution of between 85° and 115° through the tubing.

Heat is transferred from the tubing to the floor, turning the whole floor into a low-temperature radiator. Heat generated is controlled by adjusting the flow and/or the temperature of the circulating fluid. Besides being installed in a slab, the tubing can also be encased in a lightweight overpour, or snapped into grooved aluminum panels under suspended wood floors or on ceilings.

Wirsbo Company, a major system supplier that makes its own tubing, notes that radiant floor heating is installed in more than half of all new construction in Europe. A disadvantage is the relatively high cost of the tubing, which boosts up-front costs. However, the system results in a more even, comfortable heat than forced-air systems, without drafts, hot or cold spots, and radiators or duct grilles. The company, with headquarters in Sweden, reports that heating costs can be 40% to 50% less than with traditional systems.

THE HYDRONIC OPTION

The illustration shows a typical tubing pattern, which is designed to deliver heat according to the heat loss of a structure or individual room. The ⅝″ tubing, tied to the reinforcing mesh before a slab is poured, is designed to outlast the structure itself. For existing concrete slabs, tubing can be stapled above the concrete on foam insulation, after which a layer of lightweight concrete is poured. A water heater or boiler used to heat the fluid can be fueled by any available source.

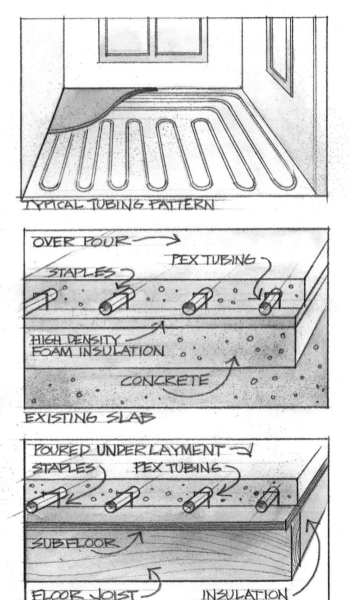

TYPICAL TUBING PATTERN

TYPES OF INSTALLATION

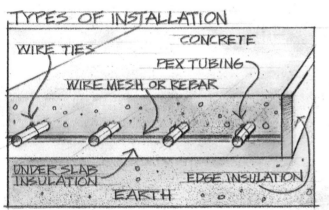

CONCRETE POUR

EXISTING SLAB

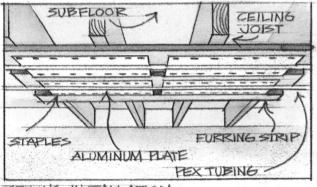

CEILING INSTALLATION

WOOD SUBFLOOR

FINISHING THE WORKSHOP

Many smaller shops operate on as little as 60-amp service with one or two electrical circuits. However, users of these shops must constantly avoid using heavier equipment simultaneously; upgrading to a larger service and additional circuits would provide great benefits from both safety and convenience standpoints. For the modern, all-around workshop that depends heavily on power tools, the minimum electrical service should be 200 amps and 240 volts. If you are planning to wire a workshop, or add to an existing electrical system, work with local building officials and follow all electrical safety precautions. Some basics:

• Circuits of 120 volts have one hot wire, one circuit neutral, and one equipment ground. The hot wire is usually black or red, the circuit neutral is white, and the equipment ground is bare or green. Do not connect the equipment ground to the circuit neutral. The circuit neutral and the equipment ground must run without interruption to all equipment.

• Circuits of 240 volts have two hot wires and an equipment ground. Circuit neutrals are not required by most 240-volt equipment. If a tool has both 120- and 240-volt circuits, both the circuit neutral and the equipment ground are required. To have 240 volts available, there must be three wires running from the power supplier transformer to the building.

• Motor circuits require special handling; the best advice is to seek out special references and/or rely on a professional electrician. In general, every circuit that supplies power to a motor must have branch circuit short-circuit protection, a disconnecting means, a controller to start and stop the motor, and an overload protection device to disconnect the motor if it should fail to start or become overloaded.

• Three-phase motors found on some shop equipment operate more efficiently than single-phase motors, but require three-phase power supply. When buying used shop equipment, check the plate on the motor. Unless you live in an industrial area, it is likely three-phase power won't be supplied, and making it available would probably be cost-prohibitive. If you don't have

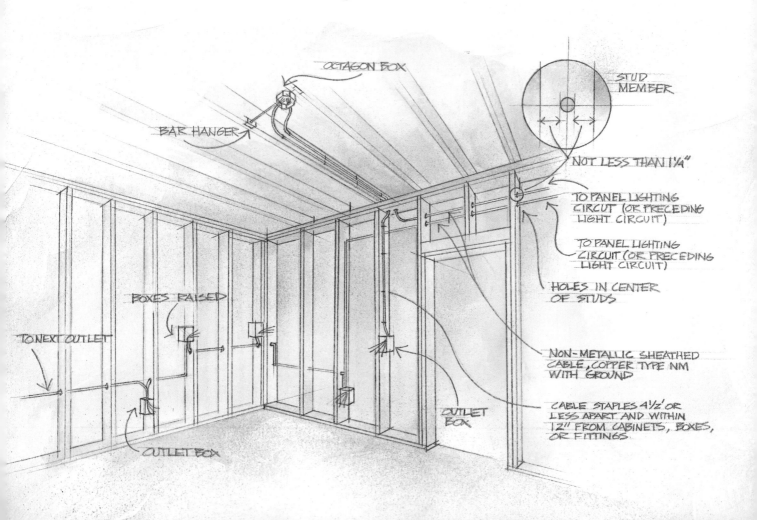

three-phase power, but need it, an alternative is to buy a roto-phase converter, which itself resembles an electric motor and converts 240 single-phase to three-phase power. They are not cheap; a 5-hp converter, for example, might cost $800.

To help map out your shop's electrical system, first add up your power wattage requirements for all lighting and tools. (Two helpful formulas are volts x amps = watts, or watts divided by volts = amps.) Generally the maximum load for one 15-amp circuit using either 14-gauge or 12-gauge wire should be less than about 1,500 watts, and less than about 2,000 watts for a 20-amp circuit using 12-gauge wire.

A rule of thumb is that you can put from 8 to 10 lights or outlets on a circuit, but check this with local officials. In some cases, duplex convenience outlets and lights can be on the same circuit, but a load on an outlet can flicker the lights. Basically you can put in as many outlets as you wish, as long as you have enough circuits to handle them. Position outlets uniformly over workbench areas, near every motor-driven tool, and around the rest of the shop's perimeter, 4′ above the floor. (One idea to minimize problems with tool cords is to attach benches to the wall and provide outlets under the front edge of the benches.) Ground-fault circuit interrupters (GFCIs) are recommended on all 20-amp outlet circuits, and are required for outside receptacles.

Nothing reduces project efficiency more than not being able to see. For most shops a minimum of 20 foot-candles of lighting at floor level is good: a minimum of ½ watt fluorescent, or 2 watts incandescent per square foot of shop floor area. Painting ceilings and upper walls a light color will also help (see Shop Wall Choices below). Above benches, provide 48″ double-tube fluorescent fixtures, mounted about 48″ above the bench surface. Hang them away from the wall, preferably over the front third of the bench. For extra light for specific jobs, consider buying trouble lights, task lights that can be clamped near areas like vises and drill presses, or newer halogen utility lights, which can flood a shop with almost more light than you might need.

SHOP WALL CHOICES. When finishing an area for a workshop, the wall material you use is a matter of personal taste and budget. Some shop owners who have used traditional drywall, and work with long lumber note that the relatively soft wall surface soon becomes scarred, nicked, and gouged. Wall material with harder surfaces can include plywood, particle board, paneling, or even dimensional lumber. Even if your shop area already has drywall installed, covering it with paneling will not only make it more nick-resistant but make it easier to hang items without searching for wall studs. If you use pegboard on shop walls, it can pay to first install spacers of wood or washers so the holes over the studs will also accept wire hooks and brackets.

Some workshop owners are installing newer-style panels of what is called either slotwall or slatwall. It's the pressure-formed 4x8′ fiberboard panel often seen in retail stores that has horizontal T-shaped tracks which can be fitted with a variety of hooks and brackets. Typically slotwall panels are rated to hold a 35-lb. load per bracket; they also can be bought with metal inserts that boost the load rating to 65 lbs. per bracket. A disadvantage of using this material in a workshop is that the horizontal slots serve as dust-catchers and take extra time and effort to keep clean.

In areas where you will be doing welding, or other work involving torches, its best to consider more flame-resistant wall materials, such as ½″ fire-retardant treated plywood or ⅝″ exterior plywood. Or cover flammable wall liners with 29-gauge galvanized steel, 0.032″ aluminum, ½″ cement plaster, or ½″ fire-rated gypsum board.

When using natural wood surfaces, keep in mind that coatings such as shellac or polyurethane can result in surface glare. If using these materials, consider selecting low-gloss versions. If the wall material is to be painted, keep in mind that dark colors absorb more natural and artificial light than lighter colors. For example, light green will typically reflect light at a rate of about 41%, while medium gray will reflect about 43%, apricot-beige about 66%, light ivory about 71%, and white about 80%.

SOUNDPROOFING THE SHOP. Besides dust control, a major disadvantage of a workshop inside the home, such as in the basement, is the problem of noise. Workshop machinery can produce noise rated as high as 115 decibels, which not only imposes a real hazard to the shop owner but can cause distress throughout the home. Even noise from a workshop set up in a separate building can bring complaints from neighbors.

Fortunately, sound-reduction strategies are available to bring noise levels under control. These include the use of acoustical tiles or panels on walls and ceiling, building walls in special ways, repositioning electrical and plumbing connections, lining and wrapping ducts, and covering floors with sound-absorbing materials. An excellent source, if you are attempting to reduce workshop noise, is *Home Carpentry: Improvements and Repairs* by Thomas H. Jones. It details, for example, several methods of building walls to reduce sound transmission, as well as the sound absorption values of general building materials and room contents.

A basic rule of thumb for a workshop within the home is to apply sound-absorbing material on at least half of the total ceiling, wall, and floor area of the room. Start with an acoustical ceiling, then add sound-absorbing areas to the walls, or cover the floor with a carpet and pad, or with carpet, pad, and acoustic underlayment. If covering the floor of a basement shop area is not desirable, cover the floor above the shop ceiling. For walls, select acoustical tiles or panels that can withstand being poked or bumped. There are more than a dozen options for building walls from scratch, starting with conventional single studs using one layer of drywall on both sides and no insulation (lowest sound control), and progressing to double-stud walls using two layers of drywall on both sides, with insulation inside the cavity against the shop-side drywall (highest sound control).

A practical approach is to insulate stud wall cavities before applying drywall, and insulating ceiling joist cavities before installing acoustical tile. If noise is still a problem, experiment by adding a layer of ½″ SoundStop board over the drywall, then another layer of drywall. Other techniques include using sound-deadening acoustical tile over hollow-core doors, dampening the vibration of workshop machinery, sealing electrical and plumbing systems with caulk or insulation, and plugging open gaps where necessary (such as by installing sweeps under workshop doors).

DECIDING ON PEGBOARD

A running controversy exists about the use of pegboard in the home workshop. Some shop enthusiasts love it, and use as much of it as possible. Others detest it, claiming it leads to a gross underuse of wall space, and pointing out that often a wall full of tools could just as well be stored in a drawer or two. As with wall-covering materials, opinions vary. Pegboard can be found with either ⅛″ or ¼″ holes spaced 1″ apart.

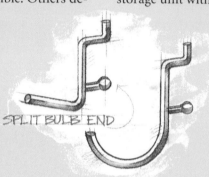

SPLIT BULB END

One reason some shop owners hate pegboard storage is because commonly available brackets have a tendency to pull out and drop off when tools or other items are removed. However, improved pegboard brackets are available by mail-order; with one style, the bracket is locked in place with the turn of a screwdriver. Several other solutions exist to solve this problem, as illustrated above. In addition, some shop owners say to heck with commercial brackets and make their own, or use appropriately sized dowels instead to make hooks and supports.

Many shop owners detest the common shop hint of tracing around tools, or making a silhouette of the tool, as an aid in remembering what goes where. If you likewise believe this makes a shop look like kindergarten class, you can simply use a labeling machine to make small labels to serve as reminders.

Even if you do not like pegboard on walls, there are other ways to use it. One is to make up a special tool storage unit with pegboard used in the style of pages in a book, as shown on page 96. Another is to use it either inside or outside storage cabinet doors, with appropriate lumber spacers under it to allow room for brackets to be inserted.

If you have access to the rear side of pegboard, discarded nylons can be used instead of brackets to hold tools and equipment. Knot one end, feed the nylon through the back, and loop through appropriate holes to wrap around brackets, or to hold the tools you want to hang there. Nylons stretch to hold various tool shapes, and will hold tools more securely than conventional pegboard hooks.

Another way to keeping pegboard hooks from coming out is to use your staple gun. Shoot a ¼″ or larger staple over the hook, as far down on it as possible. Once done, you will have eliminated that annoying fallout when removing tools or other items. Glue can also keep wire hooks on pegboard. Simply insert the hook into the pegboard, then glue the holes shut using an electric hot-melt glue gun. In a minute or so, the hook is fixed, although you can wrestle it off when you want to rearrange your tools.

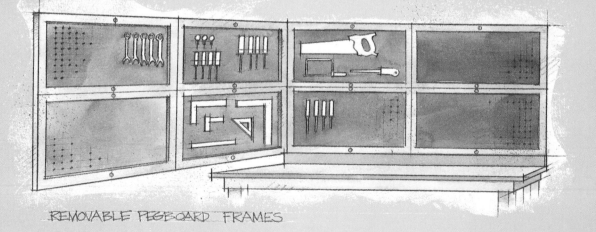

REMOVABLE PEGBOARD FRAMES

CONTROLLING SHOP SAWDUST

The first step up from the shop broom in mechanizing cleanup is the wet/dry vac. Newer versions sport higher horsepower, larger filters, variable speed, and built-in drains. A larger collector hooked to a built-in duct system, however, is more effective and convenient.

Not that many years ago, cleaning up was as much a part of shop-work as sawing or gluing. But an increased awareness of the hazards of breathing the sawdust generated in woodworking procedures (especially from some of the more exotic tropical woods) has increased the interest of woodworkers in various methods to keep it under control.

Equipment such as saws and sanders are increasingly available with dust chutes and bags to trap sawdust, or to hook up to shop vacuums. And, while small shop vacuums have come to the rescue of even the smallest shop, many home woodworkers are installing bigger equipment designed specifically for collecting dust and chips. This equipment includes more powerful and efficient shop vacs, as well as larger dust-collection machines that can be connected to individual woodworking tools or to a central duct system made up of both rigid and flexible pipe.

Besides the cost for the dust collector, a central sawdust duct system can cost anywhere from a low of about $250 on upward. But many woodworkers consider it worth more than its cost to whisk away debris from the shop environment. Not only does keeping sawdust under control make for a healthier working quarters, it can also prevent potential explosions. Even with collector and duct systems installed, many woodworkers will also wear a dust mask.

Another big advantage of a central dust-control system is that it can also save loads of time. With it you don't need to waste time moving a collector from one machine to another every time you switch to a different operation. Most of all, many shop owners enjoy not having to clean up constantly. They observe that when they head out to the shop, they want to do something other than sweep up chips and sawdust.

Shop vacuums have gotten bigger and quieter over the years, and more tool manufacturers have equipped their tools for easy hookups to them. Still, with their 1¼″ or 2½″ hoses and lower cubic feet per minute (cfm), smaller vacs are often just not up to the job of removing piles of chips and dust produced by wood-hungry tools, especially surface planers, shapers, or jointers. The minimum airflow needed to handle debris from woodworking tools ranges from about 300 to 700 cfm. Most home shop vacs provide about 100 cfm and "industrial" vacs, about 120 cfm.

Dust collectors, which operate on a different principle than shop vacuums, offer more muscle. Even smaller ones can provide from about 700 to 1,300 cfm. Their fan blades turn at much slower rpms, moving a larger volume of air at less pressure. They don't have the high-pitched "scream" of a shop vacuum either. The smallest of the dust collectors generally has motors of 1, 2, or 3 hp. The smallest will work with about 10′ of hose. But the larger are big enough to connect to a built-in duct system. They can be set in one corner and will siphon away saw debris from any power tool, regardless of its location in the home workshop.

Besides allowing a dust collector to be kept in one spot, a properly built central duct system can do a better job of collecting dust at each tool to keep a workshop cleaner and make it a better place to work. When it pays to install a duct system boils down to how many tools you have. If you have only one or two major tools, the advantage of a central duct system might be questionable. But if you have three or more major tools, a system will pay off in convenience, if nothing else. A good way to proceed is to buy the dust collector, put it on casters, and use it by rolling it to your individual tools. Then, when you get tired of rolling the collector around, consider installing a central duct system.

Setting up a sawdust collection system is getting easier. Major marketers, such as Sears, offer low-cost hood/hose kits for full-size table- and radial-arm saws, above, as well as complete manifold systems for a shop full of stationary tools, opposite page. The hood/hose kits or the manifold system can be connected to your shop wet/dry vac, or to a larger collector.

The flexible manifold system includes eight 3' sections of clear plastic tubing with elbows and five waste gates. The system mounts on the walls of the shop to draw debris from up to five free-standing tools. The hood/hose kits cost less than $50 each, while the manifold system runs less than $100.

DESIGN BASICS

You don't have to start from scratch to design a central duct collection system for your shop. Years of hard engineering work have already gone into researching and building large commercial systems. The same principles apply to a home workshop, only scaled down. Manufacturers have developed guides to help install a duct system in home shops; one prepared by Delta is called *Central Dust Collection Systems.* Check with local dealers for current guides available, or write to manfacers of collection equipment.

Air isn't really sucked into a vacuum hose or dust collector; technically, it's pushed into them. It works like this: The blower of a dust collector creates reduced pressure inside the collector. As a result, atmospheric air pressure pushes air toward the low-pressure area. In a dust-collection system, enough air current must be generated at the tool to push that dust into the duct. The velocity must be high enough to first overcome the momentum of a chip thrown off by a cutting tool, then to push that chip to the collection system. Here are some basic design suggestions:

Diameter. In a central, built-in system, try to keep the duct diameter as large as possible to get the highest amount of airflow. However, going too big can drop air velocity below 3,500 feet per minute (fpm), a point where dust can drop out of the air and clog the duct.

Material. Try to use smooth duct material, if possible, to keep airflow resistance down. You get less friction and turbulence in a smooth-wall, round-pipe duct. Friction can jump 50% in a ribbed hose.

Bends. Try to use gradually curved bends to change the direction of the airflow. At a bend, air and dust hit the duct wall, bounce back, and cause turbulent resistance. This resistance, for example, can be 100% higher in a right-angle 90° fitting than in a curved 90° elbow.

Connections. Try to avoid connecting a small duct to a larger duct, or attaching small-diameter hood connections to a large duct. These situations reduce the air entering the larger duct, possibly causing clogging. Inlets of hoods not attached to a tool cabinet should have at least a 2″-wide flange on all sides to cut down stray airflow from behind the inlet.

Inlets. Once the system is set up, keep only one air inlet open to the duct system at a time to get enough airflow at the tool you are using. You can keep the inlets at unused tools shut off with removable plugs or with slide gates, also sometimes called blast gates. (Also try to avoid rotating dampers; they create turbulence that can cause clogging.)

SYSTEM STRATEGIES

To design industrial duct systems, engineers crunch through complicated calculations on computers. To sidestep this for small shops, engineers have put together a more simplified procedure that focuses on pipe-length run, plus the extra airflow resistance caused by duct fittings like elbows, tees, and inlets. They use a chart to convert the extra resistance of such fittings into the equivalent length of straight pipe runs.

For example, the resistance of a 90° uncurved elbow, or the side leg of a 90° tee translate to roughly the same resistance found in 20′ of smooth pipe. The resistance of an unflanged hood inlet, likewise, translates to the equivalent of 10′ of pipe. Adding up all the figures, and using them with a set of curves plotted for a specific dust collector, they can figure out the cfm you could expect at a particular tool when all other inlets are closed. If it's found, for example, that the air volume isn't enough, your options would be to change the diameter of the duct pipe, change the layout to cut down the length of duct, or go with a bigger dust collector.

Usually 4″ or 5″ duct pipe will do the job in a home shop. It can be of plastic, rubber, or sheetmetal smooth-

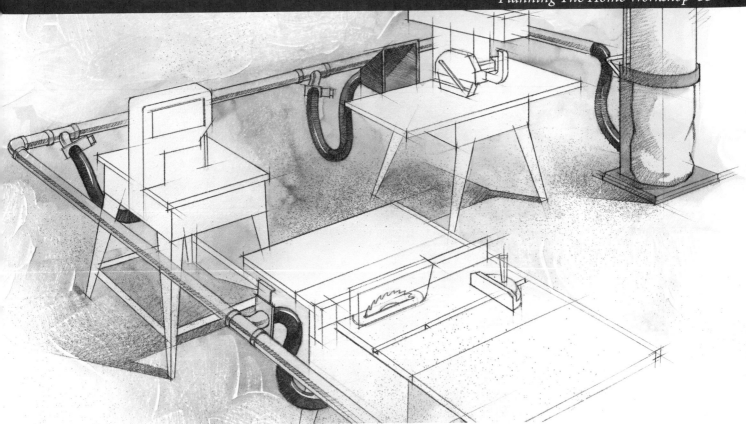

wall pipe. Each type has its own pros and cons:

• Plastic drain pipe and fittings are easy to work with and readily available in 3″, 4″, and 6″ diameters. Sheetmetal furnace pipe and fittings are available in most diameters, including 5″, but installation takes more time than with plastic.

• Some kinds of semiflexible, wire-reinforced, smoothwall rubber hose can be used for a main duct. However, you need to use plastic or sheetmetal fittings with it, which is more expensive than plastic or sheetmetal.

• Flexible ribbed hose can be used for short runs and for duct to tool connections. Dryer vent hose, not generally a good choice, can sometimes be used for little-used or low-abrasion connections.

Engineers emphasize the importance of guarding against the build-up of static electricity. There's no problem with metal "furnace" pipe, but plastic must be grounded to avoid fire hazards. This can be done by running a bare ground wire from each tool to a ground connection at the dust collector inside the plastic pipe. If the system will carry large chips, such as from a planer, the wire will need to be stretched tightly against the inside bottom wall. (Some shop owners report an alternative method is to wrap copper wire spiral-fashion around the outside instead of using a wire inside.)

The wire inside wire-reinforced, semiflexible hose provides a built-in ground system. But if plastic fittings are installed with it, an electrical ground connection must be made between two sections of the hose.

INSTALLING YOUR OWN

For home workshops, Delta engineers favor using 45° wye tee fittings for branch or drop ducts. (These are called sanitary tees in plastic pipe and wye branch tees in sheetmetal pipe.) Then, a 45° elbow can be added to the 45° branch of the wye tee to complete a 90° branch joint. Here's the general procedure:

1. Start at the dust collector and run the main duct to the first side branch or drop. Keep the duct level and use plenty of metal tape hangers to support the duct and fittings.

2. Next, attach the wye or sanitary tee fittings at branch or drop duct connections. Avoid 90° tee fittings.

3. Install any slide gates to be used at convenient locations, usually at shoulder height. You must be able to close each tool inlet or branch duct, either by slide gate or inlet plug.

4. Keep the small (male) end of each pipe section or fitting pointing in the direction of the air flow (toward the dust collector). This reduces air friction and prevents chip clogging.

5. Run the pipe as far as possible to each tool to minimize the use of branch hoses.

The next challenge is to figure out how to hook the system up to your power tools. Companies selling dust collectors will generally have hoods available for radial-arm saws, tablesaws, and jointers, as well as what they call side hoods and straight hoods. These come with collars 4″, 5″, or 6″ in diameter. Some companies, such as Murphy-Rodgers (2301 Belgrave Ave., Huntington Park, CA 90255), also sell what is called a "catcher strip," which is basically a collar on a 9x36″ metal strip. With it, you can make a dust-collection hood for any power tool. You simply cut the sides of your hood from plywood, attach the catcher strip to the edges, and seal the joints so they are airtight.

After your central duct system is installed, keep in mind that excessive dust in a collector drum or filter bag will restrict airflow and cut performance. Take time to empty collector drums when half full, and closed-style filter bags when they are a quarter full. (A drum-mounted filter bag can be run until the drum is full, but it's good to give the bag a shake at least once every 4 hours of use.) Also take care of air leaks into the system right away. Wash and dry the filter bag of the collector once or twice a year to restore filter efficiency.

Even in a smaller shop of about 13x23′, it is possible to customize ductwork to specifically handle the various tools. For example, a flexible hose on one branch could be alternated between a tablesaw and a planer. Then a second branch could go to a jointer, and a third branch to a shaper. One thing to consider is incorporating a special hood called a "floor sweep" into your system. It can be mounted at floor level, with its own slide gate. You can open it up and sweep floor dust or chips directly over to it. Once you have set up a collection system, don't throw out your shop vacuum or other dust gear; it still will come in handy.

How Much Airflow?

Below are practical airflow rates for light-duty home shops. These rates, in cubic feet per minute (cfm), are as much as 50% lower than industrial standards.

300: Jigsaw, drill press, ½″ spindle shaper, up to 16″ tablesaw, up to 6″ vertical belt sander, and disc sander up to 12″.

350: Radial-arm saw, floor sweep, and jointers from 4″ to 12″.

400: Bandsaw with a 2″ blade, planer up to 20″.

500: Lathe, and shaper with 1″ spindle.

Equivalent Length Values

Duct or fitting*	Equivalent length
Smooth-wall pipe	Actual length
Corrugated pipe/hose	Actual length x 1.5
Unflanged hood inlet	10′
90° T-fitting or 90° hose bend	10′
45° curved elbow	5′
Side leg of 90° tee	20′
Side leg of 90° wye tee	5′

* The length value for the following are 0′: Duct inlet from tool cabinet/built-in hood; flanged hood inlet; straight-through tee leg; slide gate, and 5′ ribbed hose.

How Duct Length Reduces Airflow

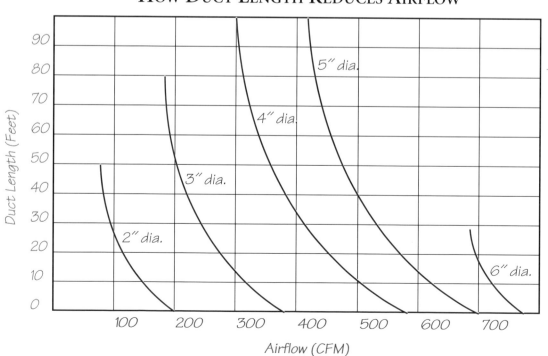

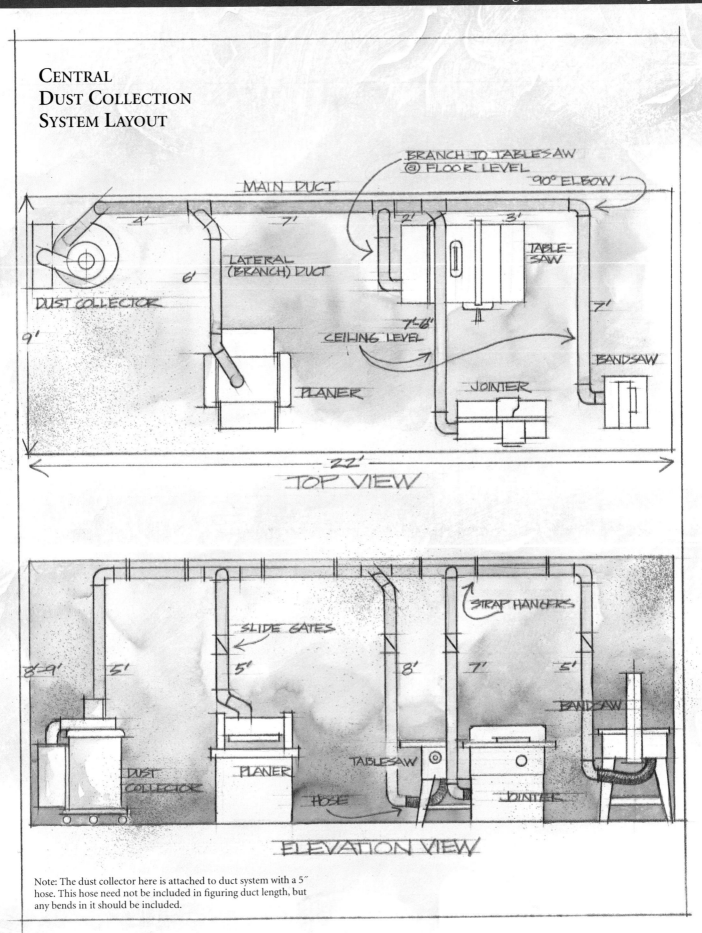

CENTRAL
DUST COLLECTION
SYSTEM LAYOUT

BRANCH TO TABLESAW
@ FLOOR LEVEL

MAIN DUCT

90° ELBOW

4'

7'

2'

3'

TABLE-SAW

LATERAL
(BRANCH) DUCT

6'

7'

DUST COLLECTOR

9'

7'-6"

CEILING LEVEL

BANDSAW

PLANER

JOINTER

22'

TOP VIEW

STRAP HANGERS

SLIDE GATES

8'-9'

5'

5'

8'

7'

5'

BANDSAW

DUST COLLECTOR

PLANER

TABLESAW

HOSE

JOINTER

ELEVATION VIEW

Note: The dust collector here is attached to duct system with a 5″ hose. This hose need not be included in figuring duct length, but any bends in it should be included.

Shop Planning Checklist

The following listing capsulizes advice from dozens of shop owners on goals to shoot for in setting up a home workshop. Many are just good common sense, others are bits of intelligence that have been learned the hard way. All echo the voice of experience that can help you think through your plan so your workshop will become the best possible.

❏ Find space other than in the basement of your home if possible. If no other space is available, be prepared to spend time and money in making the byproducts of the workshop compatible with family living.

❏ Make use of natural light and ventilation as much as possible; a guideline is that windows and skylights should make up at least 10% of your shop's total square footage.

❏ Make shop shelves and storage areas as accessible as possible. For example, keep plastic parts drawers at eye level so you can see what is inside the bins and not have to pull out 32 drawers to find a small item.

❏ Design shop components to minimize cleanup. When selecting materials for walls or building storage, keep in mind that dust will land and stay on any horizontal surface. At the bottom of shelves and benches, for example, install strips of plywood so you don't need to constantly sweep underneath.

❏ Have as much closed storage as possible, keep debris off shelves, and keep tools dust-free. Doors on cabinets or shelves make the shop look neater, and the inside of the doors can be fitted with holders or pegboard for small-tool storage.

❏ Select low-maintenance wall and floor materials, with light surface colors that will help reflect available light and make the shop area more cheerful. Because of bumping and nicking, harder materials such as paneling may be a better choice than softer materials like drywall.

❏ Avoid built-in components so that you can take your entire shop with you when you move. Separate benches and shelf units, for example, may be a better choice than those permanently attached to walls.

❏ Maintain an experimental attitude, searching the shops of others for ideas you can use. Don't think that there is only one way to set up a shop; if something might work better, give it a try.

❏ Provide space and equipment for planning, drawing, or reading plans or blueprints in a shop of any size.

❏ Set up the electrical system in the shop so that all power tool circuits can be shut off at one secondary load center. Try to have lighting fed from more than one circuit so that if one blows some light is available.

❏ Have lumber storage easily accessible and, if possible, have a separate, closed storage room so that moisture can be monitored and controlled.

❏ Design the shop so that dust collectors can be located in a separate, insulated area, or in another room, to minimize noise levels.

❏ Be generous with your electrical budget when building a shop from scratch, installing more circuits, receptacles, and lighting than you think you will need. Have receptacles protected by ground-fault circuit interrupters (GFCIs).

❏ Find and install an adequate and economical heating/cooling system; personal discomfort leads to hurrying, mistakes, and possible accidents.

❏ Have adequate work surfaces in the shop; even if you have several workbenches, space for pre-assembly and assembly will make project work more orderly.

❏ Provide a nonslip floor surface, and comfort mats for extra foot comfort in areas where you will be standing most of the time.

❏ Have the walls and ceiling of a garage workshop insulated, regardless of climate, to increase heating/cooling efficiencies and to increase your own comfort level.

❏ Standardize working heights of benches and tools wherever possible to make handling larger boards and panels easier.

❏ Categorize tools and hardware by type of activity to make it easier to locate and replace, e.g., cutting, gluing, fastening, sanding, finishing.

❏ Plan for under-bench storage of heavier items and tools; use cutouts under benches for accessories such as shop vacuums, and for tool boards, totes, or boxes.

❏ Minimize use of extension cords in the shop wherever possible; always avoid running cords permanently across floors.

❏ Develop a system to control waste and debris; plan to have at least two waste receptacles available at all times, and consider special receptacles near debris-producing machines.

❏ Size shop doors with enough height and width to allow easy moving of raw materials and finished projects. Sliding doors might offer more access without wasting space.

❏ Have a heavy, solid surface on any bench to which tools are attached; if necessary, use a thick hardwood board under bench attachments such as vises.

❏ Use latches on doors instead of knobs, to allow opening when hands are full, or in emergencies.

❏ Have safety equipment, such as smoke alarms and fire extinguishers, installed, accessible, and maintained.

❏ Provide a special area for finishing projects, with proper fans and natural ventilation available to exhaust potentially toxic fumes, closed off from the rest of the shop to help control dust.

❏ Have a first-aid safety station somewhere in the workshop; having a sink with running water available is a good idea.

❏ Install a house-to-workshop intercom; it will increase convenience and be available for emergencies. Consider a phone that lights up, as well as rings.

❏ Provide for shop layout flexiblity by using casters under tools and benches; they will allow you to change your mind on arrangements and to rearrange layouts.

❏ Minimize wasted effort by using efficient work triangles between your supplies, the tool being used, and your workbench.

❏ Allot time for shop maintenance; keeping cheaper tools in top condition is better than having expensive tools out of adjustment and with dull blades.

Section II
Setting Up The Home Workshop

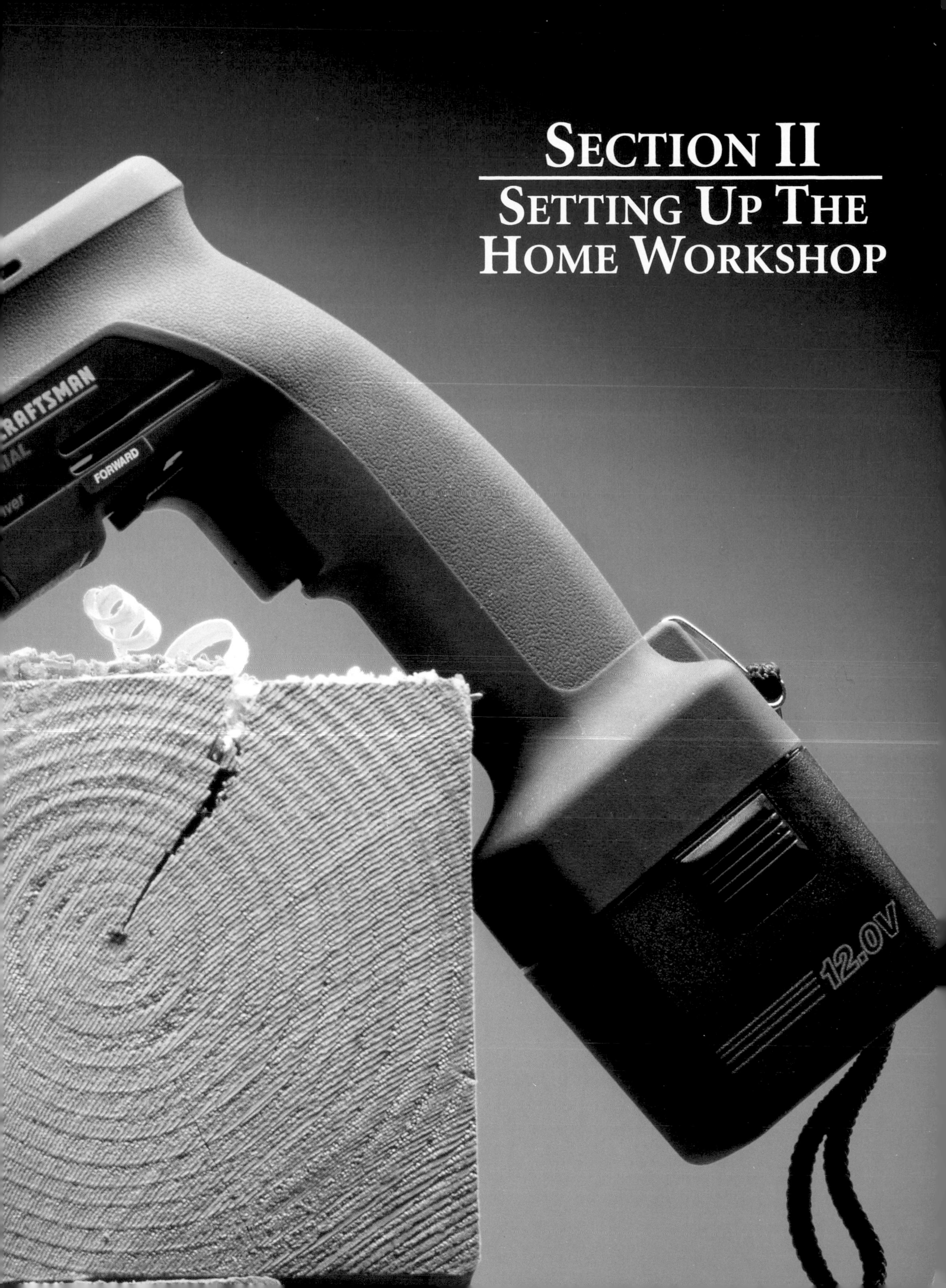

THE START-UP WORKSHOP

A basic workbench is the first order of business for even the most bare-bones workshop. It can be as simple as a supported section of plywood to start, and improved versions can be built later. The machinist's vise, above, also can be adapted to handle wood.

This example workshop, which will cost you roughly $1,000 or less to assemble, could also be called the portable shop. All the tools suggested will fit into a small cabinet or a couple of larger toolboxes, tool boards, or 5-gallon pails for both storage and easy portability. Though these tools make up a minimal arsenal, you will be able to make straight or irregular cuts, drill holes, drive screws, and sand materials for finishing or refinishing. And with the router, you can add a professional touch to your woodworking projects.

Best of all, the tools you buy at this stage can be used in your workshop no matter how complex it becomes, though you may want to upgrade them to higher-priced, heavier-duty tools as time passes and your skill increases (see Shop Tool Buying Menu, page 26). The bench grinder, a relatively inexpensive item, will serve you well in touching up blade tools, such as knives and shovels, and with proper accessories will provide motorized sharpening of edges such as chisels and drill bits.

If you are starting from scratch, the first order of business will be to build some type of workbench. Don't worry that it won't be perfect; the lumber might only cost you $20, so when you have time later to build or buy a better main workbench, the original can be scrapped or used as an extra table. Before building it, consider investing in a folding workbench like the Black & Decker Workmate or versions of it. It will give you a surface for sawing, as well as vise capabilities, and later you can use it as a portable work surface that you can take to a job site. Besides the bench, not much space is needed. Simple open shelving above or to the side of the bench should do nicely. Most of the tools can be stored directly under the bench and, if you wish, you can put a section of pegboard directly over the bench.

When you buy a portable circular saw, one in the middle of the price range will do the job, and should have almost all the better features available. The same goes for the remainder of the tools suggested; you don't need the top-of-the-line models unless you know you will be using them extensively. Be aware, however, that if you don't buy industrial-quality tools, you need to treat these tools with care; don't overload them and don't expect them to do mule-size jobs that would require tools twice their quality.

At this stage, if your budget is limited, consider buying used items at garage sales, especially hand tools and accessories that can be examined visually. Also ask around at work or at family gatherings to see if anyone has recently bought new tools and may be willing to part with its older, but workable, counterpart. Generally, don't be tempted to go to the bargain tool table you might find in a home center or hardware store; you may wish you had spent a few dollars more for a tool that will last longer or be more convenient or safer to use.

Whenever you buy a tool at this stage, try to get the owner's manual that goes with it; it will not only give you the specs and parts numbers but will also outline basic uses of the tool and critical safety information. Also be aware that no matter what you paid for a tool, its performance is dramatically influenced by the quality of blades or bits used in it. In many cases you will be better off spending a little less for a saw, for example, and a little more for the blade that goes into it.

SPECIFICATIONS

THE START-UP WORKSHOP

**SPACE: BASEMENT ROOM
OR GARAGE END WALL
AREA: 8′ X 12′ OR 96 SQ. FT.
STORAGE: OPEN SHELVING**

TOOL BUDGET SUGGESTIONS

(See page 26 for complete Shop Tool Buying Menu.)

STAGE I TOOLS

Your Budget

❑ Circular saw ($75)
❑ Sabersaw ($50)
❑ Power drill, ⅜″ ($45)
❑ Router ($75)
❑ Bench grinder ($65)
❑ Sander, pad ($50)
❑ Sander, palm grip ($60)
❑ Miter box, manual ($30)
TOTAL: $450

ACCESSORIES AND SUPPLIES

❑ Eye and ear protection ($25) ❑ Workbench ($50)
❑ Toolbox or bucket ($30) ❑ Machinist's vise ($25)
❑ Sawhorse brackets ($20) ❑ Router bits ($50)
❑ Handsaw, rip ($15) ❑ Handsaw, crosscut ($15)
❑ Hacksaw ($10) ❑ Coping saw ($10) ❑ Screwdriver set
($25) ❑ Pliers set ($20) ❑ Diagonal cutters ($6) ❑ Adjustable wrench, Crescent ($10) ❑ Open-end wrenches, reg.
($30) ❑ Open-end wrenches, metric ($30) ❑ Socket set
($50) ❑ Measuring tape ($10) ❑ Steel square ($8)
❑ Hammer ($15) ❑ Nail sets ($4) ❑ Awl ($4) ❑ Level,
24″ ($25) ❑ Level, torpedo ($10) ❑ Block plane ($10)
❑ C-clamps, four ($25) ❑ Pipe clamps, four ($40) ❑ Multimeter tester ($20) ❑ Soldering gun ($20) ❑ Putty knife, 1″
($2) ❑ Broad knife, 6″ ($6) ❑ Utility knife ($5) ❑ Paint
scraper ($5) ❑ Extension cord ($10) ❑ Other supplies ($85)
TOTAL: $725

BUDGET SUMMARY

Power Tools: **$450**

**Accessories
and Supplies:**   725

GRAND TOTAL: $1,175

SHOP CONCEPT:
Using Tool Buckets

One idea for organizing the Start-Up Shop is to use inexpensive 5-gallon plastic buckets with tool holders of tough nylon, such as the type sold under the Bucket Boss label. A pair or more of the buckets can be used to hold your portable tools. When not in use, they can be hung up neatly on screw hooks to the side of your workbench or inside a special cabinet. The tool holders come in various styles, but a basic version may have 27 pockets total, with 11 inside and 16 outside, to store assorted hand tools, such as pliers, wrenches, measuring and marking tools, and various supplies. Larger hand tools, such as saws and hammers, can be stowed inside the bucket, along with power tools and extension cords. Such buckets are easily converted to become an electric pail (see page 72). You can organize them in various ways, using one for Inside Work, one for Outside Work, another for Plumbing Work or Electrical Work. If you continue to add buckets, you can make each of them more specialized, designating a bucket for Drywall Work, or Doors and Windows, Soldering and Brazing, General Woodworking, or Glass and Screen Repair. Accessories like tool belts, parachute bags, and tool/chisel rolls help store other gear and parts in the buckets.

Starter Floor Plans

Set in a dedicated 8′ by 12′ area, this minimal shop starts with a basic workbench that can serve as the cornerstone of future shop expansion. Shelves below the benchtop can be open or closed with cabinet doors, and can serve as a catchall for portable power tools, various fasteners, as well as accessories such as a handsaw miter box. A 4′-high section of pegboard over the bench serves as home to frequently used hand tools. Tool holders for smaller items, such as various additional wrenches, screwdrivers, and pliers, can be built onto the bench itself, or can be made or purchased for attaching to the pegboard. Simple open shelves can be easily built above the pegboard, and on each side of the bench, for additional storage of tools, fasteners, tapes, sandpapers, finishes, books, or manuals.

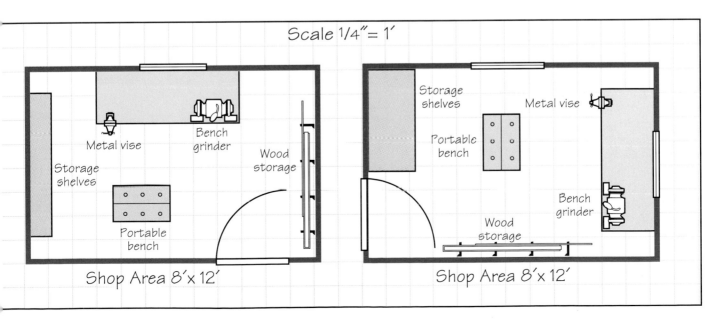

Scale 1/4" = 1'

Metal vise

Bench grinder

Wood storage

Storage shelves

Portable bench

Shop Area 8' x 12'

Storage shelves

Metal vise

Portable bench

Bench grinder

Wood storage

Shop Area 8' x 12'

STAGE I

WORKSHOP TOOL CLOSE-UPS

1 **CIRCULAR SAW.** This portable cutting tool for the beginning shop replaces the handsaw for making crosscuts or rip cuts, at angles from 90° to 45°. Sizes range from those using 5½″ to 8¼″ blades, though the 7¼″ is most common.

2 **SABERSAW.** This tool can replace a variety of saws, including the handsaw, jigsaw, coping saw, and hacksaw, as well as the knife. Important specs include strokes per minute, typically 3,000 or more; length of stroke, usually ⅝″ to 1″; and speed control, either single, two-speed, or variable.

3 **POWER DRILL.** Drills are available in ¼″, ⅜″, and ½″ sizes. The ⅜″ version, which will accept bits from ¹⁄₁₆″ to ⅜″, is a good bet for the starter shop. Drill speeds can range up to 2,500 rpm; models are available in single-speed, two-speed, and variable-speed versions.

4 **ROUTER.** For joining, edge-forming, and other professional touches, a good router is a must. It will become a key element in your shop and should be chosen carefully. A fixed-base or plunge-type router rated between 6.5 and 10 amps should be suitable for most uses, and most manufacturers offer a wide range of accessories.

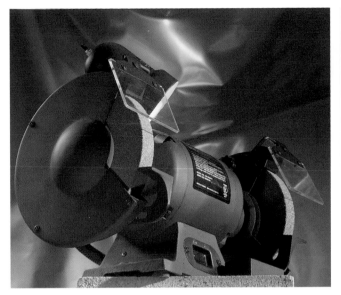

5 **BENCH GRINDER.** For general grinding and sharpening, two-wheel grinders can range from ⅕ to 1 hp, turning wheels from 5″ to 8″ in diameter. These can be fitted with a variety of wheels, plus wire wheels and buffing wheels; several accessories are available for honing and sharpening.

6 **PAD SANDER.** This tool typically accepts ⅓- or ½- sheets of sandpaper and can provide a very uniform finish. It is usually rated at between 2 and 4 amps. Look for a model with low vibration, strong sandpaper clamps, and, if desired, provision for dust collection or extraction.

7 **PALM GRIP SANDER.** Also sometimes referred to as a block sander, this tool provides a very smooth surface and can be easily controlled with one hand. It typically uses ¼-sheets of sandpaper, is rated below 2 amps, and may be available with a dust extraction system. Look for a low-vibration model that fits comfortably in your hand.

8 **HAND MITER BOX.** Varying in price from about $30 to $75, these rigs allow mitering for rough or quality finish work. Higher-priced versions incorporate more sophisticated guides with depth stops; all cut from 45° left to 45° right.

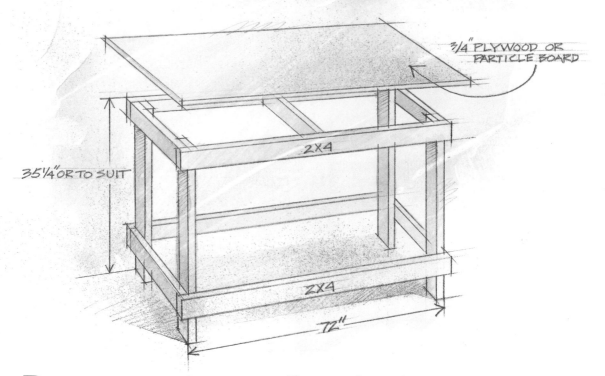

3/4" PLYWOOD OR PARTICLE BOARD

2X4

35¼" OR TO SUIT

2X4

72"

BUILDING A BASIC BENCH

The workbench is the icon of the home workshop. Until you get set up with a workbench, you can improvise with salvaged tables or desks, set up sawhorses with plywood over them, or buy small portable bench units such as the Black & Decker Workmate or similar units. Even a sheet of plywood fastened to the top of a kitchen base cabinet will work to start. However, making your own first bench can be a simple procedure, it gives you a chance to use your first tools, and later on you can use it as an extra bench or dismantle it and reuse the lumber.

There is an unending variety of workbench styles, and they vary from the most basic to ultra-sophisticated woodworking benches that incorporate every feature needed by a master craftsman. They can be built to set along a wall, or to serve as an island bench. They can be built to be freestanding, or attached directly to a wall. As your skills and needs reach levels demanding better work surfaces, you can order plans from various sources, or duplicate a style you see in stores or in the shops of others. The bench here is a basic bare-bones version that can be built quickly for a few dollars, with wood straight from the lumberyard.

The bench has a 25x72″ work surface. The base can be built completely of 2x4s, although 4x4s can be substituted for the leg uprights to make the bench sturdier. All joints are simple butt joints. Nails only can be used, though for greater strength and rigidity 3″ #14 flathead wood screws can be used in assembling the frame, and 1¾″ #9 flathead screws to fasten the top to the frame.

The top can be any sheet material, such as plywood or particle board; its thickness will depend on how you plan to use the bench, although ¾″-thick material is recommended as a minimum.

Before buying lumber, decide if you want to vary the height of the bench from the 35¼″ shown. To build, cut boards to length and lay all boards that are duplicates alongside one another to see that they match; i.e., the four legs, the four front and back rails, and the five cross braces. First assemble the end frames. Lay the four pieces for one end in place, with the legs inside the framework, 20″ apart. Position the bottom cross brace 8″ above the floor, and the top cross brace flush with the ends of the legs. Nail or screw together. Assemble the other end unit, then stand the two end units together to check for uniformity.

Next, assemble the front and back assembly. Put the two end units on the floor, or on two sawhorses, with the upper front and bottom rails in place. Line the front rails up with the end cross braces, then fasten. Assemble and fasten the back rails to the end units and check the assembled frame for squareness. Next add the top center brace by marking the center of the front and back upper rails. Position the center brace flush with the top of the rails and fasten. To attach the top, apply carpenter's glue to the top of the framing members. Place the top on the frame and fasten.

When fastening, dip nails or screws in glue before driving, then remove excess glue before it sets. If using nails, use a nail set to drive them just below the surface and fill holes with wood filler. If using screws, predrill screw holes and countersink all screwheads. When completed, sand as needed, then seal the end grain of the wood with a thin coat of white glue. Brush on the finish of your choice, such as polyurethane or varnish.

MAKING PERSONAL SHOP GEAR

Personal shop gear, what you wear in the workshop, deserves as much attention as shop machinery maintenance and adjustment. Improper or ill-fitting clothing in the shop will not only detract from your enjoyment of working on projects but also can be unsafe.

When working around shop equipment, always watch for loose clothing that can get caught in various shafts, pulleys, or blades. If you wear long-sleeve shirts or jackets, make certain that the sleeves are as tight-fitting as possible and are buttoned. Short sleeves are best. If you have long hair, make sure it is tucked up tightly under a cap. Do not wear excess jewelry, such as rings or bracelets, in the shop. If clothing, such as pants, is tattered or torn enough to be grabbed by mechanical parts, throw it away.

Pay attention to the shoes you wear; the steel-toe type is best, and try to avoid shoes without heels when working on ladders. Heels help keep your feet from slipping off the rungs. Wear gloves as appropriate and pay particular attention to both eye and ear protection. Safety glasses, goggles, or full-face shields should always be available and used in the shop, as well as earplugs or muffs. For welding, proper eye and face protection is absolutely critical.

Many workshop users wear denim cloth aprons, not only to protect clothing underneath but to carry pencils, tapes, notebooks, and other necessities in the pockets they provide, and also to have something to wipe their hands on. Denim jackets, fitted with Velcro at the sleeves and collar, can offer excellent, tight-fitting protection for woodworking, especially woodturning, which showers chips and dust. Shop aprons are easy to make and leather is a good choice for material.

First, make up a pattern; a simple way is to use a large section of brown wrapping paper. With the pattern made, you can hang it from your neck and walk around your shop to visualize how it will work, and whether any alterations may be needed. After the pattern passes inspection, trace it onto the leather with a razor blade and cut the apron out, taking care to keep the lines straight. Then give it another walk-about test. Make sure you have the straps and belt taped in place so you can be certain the apron will be comfortable to wear.

The next step is to punch the holes in the leather for the split-top metal rivets that are used as fasteners. Put the rivets through the holes, then just tap the shank of a screwdriver over the top to start the metal rolling over. You have to make sure the rivets fold over neatly, because if they don't, chances are good they eventually will come out. If you buy the leather right, the apron should cost well under $25, and you will find it was worth making. It will not only keep you clean but also may spare you from having sharp wood splinters or pieces of metal stuck in your chest or legs.

Many shop owners find that dry conditions during winter can cause a minor, but irritating problem: static electricity generated while using shop equipment, such as a bandsaw or sander. These small electrical charges snapping in the area of your head or chest don't particularly hurt, but they can come unexpectedly, causing you to lose control of your work or concentration. A solution to the problem is to buy a small clip, either one sold as a money clip or one used to clip key rings onto a belt, along with a short section of small chain. Attach the clip to the chain, then put the clip on your shoe so the chain just touches the floor to ground out errant electrical charges. It is best to put the clip directly under the ankle on loafer-high work shoes, and put it on the outside of the shoe. If put on the inside of the shoe, it may trip you.

SHOP PROJECT: Leather Shop Apron

The sketch shows a general pattern for a shop apron of leather but it can also be made of denim or other long-wearing material. A leather apron, however, will provide an additional degree of protection if you work on metal projects. It is an extra layer of skin, which is valuable when working around sharp metal, when doing hot blacksmith work, or when in an environment of flying wood splinters. The apron sketched was made of quite thick rough-side-out leather in less than an hour. To make your own, follow the general procedure explained above.

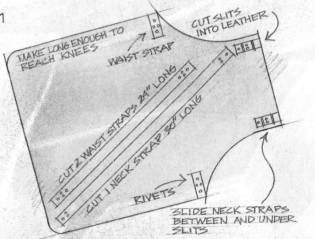

USING SHOP TOOLBOXES

When you are beginning to accumulate tools, a priority is a good toolbox, or better yet, a set of toolboxes to help keep things organized. The boxes sold in the tool sections of stores vary from cheap to expensive. When selecting a box, consider that it will probably serve you the rest of your life, so settle on one that will be as accommodating as possible. You can decide to buy a couple of larger boxes to hold frequently used tools, and supplement them with several smaller boxes for specialized tools. Another approach is to select a medium-size box and buy three or four to hold all your gear; the advantage is that they will all be the same size and can be neatly stacked under a workbench. Tip: To avoid having a mishmash of toolboxes that vary by size, color, or material, buy all the boxes you think you will need at once. You may have a problem finding the same box next year or four years down the road.

When thinking about buying toolboxes, try to decide up front if you will be using one of the increasingly popular roll-around tool cabinets of the type you see in auto garages. Available in small versions for the home shop, they can be a great aid in keeping wrenches, blades, and bits organized; if you like the idea of having one, it will reduce your need for individual toolboxes. When sur-veying the market for toolboxes, also investigate the boxes sold for fishing tackle; some larger, more expensive tackle boxes provide an amazing number of fold-out shelves and compartments which can provide an almost endless supply of places to put things.

If you would like a simple box to carry basic carpentry tools, several common styles can be duplicated. The hand-tool box shown, designed by Doug Devine, stores the hand tools used most often in special mortises and openings to keep them organized, highly visible, and within easy reach. It incorporates the concept of a "cricket," which is a simple stool that carpenters in the past found handy around the job site. With the box, you have to put tools back where they belong because there is nowhere else for them to go. When you notice an empty spot, you know you have left something behind. If you decide to build this box, the designer advises that applying a rubber stair tread to the top helps make the top less slippery. He has found that a good small pencil sharpener fitting into the edge of the box comes in handy. Also, a shoulder strap will make a long haul more comfortable.

STORING SMALL PARTS

Storing small parts in an organized fashion is one of the bigger challenges when organizing your first workshop. First consider plastic cabinets with small see-through drawers. The key to making them work is to mount them at eye level in your shop. That way you don't have to pull out a dozen or so drawers to find what you want; instead, you can see what you need in a second. For larger parts, you can make do with storage in recycled household containers until you are ready to invest in commercially available parts bins.

If you work at it, you will find an unlimited variety of possibilities using bottles, jugs, or other containers. Eyeball what is being thrown out in the trash or set out for the recyclers, and experiment. If your spouse drinks ready-mix mocha coffee by the gallons, you have an unending supply of small containers. The cost is right, and you can devise shelves to organize the containers in a handy manner. Tip: Take the time to come up with a good labeling system for small-parts containers, or use a hot-melt glue gun to fasten the nail, screw, or other item to the outside to cut down on searching time.

You can also build a bank of parts bins of standard dimensional lumber using ⅛″ Masonite or ¼″ plywood as dividers for such things as bolts, nuts, washers, screws, or nails. As shown, the wood strips across the front of the bins can be used to print out what is stored inside. Parts bins can also be kept on casters or wheels so you can pull them around the shop and end needless walking to and from parts storage areas. The parts cart shown has a pegboard storage area at the top, which provides a convenient place to hang small hand tools. A shelf below the pegboard stores tools when not in use.

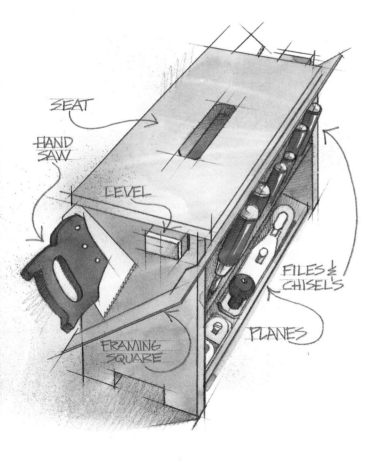

SEAT

HAND SAW

LEVEL

FILES & CHISELS

PLANES

FRAMING SQUARE

MOBILE PARTS BIN

On the side opposite the tool storage, pegs are used to hold a complete assortment of washers. Two long roll-out trays on roller bearings under the sides of the bins store fine-thread bolts, nuts, lag screws, and shields. A small-parts cabinet at the front holds fasteners, screws, and finish nails, while another rack at the rear also holds nails and screws.

MAKING TOOL CARRIERS

There are several ways to keep tools portable, either to be able to take them to the job or to help organize and retrieve them when working on various projects within the workshop. You can use traditional toolbelts and toolboxes or plastic buckets outfitted with tool holders. You can also use the concept of the tool carrier.

Tool carriers can be made almost any way that best serves your purposes. The most basic design is simply to cut out a section of pegboard to appropriate dimensions, round off the corners of the top, and make a grab-hole handle. Cut a section of dimensional lumber, such as 2x4 or 2x6, and cut a slot across one side to accept the bottom of the pegboard. You can make up several of these and store them side-by-side under a workbench, organizing tools and supplies on each as appropriate, then pull them out and set them on the workbench or take them to the job site.

You can improve on the same concept by adding boxes on either side to carry small tools or supplies like nails, screws, tape, or staples. The boxes can replace the lumber base, or they can be set on top of the base on either side. A third way is to make up tool carriers as pairs, using a box only on one side. This way you can put the carriers back-to-back and devise a locking system to keep them together when taking them outside of the shop. The advantage of this approach is that, since they are flat on one side, you can hang them separately on your workshop walls when they are not being used. For ways to hang tools from the tool boards with pegboard hooks, see page 52.

The tool carriers shown below are relatives of the basic tool board. They can be hung on the workshop wall individually, and they may be easily carried to the job site by putting two carriers back-to-back. The carriers are simply built of scrap such as plywood and ¾″-thick pine, and they can be customized with racks, cutouts, or drawers. Because they are cheap to build, you can make up as many as you need. Try to keep the contents planned for each carrier balanced and keep heavier tools toward the bottom. Window or screen-door latches can be used to lock a pair of the carriers together for easier carrying.

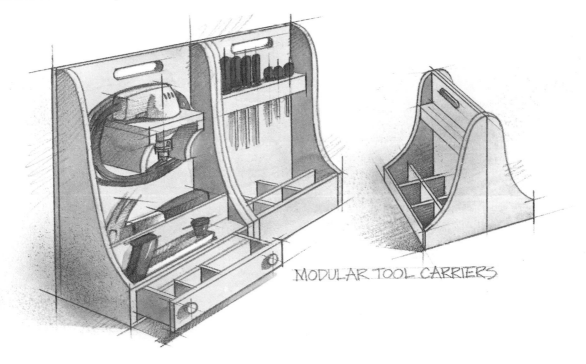

MODULAR TOOL CARRIERS

MAKING AN ELECTRIC SHOP PAIL

This electric pail doesn't light up, doesn't move, doesn't heat things up or keep them cool. But with alterations easily made in the workshop, a simple plastic pail or bucket can become a super extension cord to let your power tools reach out to where there aren't any plug-ins.

The modified pail helps keep extension cords from becoming a hassle, and also provides space for some project gear. The interior of the pail provides a place to coil an extension cord, and the cord will always be there; it is wired directly to the exterior receptacle. With a 50′ cord, for example, there will still be enough room to throw in a drill, saw, lights, or what have you, so you can carry the whole works in one trip with the pail's convenient handle.

The concept of the electric pail evolved on construction sites, particularly where the power was not in yet and carpenters needed electricity where they were working. But the best thing about making up an electric pail is that you can use a ground-fault circuit interrupter (GFCI) duplex grounding receptacle mounted in the box on the side. The special receptacle cuts off power within a split second if there is any problem with shorts or defective tools, saving you from potential serious injury.

The concept can be made as simple or complex as you wish. For example, a bare-bones version can be made with a simple hole near the bottom of a plastic bucket to snake the end of an extension cord through. Though not recommended, a single electrical pail could be made with a conventional receptacle without GFCI protection. A single receptacle can be used, or you can add double receptacles to provide four plug-ins. You also can add a switch if you need to shut power off to everything it feeds at once. You can also add receptacles and switches to the inside of the pail, instead of the outside, though doing so will make it harder to coil the extension cord inside.

Plastic pails can be purchased or salvaged from various sources; the original contents makes little difference, as long as the pail is cleaned out well. To make an acceptable electric pail as shown, buy a metal wall box and connector (about $2), the GFCI receptacle (about $14), and a 50′ outdoor 16 AWG grounded (three-wire) all-weather extension cord (about $10). First cut a hole through the pail and install the metal electrical box, using a connector through the side of the pail. Then cut off the receptacle end of the extension cord you bought and strip the exterior insulation back about 6″. Run the cord through from the inside, clamp the cord to the metal box, and strip back the wires and connect them to the receptacle.

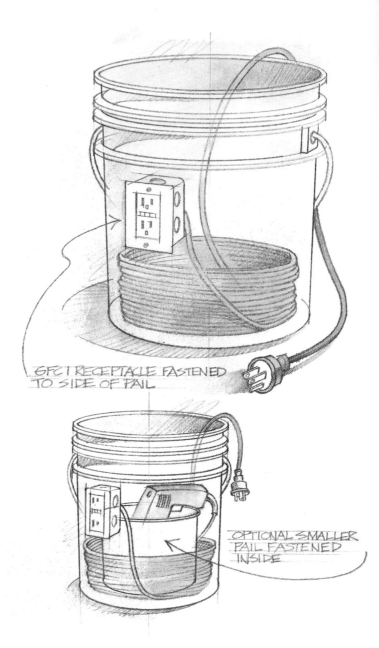

GFCI RECEPTACLE FASTENED TO SIDE OF PAIL

OPTIONAL SMALLER PAIL FASTENED INSIDE

With one brand of GFCI receptacle, the Leviton 6599-I, the wires from the extension cord connect to the bottom terminals marked LOAD, with the white wire attaching to the silver screw, the black wire to the brass screw. If you wrongly connect the extension cord wires to the top terminals marked LINE, the GFCI feature won't work. The ground wire of the extension cord connects to both the ground terminal on the receptacle and to the metal electrical box via a pigtail connection. In other words, a short wire from the grounding terminal on the GFCI, the ground wire from the extension cord, and a short wire attached under a screw inside the metal box are all connected together using a wire nut. After the components of the electric pail are together, you can test the GFCI receptacle, which has both a test button and a reset button. If you have hooked it up correctly and you press the test button, the reset should pop out, cutting off the current.

When not in use, the free end of the extension cord extending from the interior can be coiled up in the pail and the pail can be hung up out of the way in your shop or garage. If you want to make up more than one, a conventional receptacle can be used. If the second pail is plugged into the first pail with a GFCI receptacle, the ground-fault protection will be extended through to tools plugged into the second pail. Another possible modification to make coiling the cord inside easier is to bolt a second, smaller plastic bucket centered inside the electric pail. The space between the pail and the smaller bucket can then be used to coil the cord, while the bucket can be used to stow tools or materials.

Some electric pail builders prefer flat-type extension cords rather than the round type, saying the flat are easier to stuff back into the pail. The typical 5-gallon pail should handle up to 100´ of cord. Select a cord with enough capacity to exceed the amperage rating of your power tools to protect them from damage and overload. A 16-gauge 50´ cord will suffice for light-duty use, such as a smaller power drill or sabersaw. But for several tools used at once, for larger tools or motors, or for longer cords, check for the amp rating of the cord before buying. Electric motor amperage typically will be 6 amps

for ¼ hp, 10 amps for ½ hp, 14 amps for ¾ hp, and 16 amps for 1 hp (see the chart below for sample amperage ratings of other equipment). For distances up to 25´, for example, you would need at minimum a 14-gauge cord for a 1-hp motor.

Your electric pail can be modified even further by buying commercially available special pockets to slip over the top edge. Even if your electric pail is equipped with a GFCI receptacle, use all safety precautions as with any outdoor extension cord. Don't exceed electrical ratings, don't use in wet conditions, and don't use if the cord becomes damaged (replace with a new cord). Uncoil the cord before using and fully insert plugs. Keep children away from the electric pail. Unplug when not in use, don't use as a permanent power source, and store the electric pail indoors.

EQUIPMENT AMP RANGE

The ratings shown below provide a general guide only. Consult the manufacturer's specs for your power tools to determine the exact amp rating.

Bug killer	1—2	Grinder	7—10
Fan	1—3	Chainsaw	7—12
Hedge trimmer	2—3	Drill press	7—14
Weed trimmer	2—3	Belt sander	7—15
Electric drill	3—6	Router	8—13
Sabersaw	4—8	Shop vac	8—14
Vibrating sander	4—8	Air compressor	9—15
Bandsaw	5—12	Tablesaw	12—15
Sump pump	6—10	Snow blower	12—15
Lawn mower	6—12	Circular saw	12—15

EXTENSION CORD CAPACITIES

When using a power tool at a considerable distance from a power source, be sure to use an extension cord that has the capacity to handle the current the tool will draw. An undersized cord will cause a drop in line voltage, resulting in overheating and loss of power. Use the chart to determine the minimum wire size required in an extension cord. Only round-jacketed cords listed by Underwriters Laboratories (UL) are recommended.

When working with a tool outdoors, use an extension cord that is designed for outdoor use. This is indicated by the letters "WA" on the cord's jacket. Also, before using any extension cord, inspect it for loose or exposed wires and cut or worn insulation.

Ampere rating* (on tool faceplate)	0-2.0	2.1-3.4	3.5-5.0	5.1-7.0	7.1-12.0	12.1-16.0
Cord Length				Wire Size (AWG)		
25´	16	16	16	16	14	14
50´	16	16	16	14	14	12
100´	16	16	14	12	10	—
150´	16	14	12	12		
200´	14	14	12	10	—	—

CAUTION: Keep extension cords clear of the working area. Position cords used so that they will not get caught on lumber, tools, or other obstructions while you are working with a power tool.

* Used on 20-amp circuit of 12-gauge wire.

THE HOMEOWNER WORKSHOP

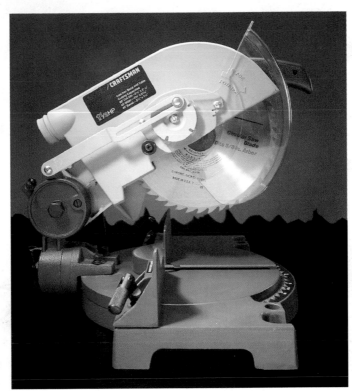

No matter what size shop you have, a set or two of sturdy saw horses, opposite, will come in handy. They can be built in a variety of styles. The relatively low-cost power miter saw, above, is handy for cutoff work on a variety of projects.

Besides the tools you bought for your Start-Up Workshop (page 63), you have now committed more space to a workshop area and are ready to start accumulating the tools that give you basic workshop capabilities: a tablesaw, power miter saw, stapler/nailer, scrolling sabersaw, drill press, belt sander, shop vacuum, and air compressor. These eight tools should cost you just over $1,000 all together.

The tool list suggests benchtop versions of the tablesaw and the drill press. Some are available in quality versions that will perform nearly as well as their floor-model counterparts. As you think through your plans, however, try to project how much use they will get; if substantial, consider going directly to the stationary models. Be aware that if you want to clear these tools from the workbench, you can buy stands or make your own to convert these benchtop models to stand-alone tools.

Also, now is the time to make a major basic decision about combination tools like the Shopsmith Mark V before proceeding to buy the additional tools suggested. Combination tools can save on space and money, but require more set-up time during a project. If you think you would be happy with a major combination tool, it will affect your buying plans throughout the evolution of your workshop, so investigate them now and make a decision.

Some of the tools added for this workshop supplement tools already bought for the Start-Up Workshop. The tablesaw and power miter saw, for example, supplement the portable circular saw, just as the scrolling sabersaw supplements the basic sabersaw already purchased. Likewise, the portable belt sander will supplement the pad sanders. Each of the additional tools may not be needed immediately, and the order that you buy these supplementary tools can be planned according to when you need them for special projects; you already have tools that can get the job done.

Among the new tools suggested is a 3″ wide by 24″ belt sander. An alternative is the 3x21″ version, though its sanding area will be smaller. The stapler/nailer will make quick work of fastening with staples or brads. The shop vacuum will help keep debris under control. The air compressor can be used with a blowgun to keep dust off motors and work surfaces, as well as with other basic accessories.

A note on the power miter saw. This saw might be the first one to buy, even before the tablesaw, especially if most of your work will be straight cuts on dimensional lumber. It is especially adept for construction-type projects, and newer models have excellent safety features, such as collapsing guards and electronic brakes. Newer models are also available that use a laser beam to indicate where the saw kerf will be. Even if you know you will want a tablesaw, consider buying the power miter saw first and see how well it serves your needs.

As you add equipment, you will need more space and more shelving for tools and storage. Besides the possibility of adding more open, board-type shelving and more pegboard, you can benefit from stand-alone shelving made of 1x and 2x lumber and plywood. Another option is to incorporate either used or inexpensive utility-grade kitchen cabinetry, which can be installed on an end wall, similar to a kitchen wall with a sink. Instead of the sink area, you can substitute a work counter with a light fixture, pegboard, or other shelving above.

SPECIFICATIONS

THE HOMEOWNER WORKSHOP

SPACE: BASEMENT ROOM OR SINGLE-CAR GARAGE
AREA: 14′ X 20′ OR 280 SQ. FT.
STORAGE: OPEN SHELVING OR CABINETS

TOOL BUDGET SUGGESTIONS
(See page 26 for complete Shop Tool Buying Menu.)

STAGE I TOOLS, UPGRADED   Your Budget

- ❏ Circular saw ($100)   _____
- ❏ Sabersaw ($75)   _____
- ❏ Power drill, ⅜″ ($60)   _____
- ❏ Router ($100)   _____
- ❏ Bench grinder ($85)   _____
- ❏ Sander, pad ($60)   _____
- ❏ Sander, palm grip ($75)   _____
- ❏ Miter box, manual ($45)   _____

Subtotal: $600

STAGE II TOOLS, NEW

- ❏ Tablesaw, benchtop ($150)   _____
- ❏ Power miter saw ($135)   _____
- ❏ Stapler/nailer ($30)   _____
- ❏ Scrolling sabersaw ($50)   _____
- ❏ Drill press, benchtop ($120)   _____
- ❏ Belt sander 3x24″ ($80)   _____
- ❏ Shop vacuum ($60)   _____
- ❏ Air compressor ($215)   _____

Subtotal: $840
TOTAL: $1,440

NEW ACCESSORIES AND SUPPLIES

❏ Workbench, extra ($50) ❏ Toolboxes or totes, two extra ($40) ❏ Ladder, 5′ step ($30) ❏ Ladder, extension ($75) ❏ Router bits, additional ($75) ❏ Drill bits, additional ($35) ❏ Saw blades, additional ($75) ❏ Extension cords, two extra ($20) ❏ Drop light ($10) ❏ Glass cutter ($5) ❏ Sharpening stones ($25) ❏ Cold chisels ($20) ❏ Deep sockets, ¼″ ($20) ❏ Tin snips ($10) ❏ Caulking gun ($5) ❏ Basin wrench ($10) ❏ Magnifier headset ($15) ❏ Face shield ($15) ❏ Combination square ($10) ❏ Wire brush, hand ($5) ❏ Spring clamps, four ($15) ❏ Tack hammer, magnetic ($5) ❏ Leather punch ($30) ❏ Wire connector set, solderless ($15) ❏ Hot-melt glue gun ($15) ❏ Other supplies ($115).
TOTAL: $745

BUDGET SUMMARY

Power Tools:	**$1,440**
New Accessories and Supplies:	745
Accumulated Accessories and Supplies:	725

GRAND TOTAL: $2,910

Starter Floor Plan

This shop provides maximum versatility within the 280 sq. ft. of space offered by a modest single-car garage, as shown, or altered to fit an available basement room. To the starter workbench it adds a second bench, plus an assembly bench. If the assembly bench is on casters, it can be easily pushed out of the way to allow vehicle parking. Both workbenches are arranged for easy access to the assembly bench. One workbench supports both a 1″ belt sander and a bench grinder, while the second workbench provides an inset for a power miter saw so its surface supports boards being cut. The benchtop tablesaw can be inset into the assembly bench; when not being used for sawing, the saw's blade can be lowered to create a fully clear assembly area. Shelves or shelf/cabinet combinations make full use of one corner, while pegs and/or shelf supports provide for narrow wood storage within easy reach of the large overhead door.

SHOP CONCEPT:
Positioning Bench Vises

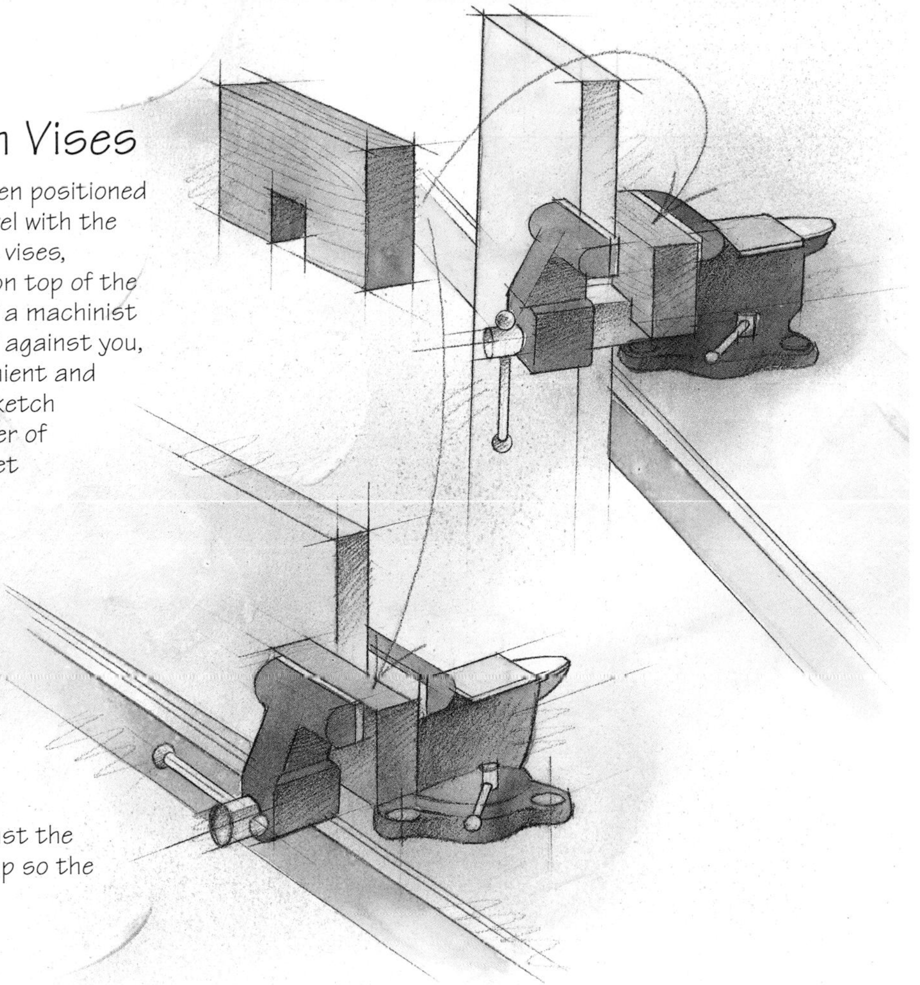

Woodworking vises are most often positioned so that the top of the vise is level with the top of the workbench. Machinist vises, however, are generally mounted on top of the workbench. Proper positioning of a machinist vise to work with you, instead of against you, will make benchwork more convenient and provide more flexibility. As the sketch shows, first make up a jaw spacer of common 2x4. With the spacer set against the back jaw, line up the front of the spacer with the edge of the bench, and fasten the vise on the workbench at that position. Doing this will allow you to set longer pieces in front of the bench, so they will reach all the way to the floor for added stability. When you want to set work on the bench itself, simply slip the 2x4 spacer against the front jaw, and the work will line up so the bench can be used as support.

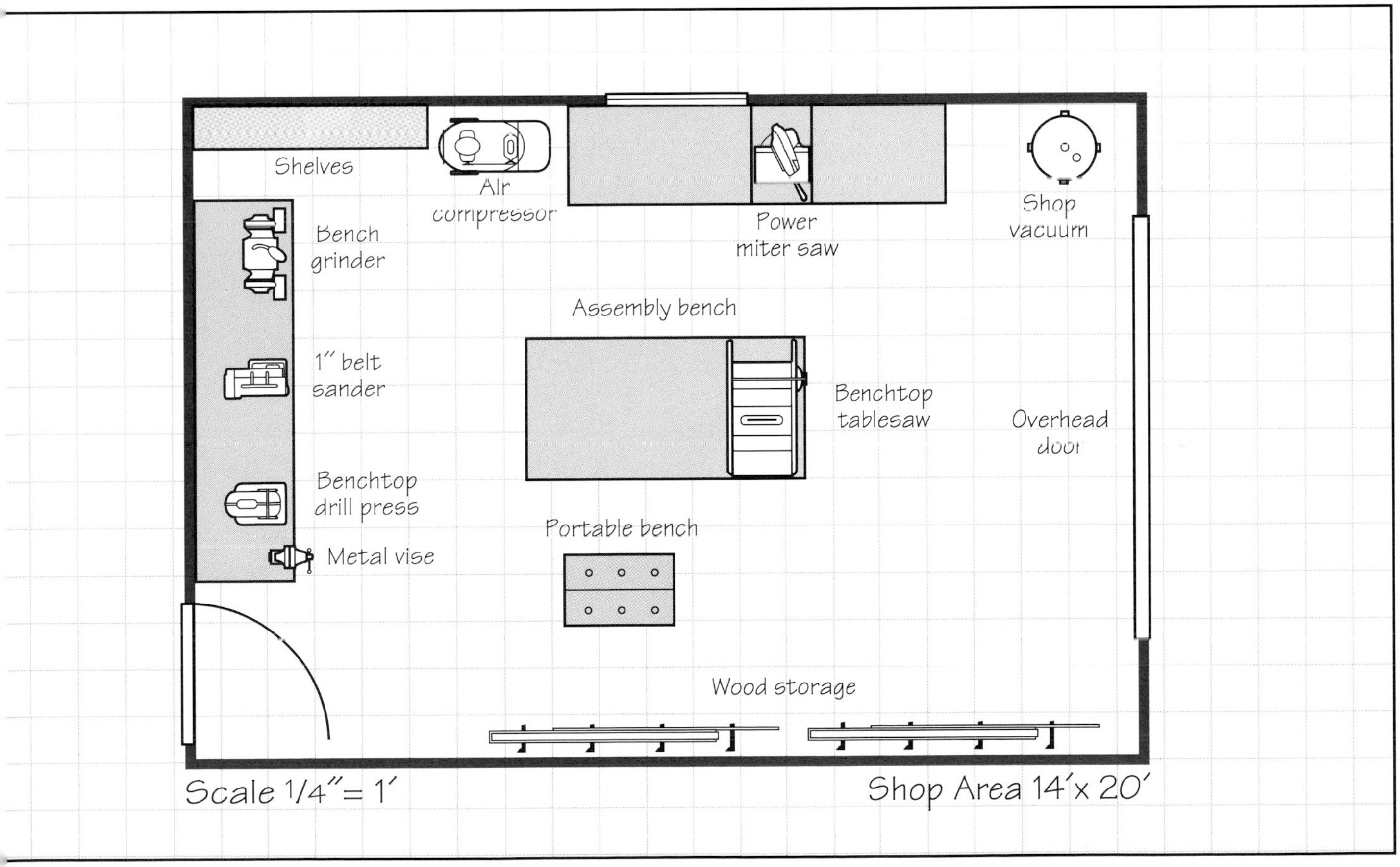

Shelves

Air compressor

Power miter saw

Shop vacuum

Bench grinder

Assembly bench

1″ belt sander

Benchtop tablesaw

Overhead door

Benchtop drill press

Metal vise

Portable bench

Wood storage

Scale 1/4″= 1′

Shop Area 14′x 20′

STAGE II

WORKSHOP TOOL CLOSE-UPS

2 **POWER MITER SAW.** A sweetheart for cutoff work, these are most often available with 10″ blades. Lower-priced models typically have a 1½-hp, direct-drive motor. Look for both mitering and beveling capability, rotating slot, and dust bag option.

1 **TABLESAW, BENCHTOP.** This saw provides tablesaw capability at lower price, smaller size, and lighter weight than stationary models. Typically it might have a direct-drive, 12-amp motor, with a 3″ cutting capacity at 90° and 2½″ at 45°, and a cast-aluminum table. Look for an accurate, self-aligning rip fence.

3 **STAPLER/NAILER.** Combining electric stapling and nailing into one tool, some models handle five staple and two brad sizes while providing dual penetration settings. Swept-back designs allow access to hard-to-reach areas.

4 **SCROLLING SABERSAW.** This tool is designed for cutting curves and patterns in thinner materials with blades that may be turned or locked into straight-line cutting. Variable speed, tilting base, sawdust blower, and fixtures for edge- and circle-cutting are usually offered. Motors are usually rated at 3 to 4 amps with a ⅝″ or ¾″ blade stroke. A wide variety of special blades are available.

5 **DRILL PRESS, BENCHTOP.** Easily movable and storable, this tool takes up little space in tight quarters. Benchtop models typically have 2″ to 3⅝″ quill travel, and can drill to the center of boards from 8″ to 14″ wide. It may have 3, 4, or 5 speeds and 7″ to 22″ of table adjustment travel.

6 **BELT SANDER, 3x24″.** Sander belts can vary in size from 3x18″ to 4x24″. The 3″-wide models generally are 3x24″ or 3x21″ sizes. The 3x24″ typically will have sanding areas from 4¾″ to 5¼″ long. Varying from ½ to 1¼ hp, most will have a provision for collecting dust.

7 **AIR COMPRESSOR.** Varying from about $200 to $1,000, lower-priced units typically may offer a 1½-hp motor, an 8-gallon storage tank, and 100 psi maximum. Air storage allows efficient use of tools, such as spray guns, wrenches, ratchets, drills, hammers, and sand blasters.

8 **SHOP VACUUM.** Essential in any shop, this basic wet/dry vac may have from a 1½- to 2½-hp motor, hose sizes of 1¼″ or 2½″, and capacities ranging from 6 to 8 gallons. Accessories, such as floor tool, dry nozzle, drain cleaner, and extension wand may or may not be included.

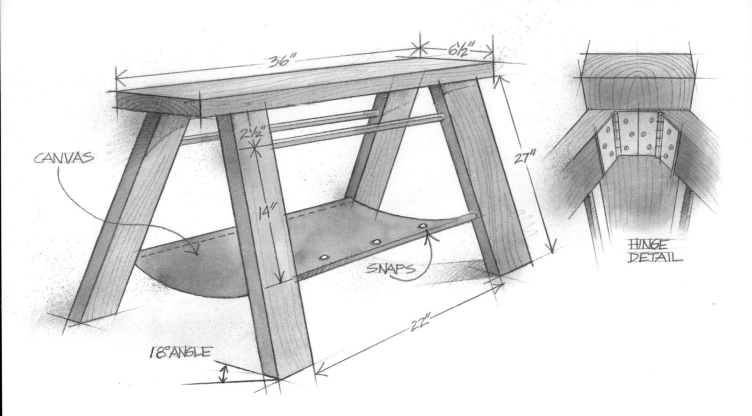

BUILDING SHOP SAWHORSES

The sawhorse, along with pegboard, can truly be called the shop owner's friend. Used as supports for sawing, or for a multitude of other uses, sawhorses have been made in hundreds of styles and versions since man began using tools. They can vary from simple to complex, low to the ground or even high enough to be used for scaffolding. You can also buy metal, folding-leg sawhorse brackets. Just cut five pieces of 2x4 to suitable length and snap into place. You can either disassemble or fold up the horses when not in use.

One disadvantage to ordinary sawhorses is that they take up storage space when not in use. The folding sawhorse shown solves this problem and easily collapses to the width of its top. It is made with 2x4 and 2x8 pine, ¾″ dowels, and four sets of loose-pin door hinges. It trades a certain amount of stability for the convenience of folding, but with modifications it can be as sturdy as solid-built versions.

The top of the folding sawhorse is a 36″-long 2x8 ripped to width. The legs are 27″-long 2x4s, with 18° cuts at each end. The hinge plates under each end of the top are positioned by butting them up against each other, and all must be installed the same way. Cross supports are of ¾″ doweling. The inside measurement between the legs of each side is 22″. The tool cloth that attaches to the lower dowel supports can be canvas or denim, fitted with four heavy-duty snaps on each side.

For each sawhorse, assemble a 36″-long 2x8, four 27″ 2x4s, four ¾x24″ lengths of dowel, and the hinges. After ripping the 2x8 to a 6½″ width, cut the legs to an 18° bevel on each end, parallel to each other. All end cuts on the legs can be made at the same time if all the legs are clamped together. To attach the hinges, butt the plates along the center of the underside of the top, 3″ in from each end, making certain they are mounted squarely so the legs will swing without binding. Each hinge will have two plates, one with two pin loops and another with three; make sure all plates mounted under the top are one or the other. Each plate will have holes for three screws. Be sure to predrill the screw holes in the top and legs to prevent cracking the wood.

The doweling is installed by drilling ¾″ holes 2¼″ into the inside edges of the legs at 2½″ and 16″ from the top hinged ends. The tool apron is 21½x33″ long. First fold ½″ of the fabric under each side and hem. Then pin a 5″ hem at two sides and test it on the sawhorse for the desired tension. After adjusting, sew temporary hems in place, then attach four snaps evenly along each side. The apron is handy for holding tools and parts when you do nonsaw work. When the horse is used for sawing, however, the apron will catch sawdust.

To make these sawhorses more stable when they will be in use for extended periods, you can tack 1x2 stabilizers across the legs on each end, just above the lower dowels. This keeps the horse from trying to fold up when you move it around or are pushing lumber over it. You can also devise a latch of 1x2 on the inside of the legs, using a piece of 1x2 screwed loosely to one leg with a notch in the other end latching over another screw or nail.

MAKING A VISE PORTABLE

Picture-framing vises (or miter clamps) have screw holes on the bottom side for attaching to a workbench. But if you attach one to your workbench for occasional framing projects, it becomes an obstacle that gets in the way of other benchwork. The only thing you can do is unscrew bolts to remove it, then reattach it when you need the vise again. One solution to avoid this inconvenience is to mount the framing vise on a wooden base that can be rapidly clamped and unclamped in a woodworking vise. With the base clamped in the wood vise, the framing vise is as solid as it would be on the bench itself.

The base becomes, in effect, a miniature portable bench for the framing vise. It can be made from scrap 4x4, 2x6, and ½″ plywood, and its assembly is very simple. To start, lock a section of 4x4 post into your woodworking vise, then make a mark on the post where it reaches the top of the wood vise. Next, decide on the approximate height that you would like the framing vise to be. Subtract 2″ and cut the post at this height. (This allows for the thickness of the 2x6 and plywood that will be fastened to the top of the post.) Consider the height of the post carefully; you may want to make it about chest high to make it easier to glue and nail framing members without bending over. If you don't want the miter clamp that high, you can use the same idea and simply cut the post shorter, even to the point where the top of the base will lay right on top of the wood vise.

After cutting the 4x4, the next step is to attach the top 2x6 into place using glue and countersunk lag screws. Then nail and glue the second 2x6 to the back of the 4x4 post and upper 2x6. Make sure that the bottom part of this second 2x6 will come down against the top of your wood vise (using the mark that you have already scribed onto the 4x4). Next, cut the piece of ½″ plywood to fit over the top 2x6, attach with glue and nails, and let dry overnight. After the glue has dried, attach the framing vise, and it is ready to use. When you get done with a framing project, you can quickly remove the framing vise and its base from the wood vise and set it out of the way in a corner.

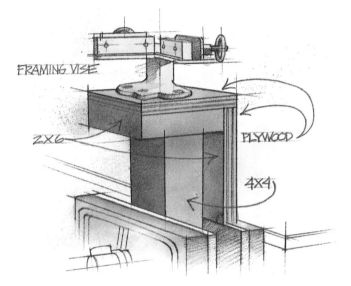

FRAMING VISE

2X6

PLYWOOD

4X4

SHOP PROJECT: Board Touch-Up Tool

Removing hardened glue squeezed out from around joints, or ripples caused by a planer or jointer, can leave a project with an amateur look. To touch up project parts, many experienced woodworkers will use a small paint scraper with a 1½″ blade more often than any other traditional wood scraper. If the paint scraper's blade is kept sharp, it takes glue or ripples off in ultra-thin shavings so you can easily tell when to stop without marring the wood.

The trick in using the scraper is keeping it sharp and knowing how to sharpen it. You don't need a grinding wheel or whetstone, just a good fine metal file and a screwdriver. Use the file across both the front and back edges, then (this is the trick) press the shank of a common screwdriver across the front edge to roll the edge over slightly toward the rear, or handle end.

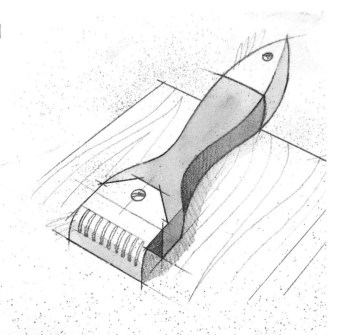

MAKING SHOP AIR MOVERS

Shop users are becoming more aware of the value of keeping down the dust and fumes while working on projects. Shown here are a pair of low-cost air movers you can rig up to make your shop a more comfortable (and healthier) place to work. The first is a simple shop air cleaner that uses furnace filters to trap dust; the second is an inexpensive and handy shop fan that can help keep fumes from building up in the workshop.

The shop air cleaner uses a recycled furnace blower fan and a simple wooden cabinet. Dust-laden shop air is drawn into the cabinet through the large opening in the bottom of the front. It then passes through a double 1x20x25″ furnace filter. The clean air is then expelled through a screen-covered opening at the back of the fan. The fan is switched on and off via a toggle switch on the front side. At the end of a day in the shop, you can shut off the fan and use a shop vac to clean the air intake area. When the filters are tapped, dust will fall

down and be picked up by the shop vac. The filters can be changed using a narrow door on the unit's side. When a change is required, the bottom filter can be thrown away, the top filter moved to the bottom, and a new filter placed in the top position.

You can make the cabinet so its top is high enough to match the height of your tablesaw. This way the cabinet can be used as a "helping hand" when crosscutting full sheets of plywood. The air cleaner will cost very little to make if you can locate a used forced-air furnace fan assembly. Put the word out in your neighborhood, and keep your eyes open. Quite often you will find that when older forced-air furnaces are replaced, all you have to do is ask the person doing the work if the blower assembly, including that valuable motor, will be available. Often they will give it to you if you carry it away.

Another way you can put a salvaged furnace blower assembly to work in your shop is to convert it into a special shop fan. Simply fasten the furnace blower to a shop-built dolly with casters, then add 1x2″ screening to cover both the belt and pulleys and the intake opening. The fan can be most useful in a garage shop to create a breeze to move finishing fumes out of the workplace.

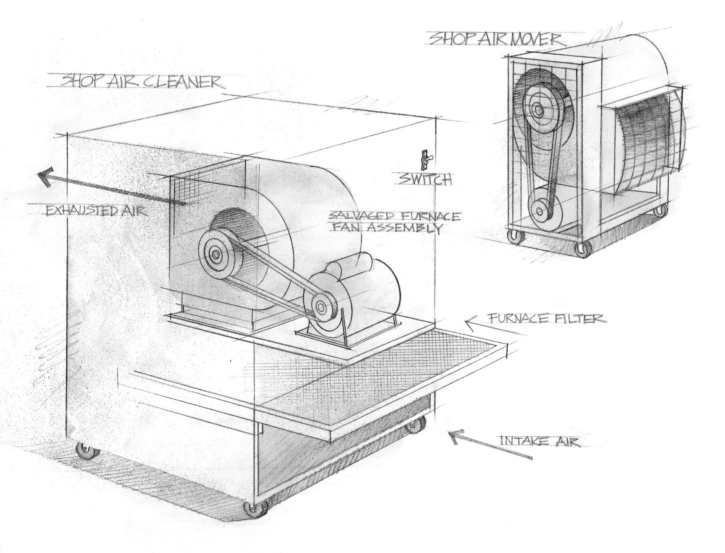

SHOP AIR MOVER

SHOP AIR CLEANER

EXHAUSTED AIR

SWITCH

SALVAGED FURNACE FAN ASSEMBLY

FURNACE FILTER

INTAKE AIR

SETTING UP FOR THIN WORK

Like any other shop tool, the average tablesaw probably performs only about a third of what it is capable of in most home workshops. The two tips below are ways to make your tablesaw work harder, either in removing a thin amount of material from stock, or in turning stock into thin strips.

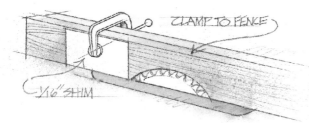

TABLE SAW JOINTING. This arrangement allows a tablesaw to be used as a jointer, making cuts of up to 1/8″ from the blade. To shave off 1/16″ evenly from even an odd-shaped piece, for example, follow this procedure: Lower the blade and attach an auxiliary fence to the saw's fence. Move the fence over the blade, leaving 1/16″ of the blade showing. Turn the saw on and raise the blade to a height that will accommodate your stock. Then add a 1/16″ shim to the auxiliary fence just beyond the blade.

As the stock is pushed through, the shim holds the workpiece out from the fence the equivalent of what the blade is removing. This set-up can also be used to straighten the edge of a board by making repeated passes, just as with using a jointer. With a wider blade, a wider cut can be made, and with a dado head installed in the saw, even wider. This arrangement can also be used to cut a rabbet by simply lowering the blade to the depth of the rabbet desired.

MULTIPLE-STRIP JIG. This jig is handy for repeated cutting of identical thin strips of any width, down to about 1/32″. As the sketch shows, it is simply a board fitted with a notch near the rear, as well as with two hold-down strips on top, to hold the board being cut into strips. The board is set in front of the notch and under the hold-downs and run through the saw. A pushstick is not needed. This jig can be set up to work with the fence on either side of the blade. If the jig is to be used with the fence on the right side of the blade, the notch and hold-downs are positioned on the left side of the jig; if it is to be used with the fence on the left side of the blade, the notch and hold-downs are positioned on the right side of the jig

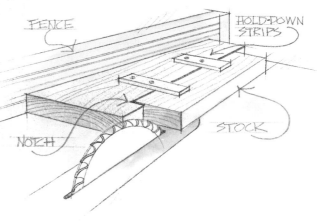

SHOP PROJECT: Finger Boards

Sometimes you may need to shape or rabbet narrow strips and require some device to hold the stock tight to the fence and (sometimes) to the table surface as well. The solution is to make up a finger (or feather) board to do this job. The finger board not only holds the work snugly against the fence, but it also prevents the work from kicking back. The fingers will allow the work to be pushed in one direction only.

To make a finger board, use a straight-grained, knot-free solid wood board from 4″ to 6″ wide, cut to a length to suit the machine(s) that it will be used on. Cut the finger end of the board at about 30° using the tablesaw. Cut the fingers in about 4″ to 5″, spacing the fingers 3/32″ to 1/8″ apart. The closer together the fingers are, the more springy they will be. To use in making moldings, clamp the finger board to the tabletop, with the ends of the fingers parallel to the fence and a little closer to the fence than the width of the stock. On some machines it is difficult to securely clamp the finger board so it won't move. In this case it is helpful to clamp another plain board at right angles to (and against) the back side of the finger board, as shown.

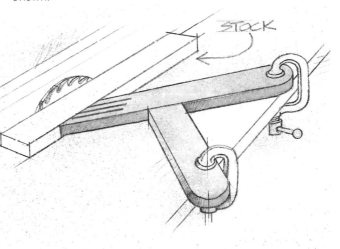

MAKING SHOP PUSHSTICKS

There are a wide variety of hold-down devices available for use with the tablesaw or jointer in the home workshop. These include rollers, rollers set at an angle, powered rollers, notched boards screwed onto the saw fence, and other devices. But often there are times when a pushstick is an absolute necessity in a workshop. Pushsticks come in all sizes and shapes, but the better pushsticks have a long toe to hold the work firmly against the saw or jointer table.

Compared with the small, aluminum bird-mouth types widely marketed, you can make your own that will be more useful, allow more control, and be safer to use. For a tablesaw, pushsticks that don't have a long toe must be used in conjunction with a second hold-down stick. If you don't use a hold-down, the work will tend to want to raise up over the blade. A single good pushstick with a long toe does the job of both an inadequate pushstick and a hold-down stick. Not only does it push and hold the work down at the same time, you can also apply side pressure on it to hold the work against the fence. The angle of the handle allows good control of downward pressure.

The designs shown here will offer you more control, especially if the wood pinches the blade, or for some other reason the work wants to raise up. To make pushsticks, oak is not recommended because it will often contain hidden splits held together by just a small amount of wood. If you attempt to make pushsticks

with oak, such pieces can split apart just as you finish making them.

Walnut and cherry woods are much better from the standpoint of internal splits. Also try to avoid using plywood for pushsticks because when you push a plywood pushstick through the blade, the blade doesn't just cut a kerf, it tends to rip out a complete ply. Avoid particleboard as well; it's quite weak and can cause excessive wear on the blade of your saw.

To avoid chewing up pushsticks too fast with saws, make them in different widths, and keep them handy near the saw to use for different widths of cut. It's better to make them a little long to begin with; then when you need to renew the notched end, you can recut it several times before finally pitching it into the scrap box. You also can make pushsticks wide enough that you can push the good piece and the waste piece through the blade at the same time. That way you won't wind up with a nib on the waste piece that can keep your work from lying tight to the fence for the second, third, or later cuts.

Pushsticks can be made as narrow as ¼″ and as wide as 1½″, for whatever width cuts you are liable to need. Start with a piece of wood 3″ wide (for a long toe), and about 12″ long (so you can recut it several times). The angle of the notch will vary according to whether you want the handle high or low. However, keep in mind that the handle should always be above the fence of the saw. To recut the notch, simply lay a square, or a piece of wood with a square end, on the end of the pushstick and make two marks. Then with just two cuts on a bandsaw you will have a new pushstick.

If a pushstick doesn't securely hold and push the work piece, it's time to renotch or throw away that stick. If

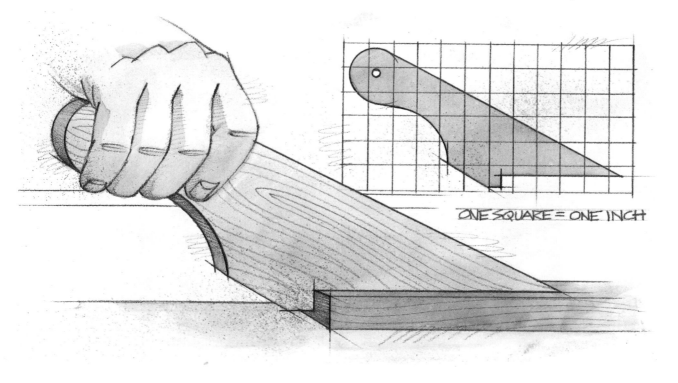

ONE SQUARE = ONE INCH

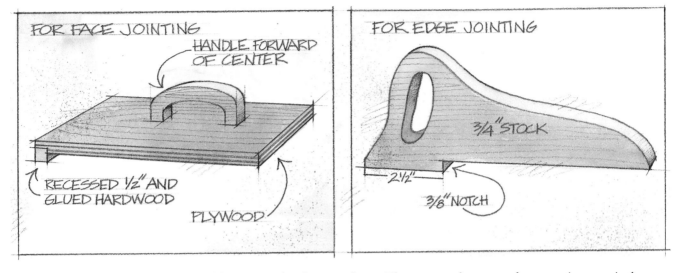

FOR FACE JOINTING

HANDLE FORWARD OF CENTER

RECESSED ½" AND GLUED HARDWOOD

PLYWOOD

FOR EDGE JOINTING

¾" STOCK

2½"

⅜" NOTCH

you make a wide pushstick and will be cutting deeply into it, make several passes instead of one deep cut. A deep cut might result in some kickback. In short, when using pushsticks, common sense and concern for safety should prevail. If it doesn't feel right, don't do it.

The specific design of a pushstick is somewhat flexible and you may want to make up a half-dozen or so to use in your shop. The important thing is that you have plenty of toe on the sticks you make so they will hold the workpiece securely to the table. Also make certain that the design of the handle allows you to get a good grip on the stick and still have your hand above the

fence. The pattern shown on the opposite page is the general shape of pushsticks used by veteran woodworker Russ Barnard with tablesaws. The thickness and notch angle of the stick can vary, however, according to its use and your personal preferences.

The pattern shown above left is for a pushstick to be used with a jointer for face jointing. It's best to make this one about 4″ wide and about 12″ long. The catch is a strip of hardwood. The pattern shown directly above is for use with a jointer for edge-jointing. It's of ¾″ stock, also about 12″ long, with a handle about 5½″ high.

SHOP PROJECT: Dowel Tenoning Jig

This dowel tenoning jig can be quite useful, especially in making furniture frames, if your router is fixed under a router table. The jig is made of a piece of hardwood about 2″ thick, 3″ high, and 14″ long. The notch in the jig should be slightly larger than the diameter of the dowel, and it should be centered with the router cutter. To cut the tenon, the router cutter must be rotating. To feed the stock into the jig, a twisting motion is used at the same time the dowel is pushed down into the cutter. For safety reasons, the jig is not for use with dowels less than ⅝″ in diameter.

DOWEL

SHAPER

JIG

THE WOODWORKER WORKSHOP

This example workshop should cost you less than $5,000 total. By adding a little over $2,000 worth of equipment to the previous shop example (see Homeowner Workshop, page 75), you will have the capability of tackling nearly any woodworking project you wish and be able to do a quality job of it.

With this workshop, you will have enough in your budget to buy higher-quality versions of the tools listed in the Homeowner Workshop, and you will also have enough in the budget to add a floor-model tablesaw, a scrollsaw, and a benchtop bandsaw. This will give you virtually unlimited sawing capability, and you will still have the benchtop tablesaw which you can adapt for specialized uses. But most importantly, at this stage you will add a jointer, which will put you into advanced woodworking capability because you will no longer be dependent on the lumberyard or other woodworkers for truing up your stock to critical dimensions.

Also, with this shop, your finishing options are enhanced by adding a 4″ belt/disc sander to your arsenal of sanders. A cordless drill/driver will make quick work of driving the buglehead wood screws now popular for wood fastening. And a minimal selection of air tools will let you start to harness your air compressor for more than inflation or cleaning tasks. After adding the floor-model drill press for greater capacity, you may decide to sell your benchtop model, or to adapt it for specialized jobs.

At this stage, you will be adding several tools that generate sawdust and wood chips. For this reason, consider all dust and chip control options available as you add equipment, such as dust pick-up chutes and bags, and waste exhaust ports. Also, with this much equipment, you would do well to consider a medium-size portable dust collector that can be moved from machine to machine. Or, better yet, consider a permanently installed

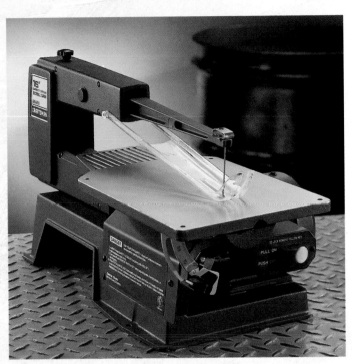

Reclaiming warped or crooked lumber is a snap with a board-surfacing jig, opposite, that you can make to use with your router. The jig comes in especially handy if you don't have a jointer or thickness planer. The scrollsaw, above, has spawned renewed interest in intricate scrollwork projects.

dust collection system, with the dust collector located in a separate room to cut down on noise.

When setting up this workshop, also consider having a separate area for finishing work, such as applying stain and finishes. By designating a specific area for these tasks, you can keep finishing supplies concentrated in one place, and you can locate the area close to a window for natural light and ventilation. It's best to have a separate finishing room, but if that is not possible you can surround the area with a canvas curtain. Besides natural ventilation, consider adding fans to speed air movement or, ideally, explosion-proof exhaust fans to keep fume build-up to a minimum.

With some project experience, you will soon find yourself paying greater attention to the raft of accessories and add-ons available for your eight new tools, as well as the other tools you already own. Besides better saw blades, drill bits, and higher-quality grinding stones and sandpapers, some major upgrades to consider include a precision rip fence for your stationary tablesaw, a vertical 1″ belt sander to help touch up blades, and an expanded selection of router bits.

The space required for the tools added to this workshop may become a limiting factor, and you may find you will have to move your shop from the basement, for example, to an area at least the size of a two-car garage, or larger. Likewise, storage space will become more valuable. Besides using wall storage, open shelving, and cabinets, look for storage opportunities under benches and on racks suspended from the ceiling. Also, at this stage, pay attention to how materials, supplies, tools, and accessories are stored. If you find yourself running back and forth when working on a project, make a note of it; a simple rearrangement might increase efficiency and make project work more pleasant.

Specifications

The Woodworker Workshop

Space: Large Basement Room or Two-Car Garage
Area: 22´ x 24´ or 528 sq. ft.
Storage: Open Shelving, Cabinets, and Under Bench

Tool Budget Suggestions
(See page 26 for complete Shop Tool Buying Menu.)

Stage I Tools, upgraded

	Your Budget
❏ Circular saw ($125)	
❏ Sabersaw ($75)	
❏ Power drill, ⅜″ ($75)	
❏ Router ($135)	
❏ Bench grinder ($100)	
❏ Sander, pad ($75)	
❏ Sander, palm grip ($85)	
❏ Miter box, manual ($60)	

Subtotal: $730

Stage II Tools, upgraded

❏ Tablesaw, benchtop* ($200)	
❏ Power miter saw ($150)	
❏ Stapler/nailer ($45)	
❏ Scrolling sabersaw ($80)	
❏ Drill press, benchtop** ($180)	
❏ Belt sander 3x24″ ($90)	
❏ Air compressor ($250)	
❏ Shop vacuum ($100)	

Subtotal: $1,095

Stage III Tools, new

❏ Tablesaw, stationary ($600)	
❏ Scrollsaw, benchtop ($250)	
❏ Bandsaw, benchtop ($140)	
❏ Drill press, floor model ($300)	
❏ Horizontal belt/disc sander, 4″ ($120)	
❏ Jointer ($300)	
❏ Air tool set ($80)	
❏ Drill/driver, cordless ($120)	

Subtotal: $1,910
TOTAL: $3,735

*Benchtop tablesaw can be used for trimming large parts and cutting small parts during assembly. **Benchtop drill press can be used with sanding drums or for horizontal boring.

New Accessories and Supplies

❏ Toolboxes, additional ($50) ❏ Tool storage cabinet ($140) ❏ Router accessories ($75) ❏ Saw blades, additional ($75) ❏ Wood countersink bits ($30) ❏ Grinder wheels, additional ($35) ❏ Sharpening stone set ($25) ❏ Multi-purpose adjustable vise ($50) ❏ Level, additional ($35) ❏ Bar clamps, additional ($100) ❏ Metal drill bit set ($75) ❏ Mechanic's socket set ($80) ❏ Allen wrench set ($10) ❏ Channel-lock-type pliers set ($10) ❏ File set ($50) ❏ Sledgehammers, two ($50) ❏ Ball peen hammers, two ($30) ❏ Battery charger ($40) ❏ Nail pullers ($50) ❏ Painting accessories, additional ($100) ❏ Industrial respirator ($45) ❏ Electrical tools, additional ($60) ❏ Plumbing tools, additional ($75) ❏ Other supplies ($110).
TOTAL: $1,400

Budget Summary

Power Tools:	$3,735
New Accessories and Supplies:	1,400
Accumulated Accessories and Supplies:	1,470

Grand Total: $6,605

SHOP CONCEPT:
Using Kitchen Cabinets

One idea that can help get your beginning shop set up more quickly is to use a basic selection of kitchen cabinets, either new or used, to arrange a work center. If you want to keep the cost low, stop by homes where lawn signs alert you that kitchen remodeling is taking place, and ask the contractor if the homeowner would be willing to sell you the old cabinets. In some cases, the contractor may have the responsibility to dispose of them and will let you take what you need for minimal cost. If you don't have any luck finding used cabinets, or simply want new ones, check with high-volume home centers, which may carry a low-end line of unfinished cabinets.

Start with a base cabinet, like a sink base unit, and add overhead wall cabinets above and utility cabinets to each side. Base units are usually 34″ high, 24″ deep, and from 12″ to 60″ wide, but utility cabinets will usually be 84″ high, 18″ or 24″ wide, and 24″ deep. Wall cabinets, including single-, double-, or triple-door units, may vary in width from 12″ to 54″, and be 12″ deep. Instead of using traditional countertops, you can cover any base units with solid lumber, flat or on edge, to provide sturdy anchoring of any vises or bench-mounted tools.

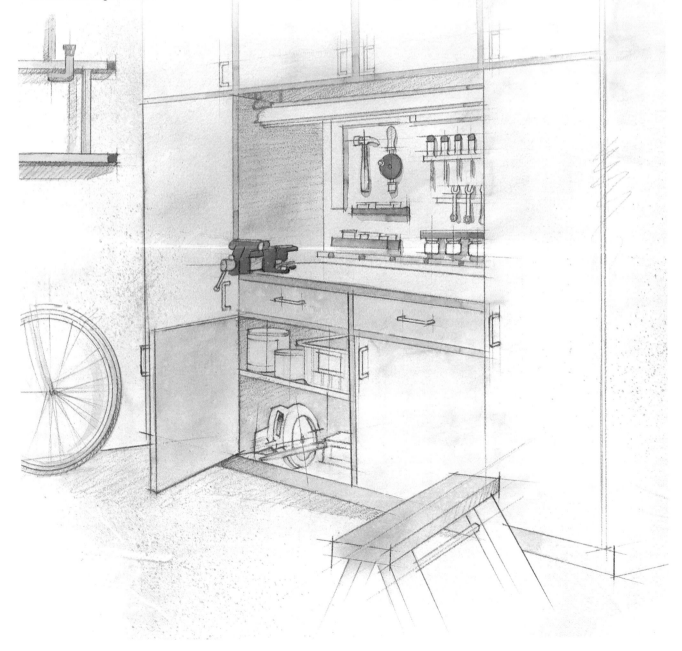

SHOP CONCEPT:
Miter Saw Support

Power miter saws work great for cut-off work, but to handle stock longer than a few feet, they need either extensions or other methods of supporting boards being cut. Extensions are commercially available if the saw will be taken often to a job site. In the workshop, however, there are two methods of creating support on either side of the saw.

One way to provide support on both sides of the saw is to create a drop-down section within the center of a workbench. If you can get by with support on only one side of the saw, the drop-down section can be made at one end of the workbench, or a shorter bench can be added on the end. Another method is to set the miter saw on top of the bench, then build raised support sections on one or both sides. With normal-height workbenches, however, this may raise the saw above what might be a comfortable working height. The supports on either side may be of any stock available. Tip: By adding an upright along the back edges of the supports, you can use sliding stop blocks to cut down on measuring for repeat cuts (see Radial-arm Saw Stop Block, page 118).

Starter Floor Plan

This shop, in space equivalent to a double-car garage, houses a full range of basic tools and provides adequate working room as well. It adds a third workbench and parts table to the two workbenches and assembly bench shown in the Homeowner Workshop. The assembly bench is surrounded by most of the equipment that would be needed while constructing or assembling a project. The assembly bench, the workbench opposite the assembly bench, and the parts table, are all kept at the same height as the surface of the tablesaw and jointer tables; this eliminates any need for outboard supports for stock being processed. One workbench is outfitted with a machinist's vise, while the assembly bench has a woodworking vise. A roll-around cabinet housing hand tools can be kept near the open working area for easy access during large-scale assemblies. Wood stored along the wall can be protected from elements and sawdust accumulation with a canvas drop front.

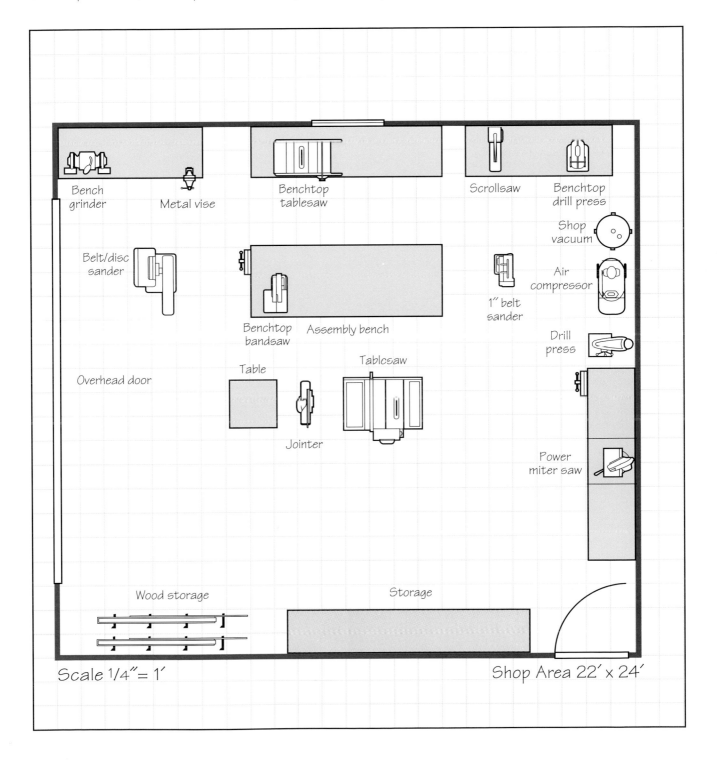

Bench grinder

Metal vise

Benchtop tablesaw

Scrollsaw

Benchtop drill press

Shop vacuum

Belt/disc sander

Air compressor

1" belt sander

Benchtop bandsaw

Assembly bench

Drill press

Table

Tablesaw

Overhead door

Jointer

Power miter saw

Wood storage

Storage

Scale 1/4" = 1'

Shop Area 22' x 24'

STAGE III

WORKSHOP TOOL CLOSE-UPS

1 TABLESAW, STATIONARY. Floor-model saws become the centerpiece of most woodworking shops. Features to consider include stability of blade mechanism and fence, table material and weight, horsepower, and whether it is belt- or direct-drive. Horsepower typically ranges from 1½ to 3.

2 SCROLLSAW. Becoming increasingly more popular for intricate scrollwork, models can cost from under $100, on up to $1,000 or more. Features to check include type of blade used, depth of cut, throat depth, table material and tilting, and speed control.

3 BANDSAW, BENCHTOP. Newer compact models offer full-size features and typically can cut wood to 6″ thick and 10″ wide. Blades usually travel over two or three wheels with rubber tires, powered by a ⅓-hp, direct-drive motor. Check for tilting table, sawdust port, and blade width capacity. Blades track better on a two-wheel design and break less often.

4 DRILL PRESS, FLOOR MODEL. Floor models allow more table travel than benchtop models, handy when using longer bits, thick materials, or mortising attachments. Features to look for include horsepower, swing capacity, quill travel range, table travel range, and speed ranges.

5 **BELT/DISC SANDER, 4″.** The 4″ refers to the belt width on these benchtop units, which resemble an inverted belt sander. Tilting tables allow bevel sanding. Belts are typically 36″ long, running at 2,000 feet per minute, while discs are usually 6″ in diameter, running at 3,200 rpm.

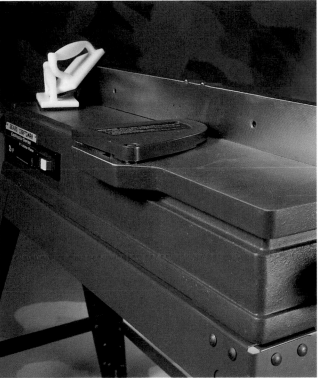

6 **JOINTER.** This tool produces the first flat side of rough lumber, which allows the truing up of the other three dimensions. It uses three or four cutting knives, an adjustable fence, and beds from about 21″ to 76″ or more long. Motors range from ½ to 2 hp. Check for adjustments possible, including tilting features, and width capacity.

7 **AIR TOOL SET.** For use with air compressors, tools can be selected according to need, including inflators, wrenches, blowguns, and brad nailer (above). Generally larger compressors are required for drills, ratchets, hammers, sand blasters, power washers, impact tools, saws, nailers, and staplers.

8 **DRILL/DRIVER, CORDLESS.** Big brother to the power screwdriver, this tool drills holes, drives screws, or turns bolts. Recharge time varies from 15 minutes to an hour, and rpm can range from 50 to 1,650. Those running on 7.2 volts will do, but 9.6- and 12-volt units have more reserve.

BUILDING A PLYWOOD BENCH

Unless you have a special reason to make a heavy workbench, consider this bench, which is inexpensive and easy to build. This design, discovered by woodworker Russ Barnard, allows you to make workbenches fast, using only 1x and 2x lumber and ¾″ plywood. The bench can be made to any size and in little time; you can make one in a half hour if you have the lumber on hand, and it may cost you less than $30 for the materials.

The best thing about this workbench is that its legs can be cut out quickly with a taper jig on a tablesaw. One 8″ or 10″ board yields both sides of one leg. Once you start building these benches, you'll discover all sorts of ways that they can be modified. Make them longer, shorter, higher, lower, even narrower. The plywood top can be used as is, or it can be covered with Masonite if you need a slick surface. The bottom shelf can be raised or lowered, depending on your needs. And you can insert drawers through one or both sides of the top frame support, which is simply a rectangle of 2x4s with a facing of 1x lumber, or you can add the drawers below the top frame.

Of course, you can make as many shelves as you want,

in any style you desire. You can paint or stain the bench, or just leave it natural. The bench is light and easy to move around, yet sturdy enough that it could be jumped on all day and still hold up. The one shown in the sketches is 8′ long, 2′ wide. If it is destined for finishing work, it can be made 36″ high, with a box/shelf at one end on top for storing supplies, such as stains, varnishes, paints, and brushes. Here is the cutting and assembly procedure:

First, make up two 2x4 frames, with the ends butting to the inside. Make up the top 2x4 frame with two 92″ 2x4s and two 18″ 2x4s. The top frame should have either one or two crosspieces, depending on how the bench is to be used. To make the bench look better, the top frame can be faced with ¾″-thick lumber before assembly. Make the bottom 2x4 frame using two 93½″ and two 19½″ lengths of 2x4. Next, make up the legs for the bench using ¾″-thick 1x8s or 1x10s. To cut the legs, you can make a jig of plywood for use on a tablesaw, or simply draw a line from end to end, marking one end 2½″ in from one edge; marking the other end 3¼″ in from the opposite edge. Then cut the stock freehand on the bandsaw. Any slight wandering from the saw line will hardly be noticeable, and will not affect the fit.

One leg side is ¾″ narrower, so the sides will be symmetrical when butted together. Flip one leg end-for-end, and join the two legs with the original outside edges butting each other. Screw the leg sides together,

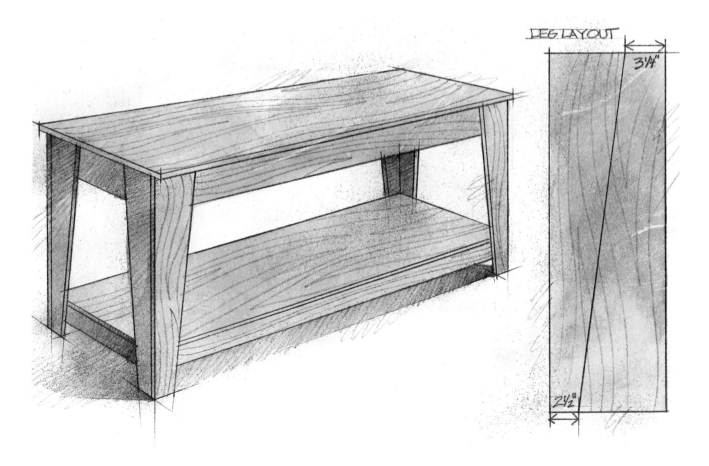

LEG LAYOUT
3¼″
2½″

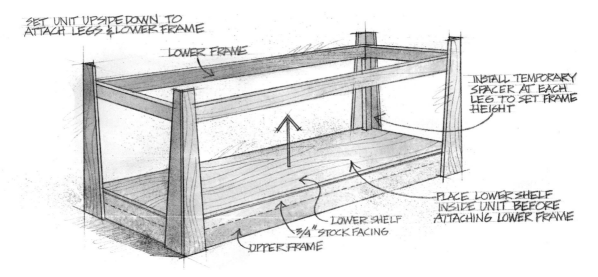

SET UNIT UPSIDE DOWN TO ATTACH LEGS & LOWER FRAME

LOWER FRAME

INSTALL TEMPORARY SPACER AT EACH LEG TO SET FRAME HEIGHT

PLACE LOWER SHELF INSIDE UNIT BEFORE ATTACHING LOWER FRAME

LOWER SHELF

3/4" STOCK FACING

UPPER FRAME

then set the top 2x4 frame upside down on a level floor. First tack the legs to both ends of the upside-down frame with 8d nails. (The legs can be any length you desire to accommodate your preferred working height.) After all the legs are nailed to the top 2x4 frame, and before attaching the bottom frame to the legs, lay the plywood for the bottom shelf inside on the bottom side of the top frame. Next, insert temporary 1x spacers in the leg corners between the plywood and bottom frames.

With the spacers supporting the bottom frame, attach the legs to it with 8d nails.

After the legs are attached to the bottom frame, turn the bench over and check the leg heights. If a leg happens to need adjusting, just pry it off and adjust to fit. With all legs checked and/or adjusted, reinforce the nails holding the legs to the frames with drywall-type bugle-head screws. After putting on the top, and any additions or finishing, the bench is ready for service.

SHOP PROJECT: T-Square Jig

A simple T-square jig is a useful shop aid for cross-cutting wide panels with a portable circular saw, especially if you do not yet have a tablesaw. This same basic T-square can also be used for routing dadoes with a portable router, as the drawing shows.

The blade of the T-square should be about 5½" wide and at least 28" long. The crossbar should be 1x3x15". The clamping block is about 2½" square and ½" thick. To assemble the jig, first draw a line across a 24"-wide panel that is exactly 90° to the edge. Then clamp the T-square blade on the line with two C-clamps opposite the end where the crossbar will be attached. Next, glue the crossbar to the blade and clamp with C-clamps. The right side of the crossbar should have enough material so the excess can be cut off with the saw. After the glue has dried, insert four wood screws into the blade and crossbar. Then glue and screw the clamping block to the crossbar.

To use the T-square with a portable saw, make a mark on the panel where you want to make a saw cut. Line up the end of the crossbar with the mark. Clamp the T-square to the panel with two C-clamps or a single bar clamp, and run the saw against the edge of the T-square blade.

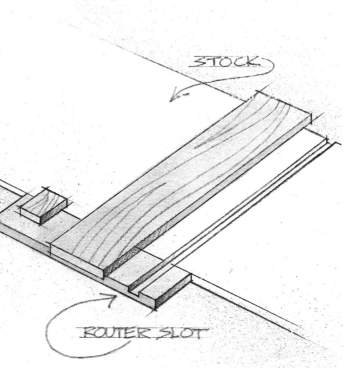

STOCK

ROUTER SLOT

STORING TOOLS BOOK-STYLE

If you don't have or want pegboard walls in your shop, but still would like the convenience that they provide for tool storage, here is an idea that can give you the best of both worlds. It's a way to hang panels of pegboard together in one place, similar to how stores display posters, and effectively gives you a "book of tools." The swinging pegboard panels can help organize your tools to cut down on chasing around the shop, even if you already have pegboard panels in other areas.

This idea was conceived to cut down on time spent hunting for hand tools in one or more toolboxes scattered throughout the workshop. To assemble similar swinging panels to organize your own tools, first decide on how many panels you would like (the illustration shows how to set up the supports for seven panels). Buy as many 2x4′ sheets of pegboard, or buy 4x8′ sheets and saw them in half. You can use either ⅛″ or ¼″ pegboard.

Next, fasten each of the panels to 5′ lengths of split ½″ thinwall conduit, using ³⁄₁₆″ machine screws. Attach the panels with 6″ of conduit extending beyond both the top and bottom of the panel. After each panel is attached to the conduit, make a panel stiffener by grooving a 48″-long piece of 1x2 with a saw on one side. Then attach the 1x2 strip over the outside edge of each panel using screws through the side of the strip. The stiffeners keep the panels sturdy as they are loaded up with tools.

After the panel sections are complete, make the top and bottom supports. Use short sections of 2x4 or 2x6 stock. Drill through ⅞″-dia. holes to accept the top ends of the conduit, and drill the same size corresponding holes in the bottom support, but drill only to a depth of 1″. This provides support for the bottom end of the conduit on each panel.

Use ⅜x4″ lag screws to mount the 2x4 supports to wall studs in your shop. If you wish, the bottom support can be placed on the top of a workbench. Either way, once the supports are attached, you can insert the pegboard panel assemblies as shown. Insert the upper end of the tubing through the upper hole first, and then swing it in and insert the lower end. Each panel is like one page of a book. The farther you space these "pages" apart, the farther they will swing to the side before they interfere with the next panel.

The assembly, set near a workbench, puts all of your hand tools within easy reach as you work at the bench vise. It can be made with as many panels as you need; just remember to drill the holes with a radius similar to that shown in the illustration. Built as in the drawing, the seven panels used on both sides will provide equivalent storage of 112 sq. ft. of wall pegboard, or the same

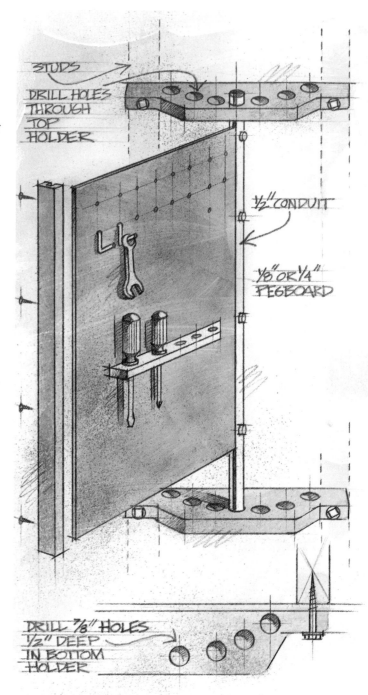

as 2′-high and 4′-wide pegboard sections running around your shop for a total of 28′.

You can use commercially available pegboard hooks in the panels. Pieces of 1x2 or 2x2 stock can also be used to make tool holders. Each strip can hold a number of screwdrivers or punches. Also, by inserting dowels in the strips, the strips can also accommodate a neatly arranged socket set. If you are good about returning items to their respective places on the panels, a quick visual check of the panels will alert you to items that are missing.

BUILDING A VENEER PRESS

As fine timber becomes more expensive and harder to get, making veneered panels can become necessary to hold down costs. If you don't trust hammer veneering, or using contact cement, which tends to leave project-marring air bubbles in the finished work, there are few alternatives to using a veneer press. Commercially available veneer presses have metal frames, but you can build your own of hardwood to serve the needs of a small workshop, at far less expense.

Before beginning to build your veneer press, you must decide what will be the largest area you are likely to veneer. The press should apply even pressure over the entire surface being veneered, and that calls for a veneer-press screw every 9″. If, for example, you will never veneer an area larger than 24x48″, you may be able to get by with four frames that each hold three Jorgensen press screws. (The ends and edges can be clamped with C-clamps, handscrews, or other clamps.) The parts required for each frame are two pieces of hard maple 2x3x28½″; two pieces of hard maple 2x3x11½″; eight bolts ⅜x2½″ with nuts and washers, and three Jorgensen #CG-1 clamps.

To start, figure out which pieces will be the tops. On the underside of each top, at the center and 9″ on either side of it, drill a 1⅛″-dia. hole 1⅝″ deep. Then drill the hole through with a ¾″ bit. Join the four pieces of maple with "through" mortise-and-tenon joints at each

PRESS SCREW

corner, made on the tablesaw, using glue. After the glue has dried, drill each to accept the bolts that keep them together when clamping pressure is applied. After the press frames are made, insert the screw collars in the 1⅝″ holes, screw in the press screws, and draw them tight.

To use the press, simply slide a couple of pieces of well-waxed fiberboard or particleboard into the frames, slip in your glued-up work, apply a well-waxed top piece, and tighten the screws. If you are using the full capacity of the press, you will want to clamp around the edges with clamps you have on hand. Four press frames may cost about $150 to build; a less expensive way is to make your own press screws of green wood instead of buying metal clamps (see Making Screw Clamps, page 124). A threading set, including a thread box and tap, will cost about $65.

SHOP PROJECT: Board-Straightening Jig

Work on the tablesaw other than straight cutting usually requires the help of jigs and fixtures that you can buy or, better yet, make up yourself. A simple jig can be used with a tablesaw to straighten the edge of a board with a side bow. Use a strip of ½″ plywood of a length that is 4″ to 6″ longer and about half as wide as the board to be trimmed. Tack the plywood strip with small nails to the top of the bowed board, with the points of the bow positioned to face toward the fence. Run the opposite side of the bowed board through the blade, using a pushstick against the plywood strip. After cutting one side of the bowed board with the jig, unfasten the plywood strip, turn the board around, and run the board through the saw again using the previously straightened edge against the fence.

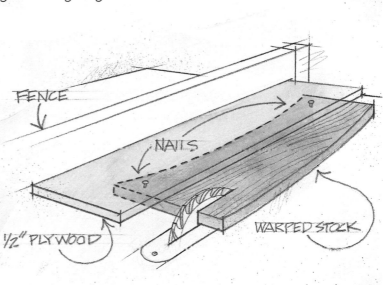

FENCE

NAILS

½″ PLYWOOD

WARPED STOCK

BUILDING A SURFACING JIG

This shop-built router surfacing jig is simple to build and can save the day when you need to restraighten boards that have become cupped, bowed, or warped. And it will never wear out.

For example, you may buy expensive wide boards and store them for your next big project, only to find later that their surfaces have become imperfect. When this happens, you can hold the board on your workbench with bench dogs and use a roughing plane, followed by a smoothing plane, to get the boards back to perfect dimensions. But the hand method is a big job, and it takes time, too. Instead of straightening boards by hand, you could use that time to build yourself this jig, which will let your router do the job for you.

As shown below, the three-part device consists of a router, a sliding router guide, and a base that holds the board to be surfaced. The board to be worked is press-fitted into the base with the aid of strap springs. The router moves across the width of the board being worked in successive passes between the rails of the top slider section, which in turn is moved over the jig base, along the length of the board.

You can build this shop helper by exactly duplicating the jig shown here or by adapting the general concept to virtually any size. The base of 1″ plywood has 2x2 pine side rails topped with ½″ hardwood slide strips. The rails are 15½″ apart, and each is 1¼″ wide. The hardwood strips are fastened to the top of the 2x2 rails with

countersunk wood screws at about every 6″. The second part of the jig is a sliding router holder that fits over the base and moves side to side over the rails of the base. The slider has a ¾″ slot that the router bit goes through. Set on the base, the slider lets the router move across the width of the board being surfaced in successive passes of small increments, and also allows the router to move lengthwise along the base as well. The slider is of ¾″ plywood. Two-inch-wide ¾″ scrap lumber is fastened on the bottom side, to fit outside the two rails of the base, and two pieces of the same lumber are used on the top side of the slider, spaced so that your router will slide between them.

To adapt some routers to fit between the slider's top rails, you may need only to grind two sides of the base to fit; for other routers you may need to make up a square router-base attachment from material such as Masonite.

To use the jig, hold the warped board in place in the base of the jig with both a spacer board and spring clips that are bent from steel strapping. For a good fit, allow about 1/16″ between the spacer board and one side of the base rails. Use small wedges under the high spots of the crooked board to prevent it from rocking as the router passes over it (see illustration). When used with a ½″ straight bit in the router, mark the slider with lines 3/8″ apart. Then, after each pass, move the router over by 3/8″; that way the bit will overlap the previous pass by 1/8″. (With this method, an 8½″-wide board will take about 24 passes, about 5 minutes' worth for both sides.) You can work one side of board, then run it through a planer, or straighten both sides on the straightening jig.

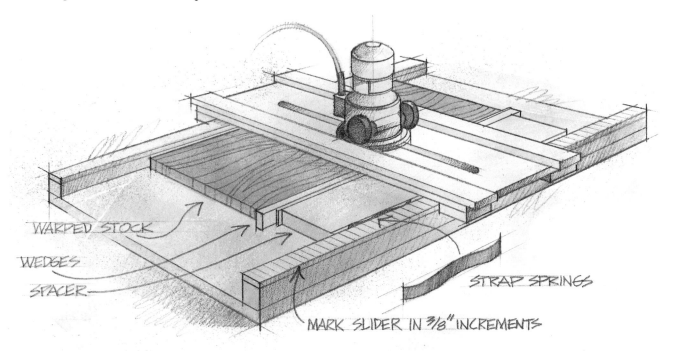

WARPED STOCK

WEDGES

SPACER

STRAP SPRINGS

MARK SLIDER IN 3/8″ INCREMENTS

MAKING A SHOP FORGE

A simple forge is often essential for heating up metal for bending when a torch won't do the job. Just as with blacksmith forges that use bellows or blowers, the key is to create some type of firebox and to fan the coals to increase the temperature of the fire. Small, temporary forges can be rigged up using either a barbecue grill, a salvaged car rim, or a flared-type truck brake drum, as shown.

Blacksmith coal is best, but barbecue briquettes can also be used. When heating metal, it is best to read up on the techniques of hardening and tempering metals, which are not the same thing. Hardening is accomplished by plunging heated metal into a water, brine, or oil bath. Tempering can be fairly complex, and how it is done depends on the type of metal being worked. Tempering gives metal more strength while retaining the desired degree of hardness.

A barbecue grill can be lined with firebricks to create a small firebox within the grill to allow a more concentrated fire. (Don't use concrete blocks, which may explode under extreme heat.) To deliver air, connect an appropriate-sized pipe to the side, using a pipe long enough so that the fire's heat won't melt the blower hose. A shop vac or a vacuum cleaner with a blower attachment can be used as an air source. To control air flow, use a rheostat switch, or drill holes into the lead-in pipe.

A car rim makes a more substantial forge. One way to use a car rim is to attach a 3″ chimney pipe under the hub opening by flaring out sections of pipe on four sides and bolting each section to the rim using the existing openings. If the first length of pipe bolted to the rim is long enough, duct tape can be used to seal the elbow. A pie pan with holes drilled in it can be used to cover the opening on the inside. Any type of blower can be used.

A flared-type truck brake drum, used with a gas burner salvaged from a water heater, makes a more convenient temporary forge. The flash pan of the burner is shimmed up away from the bottom of the drum to allow it to draw air, and the interior is lined with fire brick. A 2″ well pipe is welded to the bottom, off to one side, and a cover with holes is welded to the inside. The gas line leading to the unit should have a shutoff, and all safety precautions should be observed. The unit can be mounted on legs and air can be fed through flexible exhaust pipe from a blower controlled by a rheostat switch.

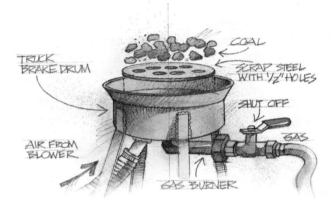

SHOP PROJECT: Radial-Arm Angle Jigs

Some woodworkers prefer using a single-purpose tool and even then prefer to use accessory jigs to minimize setups. For example, if you regularly need to cut parts on the radial-arm saw with ends at 17°, you could make up a jig to allow you to do that while keeping the saw blade at 90° to the backstop.

The jig can be positioned against the backstop and aligned with marks on both the backstop and the jig. The blade then will cut the piece at 17°, with no need to return the blade to 90°. Picking the jig off the wall is much easier than repositioning the blade of the saw each time, and you don't have to worry that the blade is exactly at 90°. Jigs can be made for different angles, marked as to their purpose, and hung on a nail until they are needed. If you need to duplicate some part with an odd angle, you can position the already-cut piece against the blade and tack a wooden strip or two against the edges of it. Then you can just use these strips to position the new piece for cutting; no need to figure the angle.

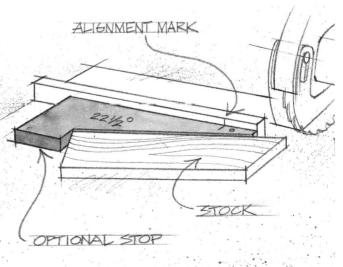

THE CRAFTSMAN WORKSHOP

When shop space becomes scarce, one way to fight the problem is to build a table with a reversible top, as shown opposite. Such a table effectively doubles the surface area available. The cordless drill/driver, above, eliminates cord hassles.

By adding less than $3,000 worth of tools to the previous Woodworker Workshop example on page 87, you will have—with minor exceptions —virtually every tool used by professional woodworkers, plus some basic tools to begin working metal. With a total price tag of less than $8,000 for tools, this workshop enhances woodworking ability by adding a stationary radial-arm saw, a stationary bandsaw, a thickness planer, a router/shaper, and a basic wood lathe. And, for working metal, it adds an arc welder, a rotary grinder, and a hefty ½″ power drill. An arbor press, not on the list, would be another worthy consideration.

The radial-arm saw is intended to supplement the stationary tablesaw already purchased. It is extremely handy for miter, bevel, and compound cuts, and can be equipped with a wide variety of accessories. Because of its versatility, it could easily substitute for the stationary tablesaw purchased for the Woodworker Workshop, as well as for the power miter saw purchased for the Homeowner Workshop. Like the benchtop tablesaw and benchtop drill press in previous shops, the stationary bandsaw added at this stage allows the benchtop bandsaw already owned to be sold or be used for specialized projects.

The router/shaper suggested is a half step between the basic router attached to a table and the stand-alone wood shaper. The router/shaper generally is a benchtop unit, and lower in price than higher-horsepower shaper machines. The wood lathe, like the radial-arm saw, is another tool that could be purchased much earlier if you have an interest in turning wood, or if your projects call for turned work. Even if it is not used that much, many woodworkers say they enjoy using the wood lathe more than any other tool in the shop.

When shopping for a welder, you will find an incredible variety of choices, starting with small 75-amp output "stick welders" that will run on standard 120-volt, 15-amp household current. Before buying a welder, try to visualize the type of work you will mostly be doing; you may want to consider one of the other welders suggested for the Professional Workshop. If, for example, cutting metal is of main concern, you may want to look at an oxygen/acetylene gas welder. Or, if working with thin metals such as car fenders will be your main activity, a metal inert gas (MIG) wire-feed welder may be the one to buy.

The addition of a welder gives you basic capabilities to work and shape metal, and you will find it handy for smaller projects, including repairing shop equipment. It will, however, influence the arrangement of your shop, both how it is set up and what materials are used for walls or floors. At a minimum, have a separate area for welding and, if possible, have a walled-off area or a separate room. Cover walls in that area with non-combustible materials and provide for adequate ventilation. A cement slab floor is best for any welding area, and fire extinguishers should be accessible.

With the addition of a welding area, it is likely you will need at least the equivalent of a two-car garage dedicated to this workshop. Even better is a structure the size of a three-car garage, or a separate building. Besides making use of all other storage possibilities, consider building permanent storage racks to help keep the shop orderly.

SPECIFICATIONS

THE CRAFTSMAN WORKSHOP

SPACE: THREE-CAR GARAGE OR SEPARATE BUILDING
AREA: 24´ X 32´ OR 768 SQ. FT.
STORAGE: OPEN SHELVING, CABINETS, UNDER BENCH, AND RACKS

TOOL BUDGET SUGGESTIONS
(See page 26 for complete Shop Tool Buying Menu.)

STAGE I TOOLS, UPGRADED   Your Budget
❏ Circular saw ($145)
❏ Sabersaw ($90)
❏ Power drill, ⅜˝ ($85)
❏ Router ($180)
❏ Bench grinder ($125)
❏ Sander, pad ($80)
❏ Sander, palm grip ($95)
❏ Miter box, manual ($70)
Subtotal: $870

STAGE II TOOLS, UPGRADED
❏ Tablesaw, benchtop* ($225)
❏ Power miter saw ($225)
❏ Stapler/nailer ($45)
❏ Scrolling sabersaw ($100)
❏ Drill press, benchtop** ($220)
❏ Belt sander 3x24˝ ($125)
❏ Air compressor ($275)
❏ Shop vacuum ($125)
Subtotal: $1,340

STAGE III TOOLS, UPGRADED
❏ Tablesaw, stationary ($850)
❏ Scrollsaw ($600)
❏ Bandsaw, benchtop*** ($200)
❏ Drill press, floor model ($400)
❏ Belt/disc sander, 4˝ ($250)
❏ Jointer ($400)
❏ Air tool set ($100)
❏ Drill/driver, cordless ($140)
Subtotal: $2,940

STAGE IV TOOLS, NEW
❏ Radial-arm saw, stationary ($450)
❏ Bandsaw, stationary ($500)
❏ Thickness planer ($450)
❏ Router/shaper ($250)
❏ Wood lathe ($300)
❏ Arc welder ($350)
❏ Grinder, rotary ($140)
❏ Power drill, ½˝ ($175)
Subtotal: $2,615
TOTAL: $7,765

*Benchtop tablesaw can be used for trimming large parts and cutting small parts during assembly. **Benchtop drill press can be used with sanding drums or for horizontal boring. ***Benchtop bandsaw can be used for small projects.

NEW ACCESSORIES AND SUPPLIES
❏ Woodworker's bench ($500) ❏ Wood vise ($125)
❏ Wood mallets, two ($35) ❏ Wooden clamps, four ($80)
❏ Bar clamps, four additional ($60) ❏ C-clamps, additional ($20) ❏ Try/miter square ($20) ❏ Dovetail square ($40)
❏ Marking gauge ($25) ❏ Sliding bevel ($15) ❏ Caliper, outside ($30) ❏ Divider ($15) ❏ Steel rule, precision ($10)
❏ Bench level ($75) ❏ Drawing tool kit ($65) ❏ Rip saw, quality ($40) ❏ Crosscut saw, quality ($40) ❏ Dovetail saw ($20) ❏ Detailing saw, fine-toothed ($15) ❏ Bench plane, short ($150) ❏ Bench plane, medium ($160) ❏ Chisel plane ($120) ❏ Trimming plane ($75) ❏ Spokeshave, convex ($55) ❏ Spokeshave, concave ($55) ❏ Drawknife ($40) ❏ Palm plane ($15) ❏ Brass plane ($30) ❏ Wood-rasp set ($125) ❏ Chisel set ($100) ❏ Carving tool set ($150) ❏ Turning tool set ($150) ❏ Circle cutter ($25) ❏ Forstner bit set ($125) ❏ Screwdriver set ($60) ❏ Other supplies ($150).
TOTAL: $2,815

BUDGET SUMMARY
Power Tools: $7,765

New Accessories and Supplies: 2,815

Accumulated Accessories and Supplies: 2,870

GRAND TOTAL: $13,450

SHOP CONCEPT:
Portable Lumber Storage

There comes a point in any home workshop when storage space for materials such as lumber becomes scarce and extremely valuable. The sketch here shows how a roll-around lumber cart will not only provide a place for raw lumber but also let you maneuver the entire inventory to where it is most conveniently used. For example, it can be kept in a room where moisture can be controlled, then wheeled out into the shop as necessary.

There are other ways to find space through the use of ceiling racks, wall racks, and portable carts. In most cases, ceiling racks are easier to install in workshops with open ceiling joists, but they can be added even if the ceiling is covered with drywall or other materials. Racks can be fashioned of wood, metal, or pipe materials. Especially valuable is a relatively narrow space reserved behind benches somewhere in the shop to store 4x8´ sheets of plywood, Masonite, or paneling.

SHOP CONCEPT:
Adapting Shop Vises

Common machinist vises in your shop can be adapted with inserts to protect expensive hardwoods. Even if you have a woodworking vise or two, the inserts can be used to add woodworking capability to your machinist vises occasionally, and, without the inserts, the machinist vises can also be used to work metal.

To convert a machinist vise, make simple wood inserts that ride the shank of the vise and provide soft jaws for holding wood. The wood inserts, as shown, are quick and easy to make, keep jaw marks off of your project, and stay in place surprisingly well. Adapt the idea to the specific vises you buy or already have. Those used on the vise shown are about 8x8", cut out to set over the vise shank, and fitted on the back side to fit the vise jaws. In some cases you can get by with only one vise insert.

Starter Floor Plan

In the space provided by a three-car garage or separate building, this workshop provides full woodworking as well as rudimentary metalworking capability. It is designed to provide efficient flow of materials. For example, from the storage area wood can be moved directly to the radial-arm saw for rough cutting to length. Then wood surfaces and edges can be processed through the jointer nearby, and next run through the thickness planer. Besides an assembly bench, the plan includes three worktables; two for wood and one for metal. One table for wood is kept handy to the jointer and planer, and the other near the tablesaw. One or both of the tables could be replaced with wheeled carts to provide more flexibility in transporting wood and projects. In this plan, the area directly behind the overhead doors can provide space for larger projects. For convenience in parts fitting and assembly work, both the benchtop tablesaw and the power miter saw used for cutting moldings have an assembly table close by. A 1" belt sander, if bought, can be near the lathe for sharpening of turning tools. The welders, drill press, and bench grinder are grouped near the metal-topped worktable, and the rolling cart for hand tools is handy to the metalworking area. Wood is stored in the corner opposite the metalworking area. For greater safety from fire hazards the metalworking corner of the workshop can be partitioned off with stud walls covered by thin-gauge steel panels. If metalworking equipment is not needed, the extra space in one corner could be used for a drafting/design center or as a fully partitioned office, as shown in the Professional Workshop plan, page 119.

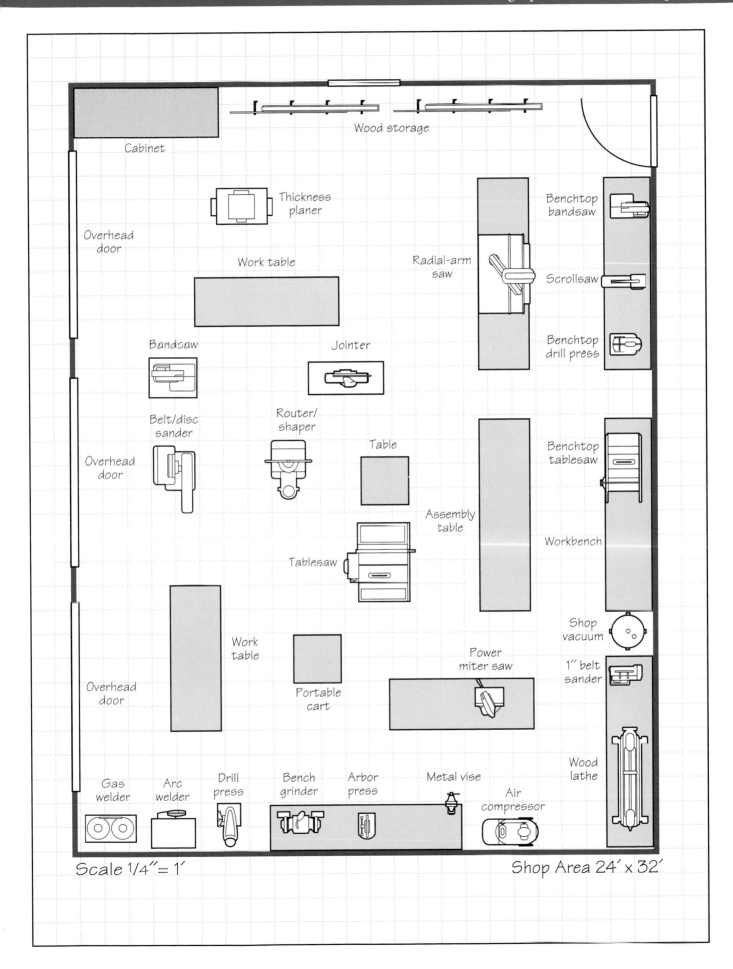

Cabinet

Wood storage

Overhead door

Thickness planer

Work table

Radial-arm saw

Benchtop bandsaw

Scrollsaw

Benchtop drill press

Bandsaw

Jointer

Belt/disc sander

Router/ shaper

Table

Benchtop tablesaw

Overhead door

Assembly table

Workbench

Tablesaw

Shop vacuum

Work table

Portable cart

Power miter saw

1″ belt sander

Overhead door

Wood lathe

Gas welder

Arc welder

Drill press

Bench grinder

Arbor press

Metal vise

Air compressor

Scale 1/4″= 1′

Shop Area 24′ x 32′

STAGE IV

WORKSHOP TOOL CLOSE-UPS

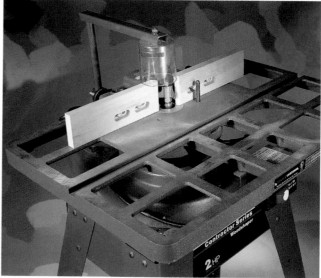

1 RADIAL-ARM SAW, STATIONARY. The most versatile of major saws, the 10″ blade version is most common. Ranging from about $250 to $1,000, it can be used for sawing or its blade can be replaced with dado or molding heads. It can also be used for sanding, buffing, grinding, shaping, routing, and some drilling.

2 BANDSAW, STATIONARY. A favorite in many home shops, this floor-model version is the tool of choice for irregular cutting. Blades from ⅛″ to ¾″ wide travel over two, sometimes three wheels. Distance from the blade to the back of the throat can vary from 10″ to 16″.

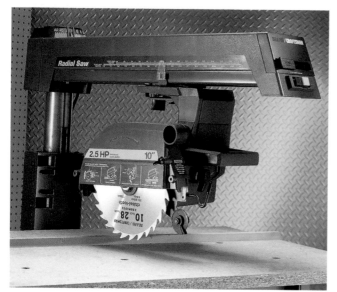

3 THICKNESS PLANER. Mostly used to smooth or reduce the thickness of stock, it's available in sizes that will accept boards from 10″ to 16″ wide, up to 8″ thick. Most have two or three knives in a cutterhead, providing from as few as 30 to as many as 1,000 cuts per inch.

4 ROUTER/SHAPER. The big brother to the router table, this machine is available in benchtop as well as floor models to shape or mold wood. A typical home shop version will cost under $400, have a ⅞- or 1-hp motor turning a cutter about 9,000 rpm, a cast-iron table, and a rear chip exhaust.

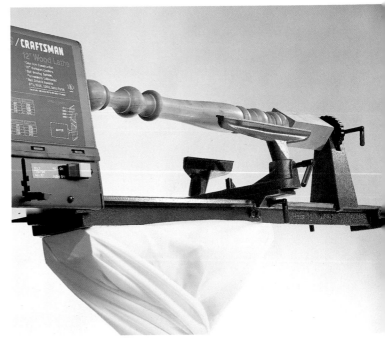

5 ARC WELDER. Compact AC welders operate on 240-volt, single-phase current for quick repairs, and for brazing or soldering with a carbon arc torch. More expensive models also offer DC current, allowing a more stable arc on difficult vertical and overhead jobs, and enough power for cutting and piercing.

6 WOOD LATHE. A typical home shop lathe will have a 12″ spindle turning capacity, a 36″ to 39″ distance between centers, a ½- to 1-hp motor, and several duplicating and sanding attachments. Step pulleys are used to provide turning speeds from about 875 to 3,450 rpm.

7 GRINDER, ROTARY. Also sometimes called a right-angle grinder, motors range from 1¾ to 3 hp to power aluminum oxide sanding and grinding discs in sizes from 4½″ to 9″. Most have a multi-position handle and will weigh from 11 to 17 lbs.

8 POWER DRILL, ½″. Hefty enough for heavy metal work, ½″ drills start at about $100 and range up to nearly $200. Variable speeds up to 1,200 rpm, as well as reverse, are common. Most offer a multi-position auxiliary handle, and ball and roller bearings.

BUILDING A REVERSIBLE TABLE

Most workshop bench or table space, no matter what size, eventually is not large enough. Or, it is taken up with mounted tools or the inevitable general clutter. Building a reversible shop worktable can give you two surfaces in the space one surface would take. A table with a reversible top allows you to bolt two tools to it, or to bolt one tool on one side and leave the other side as a large, smooth, sturdy work surface for layouts, framing, gluing, cutting, and various types of repairs.

As the sketches show, the table will double the use of the 4x4´ space it takes up in the shop. The legs are of 4x4x34½″ stock for a good, solid base, framed with 2x4 stock. A full fixed lower shelf of ¾″ stock can be added under the table for general storage. For your shop, you can duplicate the table as shown or adapt it to fit your own needs.

You have several choices for the reversible top work surface. Using ¼″ tempered hardboard will provide a tough, smooth surface on both sides. The core of the top can vary in thickness and in weight, depending on how you plan to use it. Remember that the heavier the top,

the sturdier it will be, but the more effort it will take to reverse the tabletop (turn it over). A minimum of two 4x4´ sections of ¾″ plywood is suggested as a core, faced with two sheets of ¼″ tempered hardboard. If you want a more solid top, you can add more plywood thickness or you can use 2x8 stock.

When reversing the tabletop, you will find that it is best to lift it from the end with the lighter weight. Slide the top toward you on the runners. When the back edge reaches the midpoint of the runners, lift the edge toward you up and over, always allowing the weight of the top to be carried by the runners. Depending on the weight of the top, and the tools mounted on it, one person should generally be able to reverse it. Two people can reverse the heaviest of tops.

Any tools that are mounted on the top must clear the two side runners, and must clear the bottom shelf and braces. A surface outlet box can be mounted in the center of the table, with an extension cord used to supply power to mounted tools. You can secure the tool power cords to the top so they will not hamper the reversing of the tabletop. To protect the outlet box and motor windings from metal grinder fragments and possible shorts, fasten two sheetmetal shields to protect them. If you do picture framing or cut-glass work, you can improve the work surface by cutting a piece of carpet to cover it.

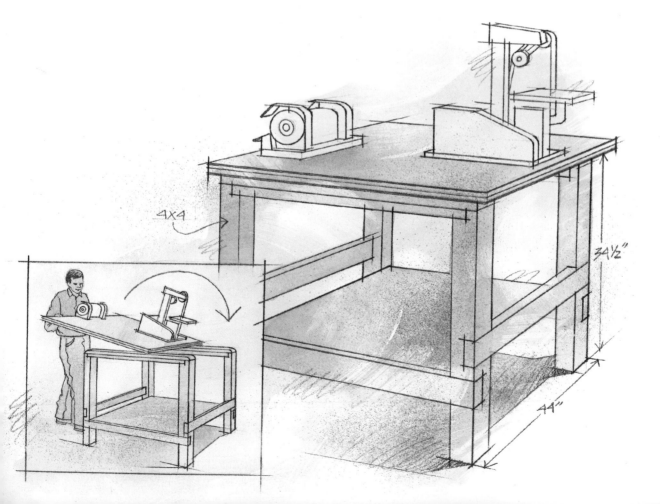

IMPROVING SHOP TOOLS

Among the many adaptations that can help you get better service from equipment, two are most helpful: (1) an extension bed for the jointer, and (2) a guide wheel for stock being rabbeted. The jointer bed extension is useful when edge-jointing a long board with a side bow. With some planning, the extension can be made to slip onto the end of the jointer with a wedging action to be held in place by friction, making it easy to attach and remove. You will need to build the extension bed to fit your specific jointer. Without an extension, the trailing end of a board with a side bow will raise up as it slides onto the infeed table, making it difficult to straighten. With the extension, the board is kept on an even plane as it passes from one end of the jointer to the other. This helps the jointer accommodate boards with a side bow, and also will work for boards with a face bow if it is not too severe.

Also, as the sketch shows, installing a guide wheel over the top of a tablesaw fitted with a dado head for rabbeting boards offers two advantages. First, the guide wheel will keep boards from raising when run through the saw. Sec-

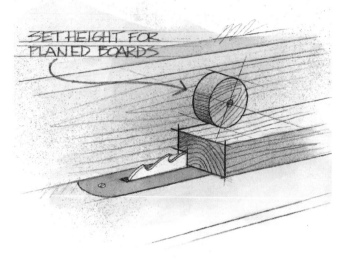

ond, installed at a specific height, the wheel will remind you if you have forgotten to run that stock through the planer before rabbeting. Cut out a small wheel of wood, and install just high enough over the table to accommodate the stock you normally run through the machine.

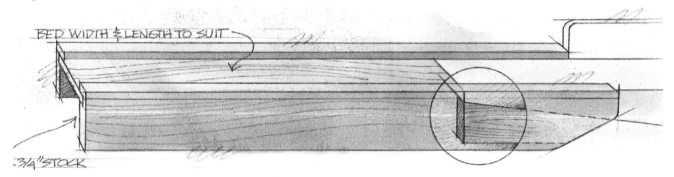

SHOP PROJECT: Clamp Improvements

Pads for pipe or bar clamps are available commercially, but you can make up your own with little effort. Scrap rubber, rubber shoe soles, or even discarded car mud guards will work. The trick is to cut the pad so the diameter of the hole in the pad is about 1/8″ smaller than the pipe or bar. You can use a sabersaw to cut the undersize circle and a slit in the top of the pad. The slit allows the pad to stretch in place over the clamp, without having to take off the end of the clamp. Make up two for each clamp in the shop and you won't have to be concerned about marring stock being clamped.

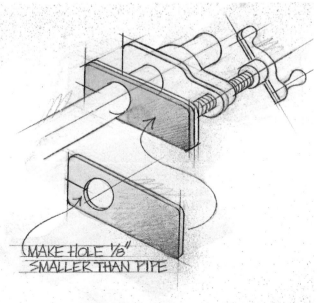

MAKING A DOWEL MAKER

Ready-made dowels, even of pine, can cost from 10 to 25 cents or more per foot of length; hardwood dowels, such as walnut, can cost $1 a foot or more. But a simple little jig you can make yourself, and operate with just a power drill, can allow you to make your own dowels at a fraction of the cost.

The materials to make the jig are inexpensive, and might be scrounged from around your shop. You need a section of 2x4 about 16″ long, and a worn-out file. With just these materials and a few screws, you can construct a dowel cutter that can produce dowels out of any kind of wood you want, of any diameter, whenever you need them. The illustrations show how this little rig works. Basically, you drill a hole through the upper edge of the 2x4, then make an angled cut in the 2x4 down so the top side of the hole is exposed. Then you insert a cutter blade made from the old file so that it is just inside the hole. To use it to make ¼″ dowels, for example, the hole in the 2x4 would be ¼″ large.

A table- or radial-arm saw is used to cut strips of stock just slightly more than ¼″ square. The next step is to put a point on one end of each strip with a belt or other type sander. If the strips are larger than ¼″ square, the other ends will require rounding to fit into the chuck of a ⅜″ drill. Then turn on the drill and, with the square stock spinning, insert it into the dowel cutter. If the blade is adjusted correctly, a perfectly round dowel will come out the other side. The dowels can be made as long as 5′ or more if you make some adaptations to the cutter, as explained below.

The 2x4 you use doesn't have to be of a precise length, but it should probably be at least 16″ long. Nail or screw it onto another board to serve as a base that you can clamp into a bench vise. To make the cutter, you must first reduce the old file to an appropriate length. If you put the file upright in a vise, throw a rug over it and hit it, it usually will break just above the vise. You can also heat the file up red hot, let it cool down, and use a hacksaw. With whichever method, use all proper safety precautions.

Next, mark the old file with some chalk where you want to make the two holes for fastening it to the top side of the 2x4. Then use a small propane torch to heat these two areas red hot to take the temper out. Doing this will make drilling holes through the file much easier. When you drill the holes, make them somewhat larger than the screws you plan to use, so you will be able to adjust the cutter after it is on the jig. Cut the file where you want the blade, then sharpen the edge to about a 30° angle, and screw it into place. Use washers under the screwheads. Make a test run and adjust the cutting blade as necessary.

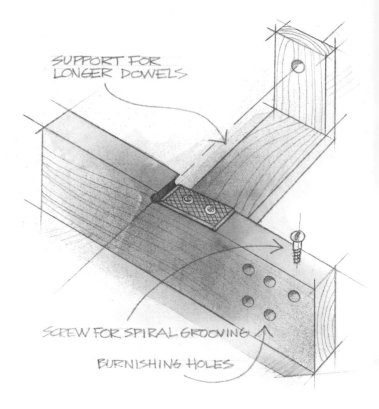

SUPPORT FOR LONGER DOWELS

SCREW FOR SPIRAL GROOVING

BURNISHING HOLES

You can make your dowel-cutting jig even more useful by adapting it to make grooves in the dowel as well. For most applications, a dowel needs to have a spiral groove or a straight notch in it so that excess glue will be able to escape when you glue it in place. So, to adapt the cutter to make grooves, simply drill another hole off to the side on the 2x4. Then put a good point on the end of an ordinary wood screw with a grinder and drive the screw down so the point just enters the hole the dowel passes through.

To make a spiral groove, insert a newly cut dowel into the hole with the screw in it and push the dowel through the hole at a relatively fast speed. With a little practice you should be able to make perfectly acceptable spiral grooves on the dowel. If you prefer a straight groove, you can also make up a little jig that you can use on your tablesaw, as shown. Basically it is just a block of wood with a wide kerf in it, made with the tablesaw blade set at about a 45° angle. To the front of this block, attach a piece of ¾″ stock and drill a hole through both it and the block. To make the grooves, clamp it to the saw fence and set the saw blade so it just barely encounters the dowel as you push it through.

To produce long dowels, the dowel-making jig can be fitted with a special wooden arm that has an upright with a hole in it. The arm can be made to extend about

TIPS ON CONSTRUCTING A DOWEL MAKER

Instructions: Drill a ¼″ hole all the way through and ½″ down from the top edge of the 2x4. Then enlarge the entrance of the hole with a ½″ or larger bit. Next, cut an angle in the top of the 2x4 so the bevel edge of the file enters near the top of the ¼″ hole. Cut doweling stock on a tablesaw slightly more than ¼″ square. Make a point on one end of the strips and round the other end to fit into a drill chuck. With the jig clamped in a vise, chuck the round end of the stock into the drill and feed the pointed end into the hole. Adjust the file to get an exact ¼″ diameter. If cutting long dowels, use a steady-rest to keep the far end of the dowel from whipping. If making spiral grooves, insert a sharpened screw just inside the ¼″ hole and run the dowel through at a slow drill speed, but push it through relatively fast.

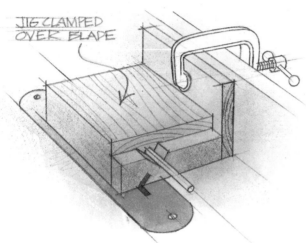

6″ back from the 2x4, so the hole in the upright lines up with the hole in the 2x4. This special "steady rest" helps keep longer dowels from whipping as they go through the jig. To make extra-long dowels with a dowel-making jig that doesn't have the steady rest, wait until you can get a helper or two. All they need to do is hold up the long dowel at one or two places so it doesn't starting whipping.

Don't forget that you can make up different-size cutters. You can make dowels the same size as any drill bit you have, and even more sizes by adjusting the cutter blade on the jig back and forth within the hole. One more way to make the dowel jig more useful is to make another tight-fitting hole on another part of the 2x4. After you get done making a dowel, you can push it through back and forth, and the friction will burnish the dowel to give it a nice finish. You can also use the jig to resize purchased dowels that have swollen slightly. Simply push them through the jig to shave off small amounts of wood so they will again fit into a ¼″ hole.

SHOP PROJECT: Dowel-Cutting Jig

This little jig works well for holding small stock, such as dowels, for crosscutting. Pieces cut off with the jig do not jump as they do when using only the miter gauge. And, as new pieces are cut, they push the cut pieces off the end of the table, away from the blade. The jig is a small sliding table of ³/₄″ stock for use with a tablesaw. It has a 90° angle V-groove across it to hold dowels in place. To make it, glue a hardwood strip to the bottom of the 10x14″ table to fit in the miter-gauge slots on the tablesaw. A piece of wood scrap fastened to the top side of the jig can serve as a handle. A strip of masking tape running along the groove can be used to make pencil marks for multiple cuts.

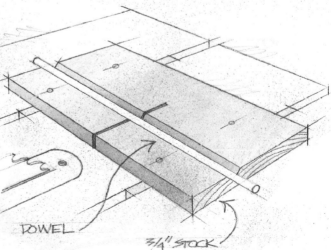

BUILDING A FOLDING BENCH

This clever design for a wall-hung workbench provides an easy answer to saving space in either a garage or a basement. Fold it out and you open up a wall of tools, plus gain a sturdy bench with nearly eight square feet of work surface.

The unit is easy to build and is compact and versatile. When not in use, just fold it up to keep your tools dust-free and to make it easier to clean the floor. You can build it with one sheet of plywood and dimensional lumber. In fact, because of its low cost, you can build more than one for different types of shop activities, such as general home maintenance work, model building, or light metalworking.

To make the workbench top, ¾″ plywood is cut to 26¼ x56½″. Then 2¼″-wide oak flooring is glued and nailed to the plywood. The cabinet is of simple box construction. A ⅛x⅜″ groove is cut on all interior faces of the cabinet frame for the pegboard. The groove is recessed ¾″ from the back side. Two cleat strips are used in mounting the unit against the wall, with holes drilled to match the location of studs. The cabinet is assembled with countersunk 2″ #10 flathead wood screws.

The leg brace support is cut from either ¾″ pine or plywood and mounted to the underside of the cabinet using four 1½″ #10 flathead wood screws. The legs are of 2x4s, with a dado ¾″ deep by 4″ wide cut across the face of each leg to accept a ¾x4x48″ rail. The rail is fastened with six 1½″ #10 screws, and the leg assembly is mounted to the bottom of the workbench with two 8″ strap hinges.

The brace is 6x32″, with a miter cut on one end. An angle block is nailed and glued to the mitered end to accept a carriage bolt (with wing nut) through the front rail. The other end of the brace is connected to the support under the cabinet with a 3½″ butt hinge. The benchtop is attached to the cabinet using two 3½″ butt hinges. A block mounted under the cabinet top provides a stop for the bench when closed.

The bench is mounted on the wall with four to six ¼″ lag screws through the cleat strips at the rear of the cabinet. The workbench is easy to finish after it is mounted on the wall, either with paint or with satin or gloss polyurethane.

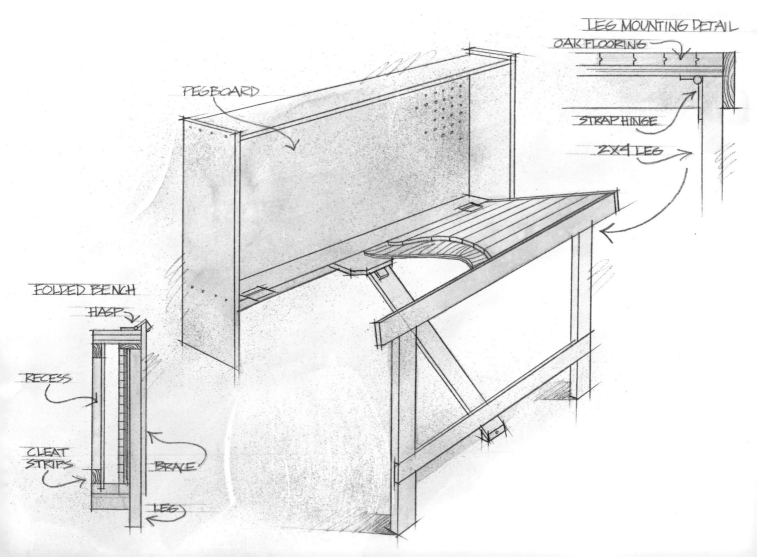

PEGBOARD

LEG MOUNTING DETAIL
OAK FLOORING
STRAP HINGE
2X4 LEG

FOLDED BENCH
HASP
RECESS
CLEAT STRIPS
BRACE
LEG

MAKING A LAMINATING JIG

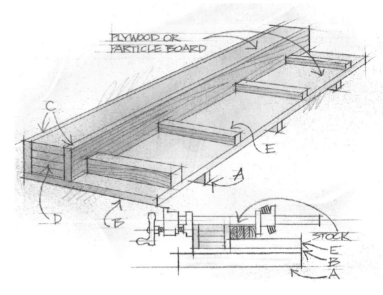

When laminating several pieces of stock face to face, it can be tricky to keep the wet glued surface from slipping out of alignment while clamping. The jig shown, originally designed for gluing up butcher-block tabletops, solves the problem. Smaller versions of the jig can be made for other kinds of laminated projects.

The material list for this particular jig is as follows: A is a piece of wood ¾x1½x20″ (three required). B is a piece of plywood or particleboard ¾x17x78″. C is a piece of hardwood ¾x3¾x78″ (two required). D is a piece of plywood or particleboard ¾x3x78″ (five required). E indicates spacers 1¼x1¼x12″. If short stock is used, it may be necessary to use more than the four spacers shown. A piece of ⅛″-thick hardware store acrylic plastic can be glued to the spacer blocks to keep glue from sticking to them. B is covered with polyethylene plastic film to receive glue droppings.

The first step in building the jig is to glue or screw together the D pieces. Then add the C pieces. The completed fence is glued and screwed to B. The A pieces attached to the bottom of B enable the jig to be clamped to a bench or table. When gluing laminated pieces that tend to ride up and down, short bar clamps can be placed under stock between the spacers to secure the stock until horizontal clamps are fastened to prevent further movement. A good procedure is to glue about four thicknesses of stock at one time, using a 3″-wide paint roller to spread the glue. Glue two of these assemblies together, run them through a planer, and then glue all the double sections together, using dowels to help line up the joints so they are flush.

SHOP PROJECT: Grinder Tool Support

The tool supports on most lower-priced bench grinders are narrow and may be limited in adjustment possibilities. The sketch shows how to make up one of your own that will be wide enough to handle most all items that need sharpening, and that will offer nearly infinite adjustment.

This support, made of plywood, provides a working width of 16″. The tool rest is 3½″ wide and ¾″ thick, and is carved out where it meets the grinder wheels to minimize the gap between the rest and wheels. Toilet bolts, screwed into the ends of the tool rest, are set in holes drilled in the end brackets. Wing nuts are used on the ends of the toilet bolts. The end brackets are made of 1″-thick plywood, and are slotted for front-to-back adjustment where they attach with wood screws to either the end of a workbench or to a block of wood on top of the bench.

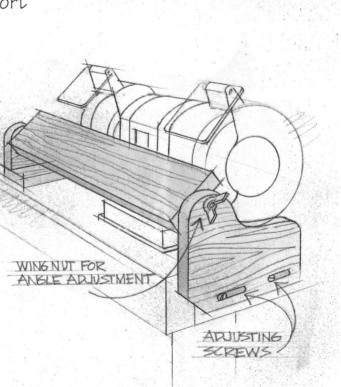

THE PROFESSIONAL WORKSHOP

Sliding saw tables, opposite, can be easily made up of low-cost materials in several versions to help cut down on measuring time when making crosscuts. The rotary grinder, above, is indispensable for metalwork.

This workshop comes the closest to what you might consider a dream shop. With full woodworking and metal-working capabilities, the price tag will be about the equivalent of a decent new car. But many would view it as a bargain, considering its full-range possibilities.

For about $12,000 additional tool investment over the Craftsman Workshop example on page 101, it adds equipment to achieve greater capabilities with wood, metal, or other materials. It boasts three additional woodworking tools: a random orbit sander for quickly removing material, a surface sander for sanding wide, flat panels, and a power planer, allowing the flexibility to do planing work on a portable basis. Likewise, it adds a slide compound miter saw for complex cutting either in the shop or on the jobsite. Among the tools added is a metal inert gas (MIG) wire-feed welder (a choice tool for thin metals), a big-league sawdust collector, a reciprocating saw, and a hammer drill.

If you have followed the tool-buying suggestions for the Craftsman Workshop, you already will have experience with the arc welder. Some shop owners get along fairly well with only an arc welder or a gas welder. At this point, you also could decide that what you need is a bigger arc welder with more capacity and output range, rather than the smaller one originally purchased.

This workshop provides plenty of opportunity to buy in stages. At this point you might consider a separate motorized grinder with wire wheels, but you could get by with a wire wheel on your original bench grinder. Likewise, you can wait on a metal bandsaw until your projects would make it pay. If the hammer drill suggested would be rarely used, then use the money for other specialized tools that will get more use, such as a hollow chisel mortiser, prized by many wood-workers. Or, you may opt for an oscillating spindle sander, or add more air tools, such as a pneumatic nailer/stapler.

If no other tool is on your wish list, spend any spare money to buy needed hand tools or accessories, to upgrade the blades and bits in the tools you already own, or to invest in metal-machining equipment, such as a metal lathe. With a metal lathe, you will be able to duplicate parts that are either expensive or no longer available, or to machine new parts to build your own tools or other needed jigs or fixtures. If you follow this pursuit, you will eventually need specialized tools, supplies, and accessories. Some examples include: a precision scale, a metal brake, die-maker files, a bead blast cabinet, a telescoping gauge set, a protractor, an internal pipe wrench, a tachometer, specialized pliers, a slag grinder, a swivel vise, and a deburring tool.

The tool suggestions for this workshop do not take vehicle work into account. If you intend to work on engines and automotive-related projects, you will need to plan to accumulate the metalworking and air tools listed, reduce the tools for working wood, and add such equipment as jacks, stands, engine hoists, electronic diagnosis equipment, a good cabinet full of specialized wrenches, and lubrication gear.

Because of the full-range capacity of this shop, an area equivalent to a three-car garage will likely be necessary to provide comfortable working space as well as material storage. A separate building is best, particularly because of the ever-present possibility of fire in a shop that accommodates welding and metalwork.

Specifications

The Professional Workshop

Space: Separate Building
Area: 26′ x 36′ or 936 sq. ft.
Storage: Open Shelving, Cabinets, Under Bench, Racks, and Office

Tool Budget Suggestions
(See page 26 for complete Shop Tool Buying Menu.)

Stage I Tools, upgraded

Your Budget

- ❏ Circular saw ($150) _____
- ❏ Sabersaw ($100) _____
- ❏ Power drill, ⅜″ ($125) _____
- ❏ Router ($235) _____
- ❏ Bench grinder ($140) _____
- ❏ Sander, pad ($90) _____
- ❏ Sander, palm grip ($100) _____
- ❏ Miter box, manual ($75) _____

Subtotal: $1,015

Stage II Tools, upgraded

- ❏ Tablesaw, benchtop* ($250) _____
- ❏ Power miter saw ($430) _____
- ❏ Stapler/nailer ($45) _____
- ❏ Scrolling sabersaw ($140) _____
- ❏ Drill press, benchtop** ($280) _____
- ❏ Belt sander 3x24″ ($180) _____
- ❏ Air compressor ($500) _____
- ❏ Shop vacuum ($190) _____

Subtotal: $2,015

Stage III Tools, upgraded

- ❏ Tablesaw, stationary ($1,700) _____
- ❏ Scrollsaw, benchtop ($800) _____
- ❏ Bandsaw, benchtop*** ($250) _____
- ❏ Drill press, floor model ($600) _____
- ❏ Belt/disc sander, 4″ ($375) _____
- ❏ Jointer ($700) _____
- ❏ Air tool set ($350) _____
- ❏ Drill/driver, cordless ($170) _____

Subtotal: $4,945

Stage IV Tools, upgraded

- ❏ Radial-arm saw, stationary ($600) _____
- ❏ Bandsaw, stationary ($750) _____
- ❏ Thickness planer ($1,000) _____
- ❏ Wood shaper ($450) _____
- ❏ Wood lathe ($750) _____
- ❏ Arc welder ($450) _____
- ❏ Grinder, rotary ($180) _____
- ❏ Power drill, ½″ ($200) _____

Subtotal: $4,380

Stage V Tools, new

- ❏ Sander, random orbit ($140) _____
- ❏ Sander, surface ($1,050) _____
- ❏ Power planer ($140) _____
- ❏ Compound miter saw**** ($450) _____
- ❏ Wire-feed welder ($750) _____
- ❏ Sawdust collector ($300) _____
- ❏ Reciprocating saw ($150) _____
- ❏ Hammer drill ($125) _____

Subtotal: $3,105
TOTAL: $15,460

*Benchtop tablesaw used for trimming large parts and cutting small parts during assembly. **Benchtop drill press used with sanding drums or for horizontal boring. *** Benchtop bandsaw used for small projects. **** First power miter saw used for basic cutoffs.

New Accessories and Supplies

❏ Professional tool set ($2,400) ❏ Rolling tool cabinet, 15-drawer ($500) ❏ Welding table ($100) ❏ Arbor press ($200) ❏ Machinist's tool chest ($180) ❏ Anvils ($75) ❏ Snap-ring pliers ($8) ❏ Gear pullers, two sizes ($60) ❏ Snap-ring assortment ($20) ❏ O-ring assortment ($15) ❏ Blacksmith hammers and tongs ($100) ❏ Tap and die set ($100) ❏ Wire brushes, extra ($10) ❏ Strap clamp set ($25) ❏ Countersinks, 60°, 82°, 90° ($30) ❏ Carbide metal drill bits ($75) ❏ Center drills, #1, #2, #3 ($30) ❏ Cant-twist clamps ($20) ❏ Grease gun ($20) ❏ Specialized screwdrivers ($40) ❏ Other supplies ($250).
TOTAL: $4,258

Budget Summary

Power Tools:	$15,460
New Accessories and Supplies:	4,258
Accumulated Accessories and Supplies:	5,685

Grand Total $25,403

SHOP CONCEPT:
A Workhorse Workbench

There are several ways to harness a workbench to
be more useful for general-purpose shop work, as this
sketch shows. This workbench has an under-bench area
for slide-in tool carriers made of pegboard and dimensional lumber; each tool carrier is organized for specific types
of jobs. The removable insert over the two banks of drawers along one end provides instant access to the top
drawers. If the contents of a specific drawer are needed
for the project at hand, those drawers are simply moved
to the top of the banks, directly under the removable insert. The back side of the bench has conventional shelves
behind cabinet drawers, along with space for two smaller
file drawer cabinets for keeping project plans, tool manuals, and the like. The top of the bench, of laminated hardwood strips, has a metalworking corner that provides the
services of an anvil, and more. It is made of a short section of large angle iron, approximately 3/8x6x6", which is
fastened to the corner of the benchtop. Assorted holes
drilled into the plate are used for bending round metal.
Several of the holes are customized with lips to allow
a fast way to punch glue grooves in dowels. A large-
diameter shaft stub is welded to the outside
edge of the plate, level with the
top, for smaller round-
ing jobs.

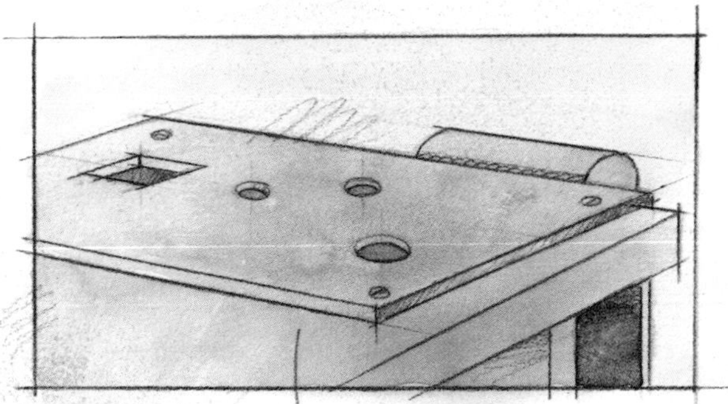

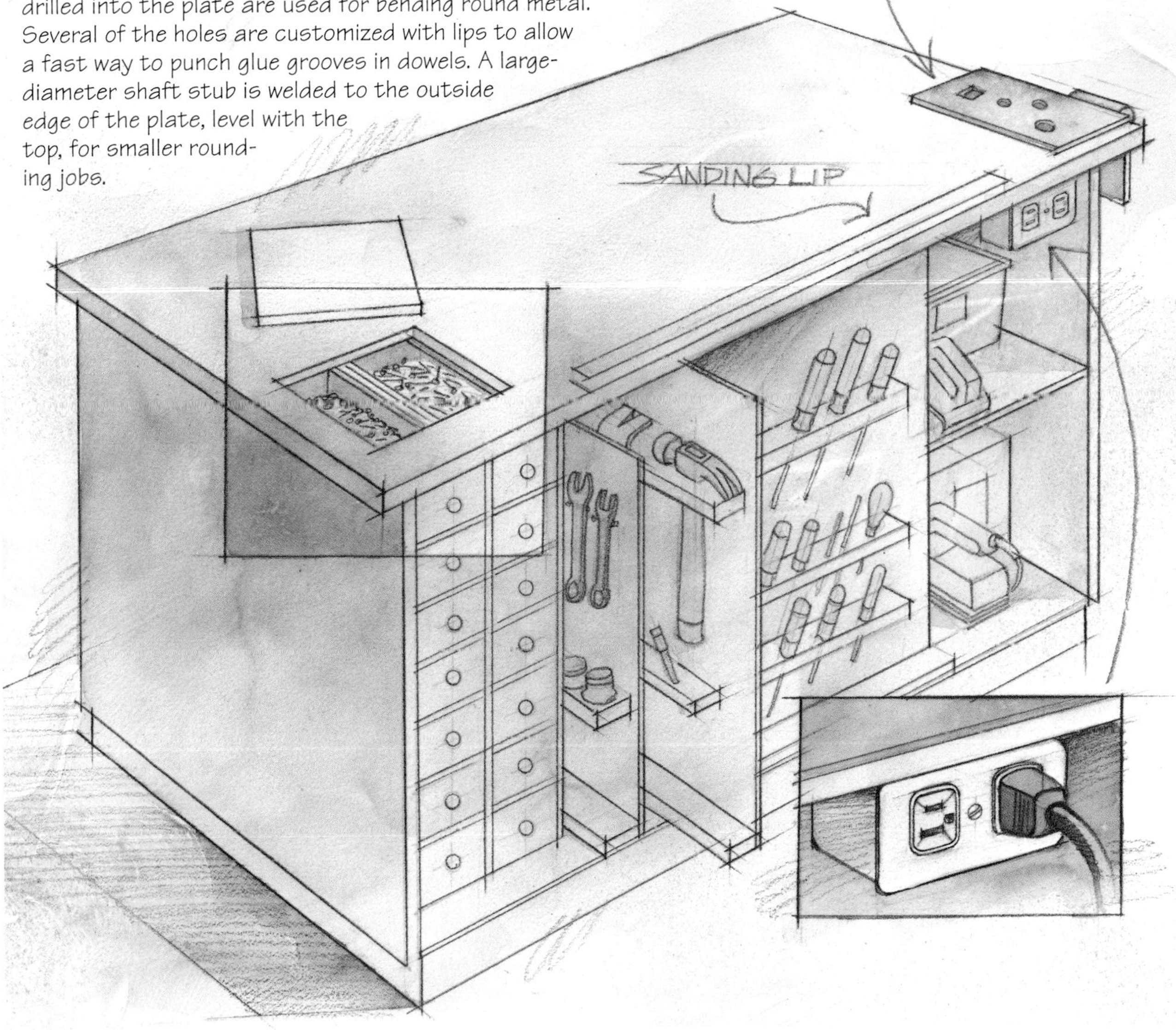

SANDING LIP

SHOP CONCEPT:
Radial-Arm Stop Block

This idea saves measuring time when cross cutting boards to predetermined lengths on the radial-arm saw. The same idea can be adapted to power miter saws. As shown, a simple stop block made with a short bolt fits over, and slides along, the top of the back wooden fence. To make a handle, a rosette of wood can be cut in half and glued back together over the head of the bolt.

Measuring marks can be penciled onto the back fence as required. For example, if you need to cut boards to exactly 32" lengths, set the block so when the board is pushed against it and cut, it will be 32". Make a mark to the blade side of the block indicating that the mark will produce a 32"-long board. If blades of different widths are used, measure from blade to block.

It is important that the end of the bolt pressing against the wood fence is flat and not sharpened to a point, so the bolt won't make indentations in the fence and cause slight changes in position. Be sure to hold the wood between the block and blade down and against the fence while cutting.

BOLT HEAD RECESSED AND EPOXIED INTO SPLIT KNOB

NUT RECESSED AND EPOXIED INTO SIDE

BOARDS CUT HELD AGAINST STOP

Starter Floor Plan

This ultimate shop is best set up in a clear-span building and is designed to provide a smooth flow of materials, from rough stock to finished product. Wood from storage can be either carried or carted to the radial-arm saw for rough cutting. From there, if boards are to be edge-jointed for ripping into strips, they are carted to the tablesaw to be ripped. Or, if boards are to be planed after jointing, they are face- and edge-jointed and carted to the planer. After planing, they can be carted to the surface sander, then moved to the tablesaw for cutting the pieces to final dimensions.

Other advantages of this plan include having the assembly bench located close to tools that may be used during assembly, such as the drill press, belt-disc sander, power miter saw, and bandsaw. The scrollsaw and benchtop drill press are near each other so that holes can be readily drilled for internal cuts. The lathe is between a 1" belt sander and bench grinder for sharpening tools used for either cutting or scraping work. The bandsaw, spindle sander, and router/shaper are within 10' of each other for sawing, sanding, and shaping work. As with the Craftsman Workshop, consider enclosing the metalworking area with thin-gauge steel panels for spark and fire protection. In this area, the metal bandsaw is near the metal storage area for convenience when cutting stock to length. Cut metal is then easily loaded onto a cart and wheeled to the welding bench for grinder or wirewheel work. The welders are located near an overhead door so they are available for working on large equipment, which can be kept outside. The storage and pick-up area, intended for storing finished projects, is near the office. After inspection and payment, the projects are moved through the nearby exit door. Larger objects, after acceptance, can be carted through the overhead door.

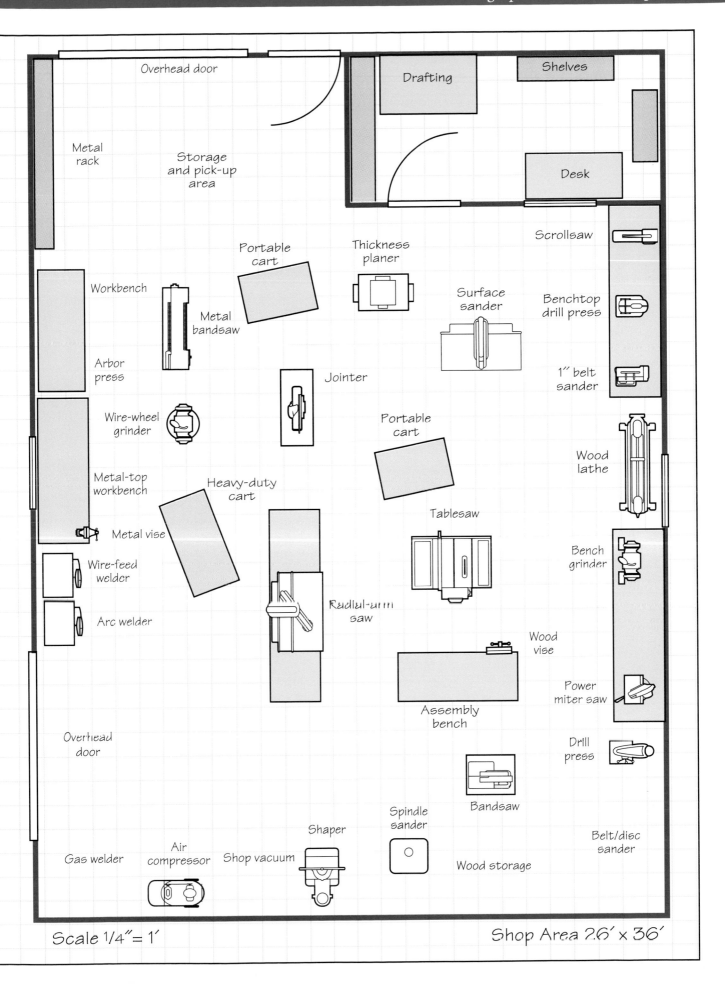

Overhead door

Drafting

Shelves

Metal rack

Storage and pick-up area

Desk

Scrollsaw

Portable cart

Thickness planer

Surface sander

Benchtop drill press

Workbench

Metal bandsaw

1″ belt sander

Arbor press

Jointer

Wire-wheel grinder

Portable cart

Wood lathe

Metal-top workbench

Heavy-duty cart

Tablesaw

Bench grinder

Metal vise

Wire-feed welder

Radial-arm saw

Wood vise

Power miter saw

Arc welder

Assembly bench

Drill press

Overhead door

Bandsaw

Belt/disc sander

Gas welder

Air compressor

Shop vacuum

Shaper

Spindle sander

Wood storage

Scale 1/4″= 1′

Shop Area 26′ x 36′

STAGE V

WORKSHOP TOOL CLOSE-UPS

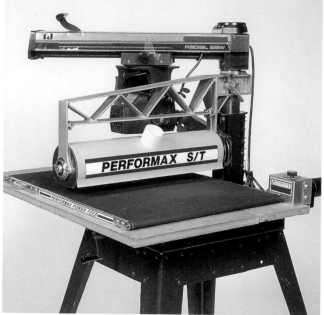

1 **SANDER, RANDOM ORBIT.** This versatile tool performs many roughing, finishing, and even polishing operations. Both 5″ and 6″ versions are available with auxiliary handles, variable speed, dust extraction, and other options. Smaller machines with 1½ to 2½ amps perform well in finishing applications, but for heavier work more powerful versions remove material nearly as quickly as a belt sander and provide a swirl-free finish.

2 **SANDER, SURFACE.** Designed to surface-sand wide pieces, it's available as a separate machine or radial-arm saw attachment. It can be used for surface- and finish-sanding, removing planer ripples, or surfacing rough or resawn boards. With open-sided design, stock as wide as 44″ and 4″ thick can be handled.

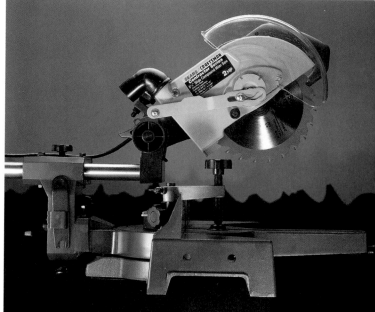

3 **POWER PLANER.** For portable planing a typical ¾-hp version can smooth and plane boards up to 3⅝″ wide, with settings to 1/16″. They rev up to 15,000 rpm no-load speed and provide up to 30,000 cuts per minute.

4 **COMPOUND MITER SAW.** With abilities rivaling the radial-arm saw, the slide compound miter saw allows compound miter/bevels up to 1¾″ x 8⅝″ and bevels up to 1¾″ x 12″. Typical models offer a 2-hp motor powering an 8¼″ blade.

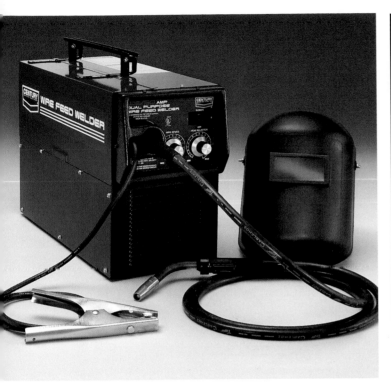

5 **WIRE-FEED WELDER.** Wire-feed MIG (metal inert gas) welders are used for welding lighter, thinner metals from 26-gauge to ¼″-thick steel. Typical welder packages include helmet, gun assembly, gas hose, gas pressure regulator, ground cable and clamp, and welding and spot-welding nozzles.

6 **SAWDUST COLLECTOR.** Hooked either directly to tools or to a central duct system, dual bag 1-hp systems operate at over 900 cu. ft. per minute. The upper bag filters dust while the lower bag collects larger particles. Casters allow easy moving between tools.

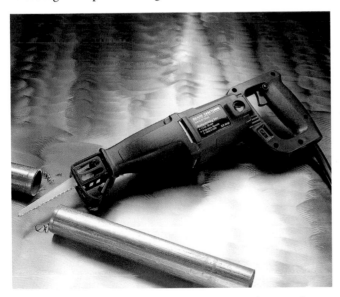

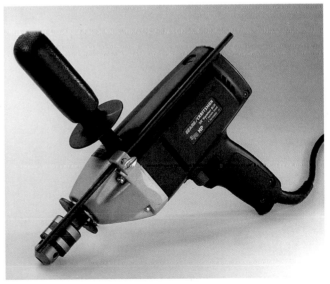

7 **RECIPROCATING SAW.** Heavy-duty saws have ¾-hp motors with dual variable speed ranges of 0 to 1,800 and 0 to 2,400 strokes per minute. They boast spiral bevel gears, 100% ball and roller bearings, and provide 1⅛″ stroke cuts.

8 **HAMMER DRILL.** Rotary hammer drills typically provide variable speeds to 1,200 or 2,500 rpm in drill mode, and 25,000 or 50,000 blows per minute in hammer mode to drill concrete with minimal effort. Typical drills accept ⅜″ bits and are reversible.

USING SLIDING SAW TABLES

If you find that you are making repetitive saw cuts for multiple project parts, consider making and using a sliding table on your tablesaw. It will save considerable time compared with setting up equipment from scratch over and over for 90°, beveled, or mitered cuts.

The table is an appropriately sized sheet of ½″ or ¼″ plywood, depending on the depth of cut needed and the diameter of the blade. The plywood has a narrow strip of stock fastened beneath it to fit the miter-gauge groove in the saw table. The guide strip is glued to the bottom, then nailed from the top. If the bottom guide strip is deliberately made ¹⁄₃₂″ narrower than the miter gauge slot, the sliding table can be maneuvered for more precision. You can make the initial cut bearing away from the blade, then by bearing toward the blade, an additional ¹⁄₃₂″ can be removed for a smooth trimming cut or when fitting moldings.

For a closed-end table for 90° cuts, strips of 1x2 are screwed to the plywood from the bottom to function as stops on both the edge to the front of the saw and the edge opposite the blade side. This version can be used with spacer blocks for repetitive cuts, as described below. For an open-end version for 90° cuts, only the stop along the edge to the front of the saw is attached, using screws from the bottom side. This version works well for squaring the ends of long boards. Either version can be used to make bevel cuts from 0° to 45° by tilting the blade.

Similar sliding tables can be made to make either 45°

or 22½° cuts, as shown. One arranged for 45° cuts can be used to cut perfect miters, provided you use the guides on each side of the jig to make matching cuts. (This is important because if only one guide or the other is used, any variation from 45° will be multiplied when fitting the two halves of the miter together. If both guides are used one at a time to make matching miter cuts, any deviation from 45° or 22½° will be self-correcting.) On the table for either 45° or 22½° cuts, the legs can be made adjustable to accommodate occasional odd angles. Sandpaper can be applied along the edges of the stop or guide strips on any of the tables to supply added friction.

The key to using the closed-end sliding table for repeated cuts are spacer blocks of wood of various lengths that are inserted as required for cuts of specific measurements. The blocks essentially function as miniature "story poles" that, when inserted by themselves or with other spacer blocks, instantly provide the width of cut needed. For example, one spacer block set on the sliding table can be used to make a cut of one width. That same block, plus one or more additional blocks, can be used to make predetermined cuts of other widths.

To make up the blocks, use plywood or cut from stock so the grain runs lengthwise to minimize any dimensional change. As you accumulate spacer blocks for various-width cuts, write on the block the cut that it is used for, along with what other spacer blocks are used with it, if any, and other information pertinent to the cutting procedure. Be aware that during winters the spacer blocks may sometimes shrink enough to throw off the measurements. So occasionally use a rule to double-check the cut made and, if the block needs it, use layers of tape on one edge to shim back to the precise length.

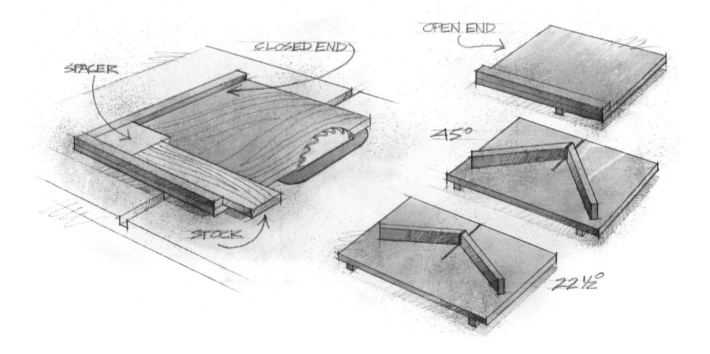

MAKING TABLESAW INSERTS

Most tablesaws come with a metal or plastic insert that fits in the recess in the area around the blade. The inserts can be taken out for removing or installing blades or dado heads. Saw manufacturers warn that you should never operate the saw without the proper insert in place, either a saw-blade insert when sawing, or a combination insert when doing dado or molding work. The insert helps keep small pieces of wood from getting wedged in beside the blade.

The problem with using only one insert for sawing is that the hole for the saw blade must be wide enough to accommodate the full range of saw blade angles. Therefore, for a particular angle, the open area around the blade will be larger than necessary. Professional woodworkers like to make their own inserts to keep the open area around the blade to an absolute minimum, one for each common setting, such as 90°, 45°, and 22½° blade angles.

The tight-fitting inserts are easy to make. Use stock selected to precisely match the height of the table. First cut the shape on a bandsaw. Then lower the saw blade

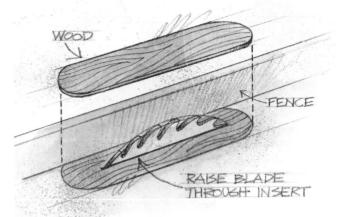

and position the blank insert into the recess of the saw table. Move the fence on top of the insert, making sure the blade won't come up under it. Clamp the blank insert down onto the saw table and then raise the blade (set at a chosen angle) on up and through the insert. By making up custom inserts for all angles commonly used on the saw, each will allow just enough room for the blade, rather than allow gaps at both sides like a common insert. They will also help prevent splintering on the bottom of boards being cut.

SHOP PROJECT: Bandsaw Helpers

Many helpful jigs can be made for the bandsaw; the ideas below are only two examples. You can use a simple piece of plywood and pegs to cut discs. Line up the center of the peg to the bottom of the saw gullet (some adjustment may be necessary), then clamp a stop block to the rear of the table. Slide the jig back, place the stock on the peg, then push the jig into the

blade until it touches the stop block. Then turn the stock. A bandsaw also works well for resawing thick wood for book matching or for projects that call for thin wood. To resaw, you can use a fence, which must be properly aligned, or a single contact point that allows you to steer the wood being cut. The contact point can simply be a block clamped to the table.

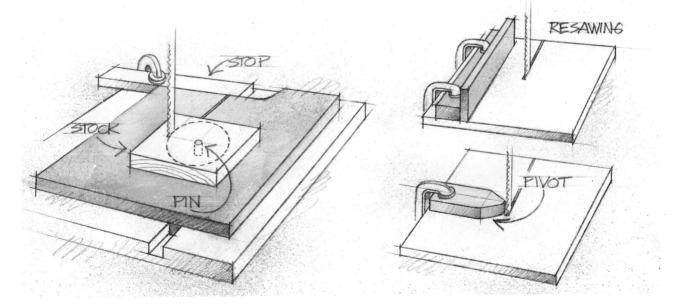

MAKING SCREW CLAMPS

Commercial hand screw clamps can cost between $11 and $30, depending on size and where you buy them. But you can make your own for virtually nothing, and several can be made up in an afternoon. Kits available for making metal-threaded hand screws cost around $11 and will require drill bits in sizes you likely won't have. The price of five such kits will get you a new wood-threading kit and enough wood to build five clamps. While lacking the bidirectional threading of commercial hand screw clamps, making your own will provide enough clamps for virtually any project, plus an opportunity to practice some precision joinery during slow times in the home workshop.

To make each of these clamps, you need two pieces of scrap hardwood stock, nominally 2x2x10″, and two pieces of freshly cut "green" hardwood stock, nominally 1½x1½x17″. This green stock must be fairly recently cut from the tree because wood that has dried doesn't thread well. You'll need a tablesaw with a dado blade, a drill (press or hand type) with ⅝″ and ¾″ bits, and a matched pair of threading tools.

For each clamp, cut a 30° notch off one end of either side, and lay out for the drilling, 1″ from the un-notched end and 4″ on center from that. In one piece, drill two ⅝″ holes for tapping, and in the other piece, drill a ⅝″ hole nearest the end, and a ¾″ hole nearest the middle. Threading the pair of holes is a simple matter of inserting the tap in the hole and turning slowly and evenly. These blocks can be fully dried material; internal threads seem to hold up better in the making that do external threads.

The threaded portions of the clamp are first shaped on the tablesaw. After stock has been cut and sawed into usable strips, make a jig to use on your tablesaw; it will permit its dado head to function as a rough lathe. This jig will make a straighter and truer piece of threading than most woodworkers can probably make on the lathe. The jig consists of a pair of centers mounted on a pair of endboards fastened to a piece that can be slid side to side in a standard tablesaw "cut-off" box. The jig can be made entirely of scrap stock. But mount the screws exactly opposite one another, like the centers on a lathe, low enough to the saw table so the dado head will reach it enough to cut the stock to ¹¹⁄₁₆″ diameter (which is perfect for cutting a ¾″ thread). If desired, a pair of sawn or routed slots can assist in lining up the parts of this jig squarely.

Screw the first of your pieces into the jig, and set the dado head so it will turn a diameter of about 1¼″. The jig works by hand-turning the stick over the dado head. Since the piece is 1½′ long, your hands will be far enough from the cutters to be safe. The handle portion should be about 4½″ long. After the handle is turned, raise the cutter so only ¹¹⁄₁₆″ remains on what will be the threaded surface. Turn the balance of the stick down to that diameter. After you have made several such pieces, take them all to a vise.

Mount one of the pieces in the vise, and begin threading it by putting the thread box over the end and turning slowly and evenly. Expect some chip-out even in the "wettest" wood. Up to about 20% chip-out is perfectly acceptable and will not affect the operation of the clamp. After the threading is done, and you have turned the thread box back off the piece, use a stiff wax (such as Door Ease) to prevent the threaded piece from drying out too fast. Because you're working with green wood on these threads, some percentage of loss is inevitable.

After you have threaded two pieces, whittle the threads off the first inch or so of one piece. At that point, you are ready to assemble the clamps. The piece with the whittled end goes through the end hole of the threaded piece into the ⅝″ stopped hole in the other piece. The other threaded piece goes through the ¾″ hole in that piece and into the threads in the first piece. That is all there is to assembling the clamp. At first the clamp's threads may seem almost too tight and squeaky to turn. But as time passes and they dry a bit, their fit becomes more nearly perfect. Apply a coat of wax or some other light finish to the whole clamp, and it is ready for use. After you have spent an afternoon learning how easy these are to make, you may well take a bit of extra time on the next batch to make them fancier.

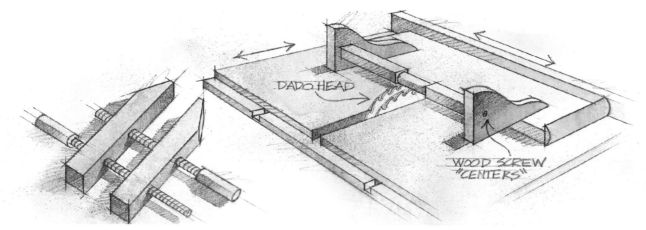

DADO HEAD

WOOD SCREW "CENTERS"

BUILDING A GRINDER-POLISHER

This rig may be one of the handiest tools you may ever build in your home workshop. Equipped with shop-built wheels, covered either with sandpaper of various grits or with leather, the setup works well for all kinds of sanding, sharpening, and polishing tasks.

If you already have an electric motor and some scrap hardwood, building the grinder-polisher shouldn't cost you more than about $25 all together. Unless you have them, you will need to buy the shaft, the pillow blocks used on the shaft, a pulley for the shaft, the motor, and a pulley for the motor. A motor from a discarded appliance will work fine.

The housing for the unit shown measures 30″ long, 12″ wide, and 12″ high. The wheels on the shaft are 8″ in diameter, and can be made in the shop. They are pulleyed to turn in a clockwise direction, as viewed from the right side, at a low speed of between 500 and 600 rpm. (In other words, the top half of the wheel turns away from you as you stand in front of the wheels.) A horizontal rod across the front of the housing is used as a tool rest. Though the sketch shows four wheels being used, you can set up more or fewer, depending on how wide you build the unit. Consider how the wheels will be used; you may want to space the wheels to allow more elbow room when using one specific wheel.

Of the four wheels shown, one is equipped with coarse-grit sandpaper, another with medium-grit sandpaper, another with emery cloth, and one with leather. The grinder-polisher can be used to sharpen and polish tools or metals, or for polishing and sanding small wood pieces. A wheel with leather can be used with

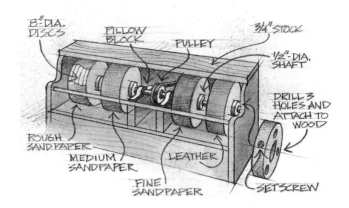

jeweler's rouge to make it work like a leather strop to put a mirror-like finish on whatever you put against it.

To make your own wheels, you can use ¾″ stock, glue three layers together, then cut the circular shape with a bandsaw. To round the rough-cut wheel, you can put it in a wood lathe, if you have one, or you can put it sideways in your post drill and clamp down a piece of metal to lay a chisel against. The trick is to get the surface of the wheel as smooth and flat as possible. High spots on the wheel will wear out and require a premature overhaul. It is best to use flat rubber over the wheel before attaching the sandpaper (⅛″ thick is best). You can buy 3″-wide sanding belts, cut them in half, then use contact cement to put a strip on a wheel. Roll the sandpaper on until it overlaps, then cut it so the ends just meet. Then use a hacksaw to cut off the excess width (about ½″) on one or both sides.

If you don't want to make your own wheels, check with lapidary supply houses for wheels or drums of aluminum, padded with rubber, with a special clamp for attaching sandpaper.

SHOP PROJECT: Radial Blade Support

Generally when a radial-arm saw is first set up, a ¾″ plywood or particleboard top is installed for the table surface. As the saw is used, the slot that the blade makes in the top becomes widened. Then, when you cut veneer or plywood, it splinters on the bottom side because there is no support on each side of the blade. To solve this problem, put a ¾″-wide dado head on the saw and cut a dado ½″ deep into the top. Next cut a strip of hardwood ¾″ wide and ½″ thick to fit into this slot. Then put a regular blade on the saw and make a cut ¼″ deep down the length of the strip. When, after it has been used awhile, the cut becomes too wide for a clean cut in plywood or veneer, simply pick it out and install a new strip. Don't glue it in; just cut it so it is snug enough that you have to tap it in.

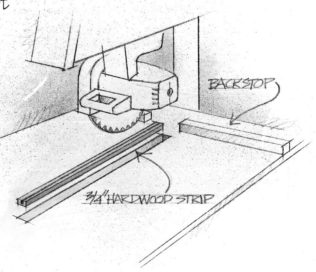

BUILDING A SHAVING HORSE

By whatever name you call it, either a shaving horse, peeling bench, or schnitzelbank, this is a handy device if you need both hands free, a quick release, and a powerful grip on your material. There are different sizes and designs. But all of them work on same basic principle, which uses a foot-operated vise with an off-center pivot post for a quick gravity release.

The shaving horse is a folk tool that has been in use for centuries by coopers, shingle makers, log peelers, basket makers, and craftspeople in countries all around the world, including England, Switzerland, Germany, and the Scandinavian countries. At the colonial village restoration in Sturbridge, Massachusetts, there are several long three-legged models dating from the 1830s in the cooper's shop. These are all-wood, pegged models that are still used to demonstrate the shaping of oak barrel staves with various drawknives and spokeshaves. Some early rustic shaving horses were constructed with a seat from a log split lengthwise, legs from round posts, and a pendulum hewn from another log.

All kinds of modifications are possible. The size can be adapted to the individual and to the space available. The function can be accommodated by designing the gripping head to handle materials of different shapes and thicknesses. You could even make a fancy one for show, to use as a coffee table or conversation piece. The version shown here was constructed after researching critical dimensions and angles used by early designers. It uses dimensional lumber (one 8′ 2x10 and two 8′ 2x6s) and modern fasteners.

To build this shaving horse, pay attention to its critical dimensions. The legs are angled for stability (11° out front and back). The ramp angle is 15° and its length is 22″ for a 48″ model or 24″ for a 54″ model. Holes in the pendulum are ⅝″ from edge to center of the hole, perpendicular to the flat surface of the pendulum. The hole through the ramp is aligned and perpendicular to the edge of the ramp. The slots in the seat and ramp should be cut accurately to prevent binding. Also the pendulum should swing freely with a minimum of side-to-side wobbling. Here are the steps of construction:

First, cut the legs to the desired length, using 11° angle cuts as shown in the diagram. Cut the seat to size; notch for legs (11° again) and cut the slot for the pendulum. Next, cut the ramp at a 15° angle and drill the hole for the pivot post. Then cut the ramp support with a 15° angle on top. Assemble the seat, ramp, and ramp support, positioning the ramp support just ahead of the slot in the ramp; countersink the screws. Next, attach the legs, then cut the end braces to fit, and attach.

Make a pattern for the pendulum and cut it from 2x10 material. Next, drill the pivot-post holes. Position

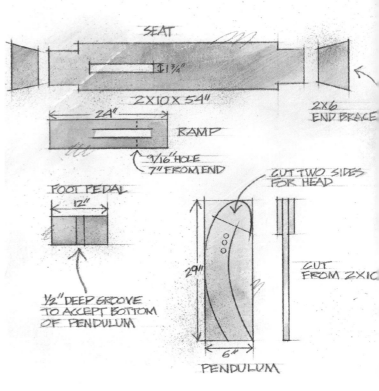

the first hole 3″ down from the lip of the head; put two or more others ¾″ on center, each one ⅝″ from the edge of the pendulum to the center of the hole. Cut out the two head pieces using the top of the pendulum as a template, then attach them. Cut a ½″ groove in the center of the foot pedal to fit the bottom end of the pendulum. Then slide the pendulum through the slots, line it up, and insert the pivot post through the holes in the ramp and the pendulum. Secure with hitch pins or cotter keys through the holes in the ends of the pivot post.

Finally, fit the foot pedal to the pendulum and secure with drywall-type screws. Note that if you use legs shorter than 20″, you may have to cut a little off the bottom end of the pendulum so that it will clear the floor. Now all you need is something to shave or peel, and you can put the shaving horse to work.

Materials List:
1 Seat 48″ to 54″ 2x10
1 Pendulum 30″ 2x10
4 Legs 24″each 2x6
2 Head Pieces 10″ each 2x6
2 End Braces 8″ each 2x6
1 Ramp 22 or 24″ 2x6
1 Ramp Support 6″ 2x6
1 Foot Pedal 12″ 2x6
1 Pivot Post 7″ Steel Rod ½″
2 Hitch Pins or Cotter Keys

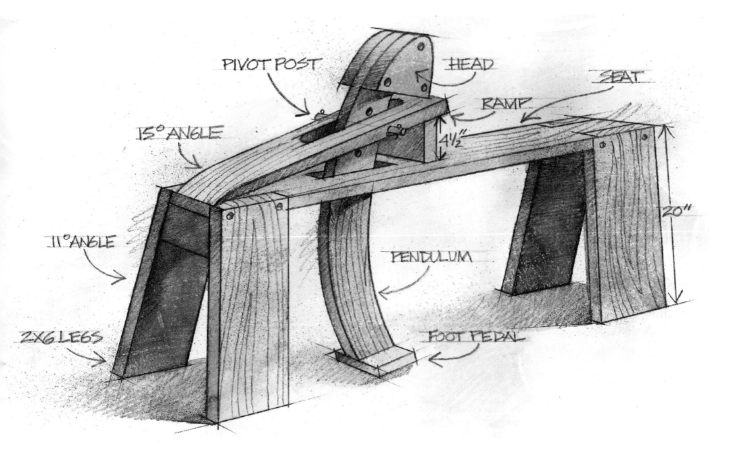

PIVOT POST

HEAD

SEAT

15° ANGLE

RAMP

4½"

11° ANGLE

PENDULUM

20"

2×6 LEGS

FOOT PEDAL

SHOP PROJECT: Square-Stock Tenoning Jig

This jig is designed for putting a round tenon on the end of square stock, and it is used with a dado head replacing the blade in the tablesaw. As the sketch shows, the jig is simply a base, fitted with a strip beneath to fit the miter gauge groove in the saw, and two uprights on top spaced approximately 8" apart. A curved notch is made in the center of each of the uprights to serve as a cradle support for the square stock. To use, the square stock is positioned in the cradle notches, and the jig is moved into the dado head while the square stock is turned to make the rounded end. The specific dimensions that are required and the height of the dado head in the saw will depend on the specific size of square stock and the diameter of the round tenon you wish to make.

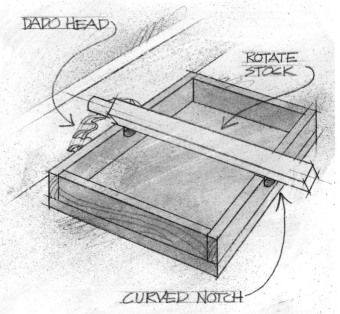

DADO HEAD

ROTATE STOCK

CURVED NOTCH

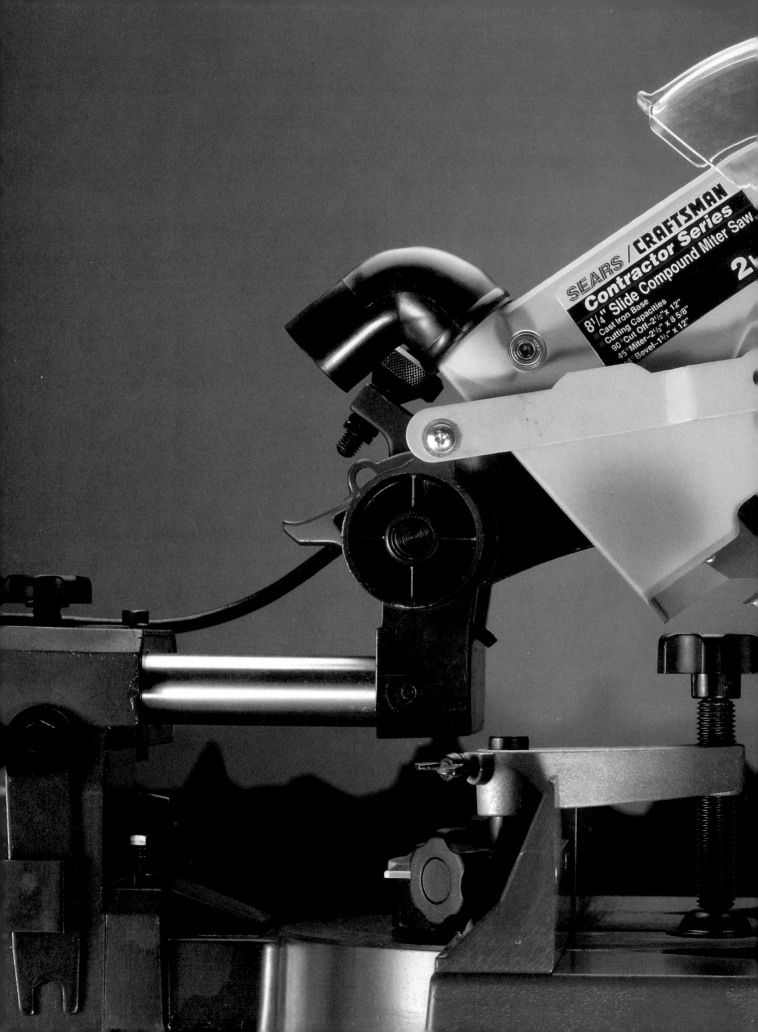

SECTION III

EQUIPPING THE HOME WORKSHOP

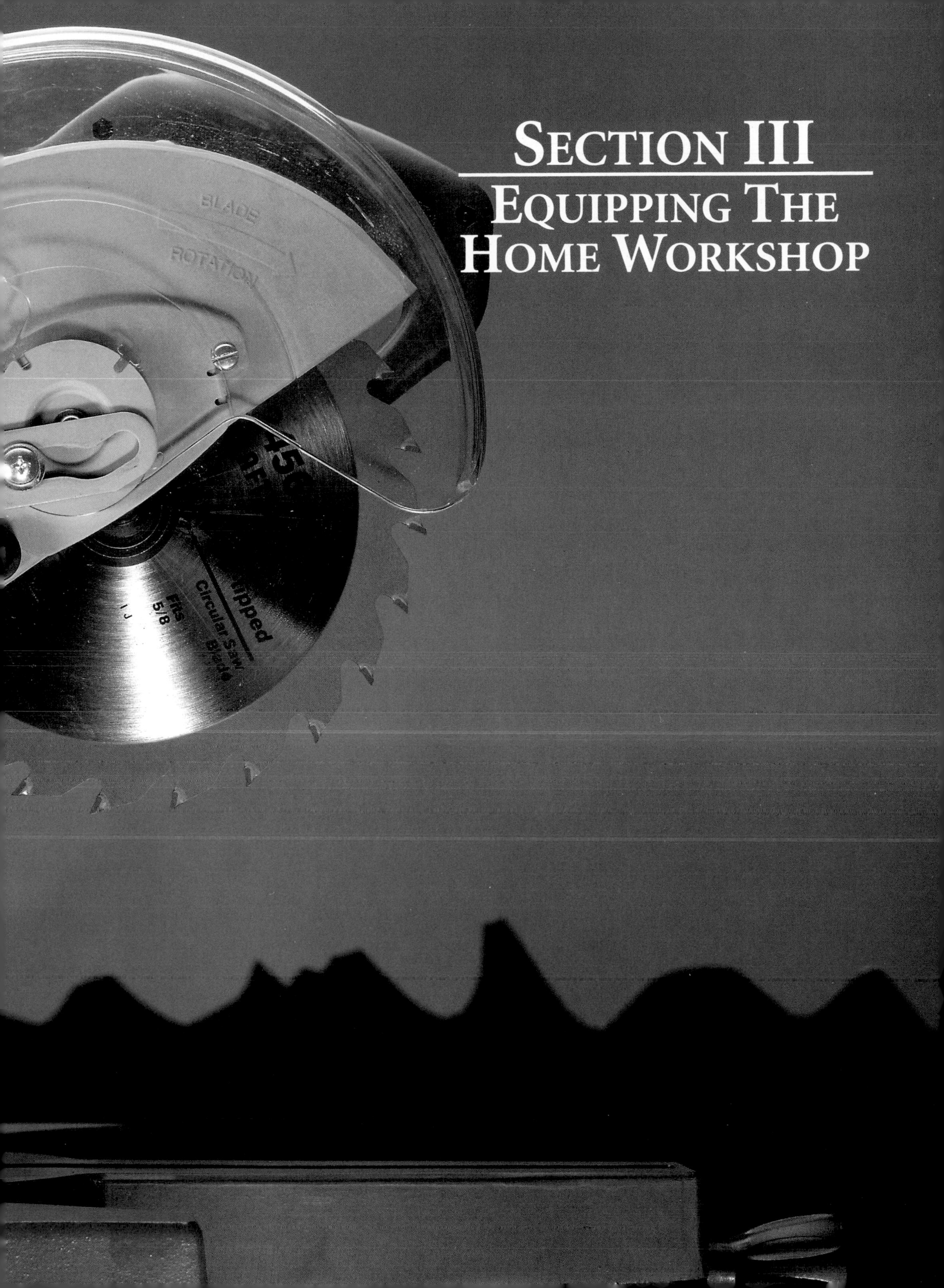

SHOP TOOL BUYING OPTIONS

Setting up a shop can be a lifelong pursuit, and it can be expensive. A shop with a top-grade example of each major shop tool and minimal hand tools and accessories can cost $5,000 and upwards. The payback from this investment can come in many forms. However, there is no reason to waste money; the goal is to invest in your shop as wisely as you can and do as much as you can to keep costs down. Here are tips from woodworker Hugh Foster that can help you decide which tools to buy, and when to buy them.

1 Know what you want to do. Then buy those tools you need to accomplish your goals. Realistic planning is important unless you are one of those rare folks for whom money is no object. It is probably cheaper to get the right tools for the job the first time rather than to have to buy another tool at a later date.

2 Try to avoid being known as a "tool borrower." It is fair to borrow a tool once; after that, buy it. If you don't need it enough to buy it, you don't really need it.

3 Consider buying the best tools you can afford. Quality tools are a joy to work with, but there are also other reasons to buy quality: It is also cheaper to buy the right one the first time than to break its inferior likeness. Also, you're less likely to get hurt with first-quality tools. (In the same vein, keep your cutting tools sharp. Well-maintained second-quality tools are safer than dull, unmaintained top-quality tools.)

4 Consider the advantages of buying used equipment. It's one of the most cost-effective ways of building up a shop. For approximately one-half of the new price you can get a good, serviceable piece of equipment that will last a lifetime if you select a quality machine and clean,

When considering a used workshop tool, check to see if the original owner's manual comes with it. The manual can be indispensable when ordering replacement parts, and in understanding how the tool works and any special safety precautions.

repair, lubricate, and adjust it before placing it back in service. You'll also be able to afford larger and heavier equipment than you'd be able to buy new.

5 Shop garage sales, estate sales, and the local shopper papers. Try to arrange for a "pre-sale" even if it is at a premium price. You'll likely be one of hundreds of callers for most tools, and it won't do you much good to try to dicker on price very much. Used workshop tools can often sell for more money (though less value, if inflation is factored in) than was originally paid for them. Still, most buyers get a verifiable bargain.

6 Besides shopping the classifieds, consider placing a classified ad in the paper yourself, advising others of what you are looking for. That low-buck investment may work wonders in helping you connect with others who want to sell tools for a wide variety of reasons.

7 Know how to inspect your used tool purchases for wear and needed maintenance. If you can keep it in adjustment, the older tool, by virtue of its extra weight and anti-vibration tendencies, might be a very wise investment, especially if you have a lot of room in your workshop.

8 Whether buying new or used, pay attention to the design of the tool. Is it simple enough that you will be able to repair it when it breaks down? You may not want to be a machinist, but mechanical skill and patience are required if shop machinery is to be kept running smoothly. Another question is whether, assuming you are able to fix it if it breaks down, you will be able to get any necessary parts.

9 Some of your most favorite hand tools can come from garage sales if you get to them early. For instance, a 50¢ handful of chisels might take you a day to sharpen, temper, and re-handle. Since the out-of-pocket costs are next to nothing, the non-cash "profit" might be well over $100. (The process of keeping even new tools in condition is too often ignored, though they require care and maintenance regularly.)

10 If you have three-phase electrical service available, you can investigate buying used industrial-duty tools, which occasionally can be purchased at home-shop prices.

11 Take the woodworking classes at your local technical school. They are usually inexpensive, perhaps a few dollars an hour for the course. You will meet good people there. The shops will be well equipped with a variety of tools. Sample them. Learn what you like and don't like. The talk there will provide sources of tools, and comments about the various brands may help you find a bargain and/or avoid a lemon. Sharing chores in the class is also bound to teach you some new techniques, too.

12 Visit local tool dealers, apprise them of the prices advertised in magazines and catalogs, and ask if they will negotiate a discounted price. Or, ask them what services they provide to justify their higher prices. Most advertisers in magazines are honest and reputable and provide fast delivery of items that can't be bought locally. However, remember that it isn't fair to use up your local dealer's time and then buy mail-order to save a couple of dollars. Similarly, it isn't fair to expect your local dealer to provide first-rate service on tools that you bought from somewhere across the country. If the dealer has the expertise, buying there may well be worth the extra cost.

13 Visit the home workshops of others. Try out their equipment if you can. However, insurance premiums being what they are, you may have to settle for watching the owner use the tools, or just listening to any opinions on how well they work.

14 Be sure to get some good, comfortable eye, ear, and lung protection. Be sure to wear ear protection whenever you are in a shop where power equipment is running. Noise pollution is an underrated problem with all power tools.

15 Buy your hand tools first, or at least as you progress. With them, you do the finest of your work. Another reason to buy sooner rather than later is that their cost is escalating faster than the cost of power equipment. Hand tools are safer and, for many jobs, not that much slower to use.

16 Don't buy any tool without trying it out. Eventually you may just want the best, period. But, remember, price isn't the only indicator of quality; it is not great tools that turn out professional work, but what you do with the tools that you have.

BENCHTOP OR STATIONARY?

If your workshop space is limited, using combination tools is one way to provide a maximum of tool capability in that space. Another way is to favor benchtop tools over stationary tools. Most tools available in stationary floor models can also be purchased in versions designed to sit on top of the workbench, including the tablesaw and the bandsaw. However, the most common benchtop tools found in workshops are the drill press, the power miter saw, the belt/disc sander, and the bench grinder. Besides saving the space taken up by tool stands, other major advantages of benchtop tools are lower cost and greater portability.

Of those people buying benchtop versions of major tools like saws and drill presses, studies show that about 4 out of 10 believe they perform as well as stationary models, while 6 out of 10 plan to eventually trade up to a stationary model of that tool. If you opt for benchtop tools and want to get them off the workbench, it is easy enough to mount them on tool stands, either commercially available or made in the shop. Tool stands can be made of wood or metal. Special stands are also available that allow attaching up to three benchtop tools onto a revolving turret mount.

THE WORKSHOP BIG EIGHT

If you are serious about setting up a home workshop, chances are eight out of ten you probably already own some assortment of smaller shop tools, such as power drills, circular saws, sabersaws, and sanders. You may or may not have already purchased one or more of the most essential major home workshop power tools discussed in this section, which are ranked in relative importance to project work: (1) tablesaw, (2) radial-arm saw, (3) bandsaw, (4) jointer, (5) wood lathe, (6) drill press, (7) thickness planer, and (8) shaper.

These are the tools that can bring you out of the average fix-it category and put you into the ranks of the well-equipped shop owner with professional capabilities. Studies show a typical progression starts with portable tools, such as a ⅜″ portable drill, a 7¼″ circular saw, and some type of sabersaw. The next step involves not only more expense, but dedicating some sort of space to a shop area. Whether you go with benchtop tools or with stationary floor-model tools becomes a matter of preference, budget, space availability, and your overall tool-buying plan.

Benchtop tools are a half step after portable tools; for example, a benchtop tablesaw will augment or replace a hand-held circular saw. A benchtop drill press will augment or replace a portable power drill. A benchtop bandsaw will augment or replace a hand-held sabersaw. A portable router fastened to a router table leaves the category of portable tools and becomes a benchtop tool. For more on making these second-step decisions, see Benchtop or Stationary, opposite page, and Buying Combination Tools, page 162.

This section highlights the flagship tools of the home workshop and discusses the most common operations of each of these tools. All in all, the following pages will give you an overview to help familiarize you with major tools so you can better plan your tool buying. One tool not included here but increasingly popular in home workshops is the power miter saw, also sometimes called a motorized

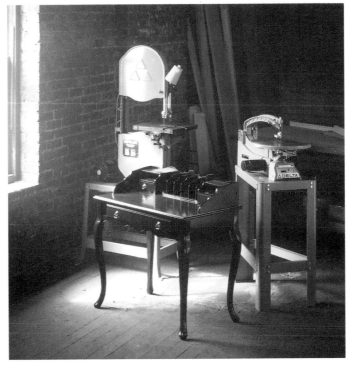

Fine furniture builders regularly demonstrate what can be done with good wood and good tools. The total cost of the eight major tools on the following pages can range from about $3,000 on up to $6,000 or more, depending on quality and features.

miter box, compound miter saw, or cut-off saw. Some shop owners say that if they were starting over again, this would be the first saw they would buy.

By whatever name, its main function is crosscutting, replacing portable handsaw miter boxes. If you plan to use a radial-arm saw mainly for crosscutting, then you may be wise to consider the more economical and specialized power miter saw. Standard models offer blade sizes ranging from 8¼″ to 15″, with powerful motors for quick, clean cuts of 2x6s at 90° or 2x4s at 45° in a single pass, plus electronic braking to stop the blade in as little as one second. Newer compound power miter saws offer quick and easy bevel and compound angle cutting. Some versions, called slide compound miter saws, have a motor/blade assembly mounted on a sliding arm to provide versatility that rivals a radial-arm saw.

You will notice that the complete list of the Big Eight tools presented here is not included in any example shop in this book except the most complex, the Professional Workshop. While the listing represents the ultimate capabilities, many fairly well-equipped home workshops may be missing at least one of these major tools. If you disagree with the listing of the tools in this section, be aware that it is a compromise. Arguments for the inclusion of other tools, or different rankings for the specific tools presented, will in most cases be perfectly valid for you. Much depends on what tools you already have, what projects you are working on now, and what you will be working on in the future. If your interest is in shaped craft projects, for example, a bandsaw might be your first priority. Or, if these projects are small, you might opt for a scrollsaw, and, depending on what else you do, you might not have need for any other major shop saw.

1. TABLESAW

The tablesaw is the workhorse of most shops where serious woodworking is done. It can be used to rip, crosscut, miter, and bevel, or to make rabbets, dadoes, or other cuts for most all woodworking joints. Even with a conventional saw blade, it can produce moldings and dress up boards like a jointer. Or, the saw blade can be replaced by a dado head, molding head, sanding disc, or even special blades to cut metal or other materials.

The tablesaw consists of (1) a flat cutting surface, (2) a circular blade, and (3) a motor and drive beneath the table. The blade can be adjusted up and down, or at an angle. Tablesaws are available in benchtop and stationary models. Some benchtop models have been improved enough to be considered for a primary shop saw. When buying, check for rip fence adjustment and alignment, distance between the fence and blade (rip capacity), and the distance from the front of the table to the blade. Note which way the blade tilts (left or right), table material, horsepower, and type of drive train (belt or direct drive). Also check cutting depth with the blade at both 90° and 45°, and power source options (either 120 volts, 240 volts, or both).

Tables traditionally are of cast iron, but also may be cast aluminum.

They have two guides: the rip fence, which is parallel to the blade and can be adjusted toward or away from the blade, and the miter gauge, which slides in slots parallel to the blade to push work into the blade when crosscutting. Motors will range from 1 to 3 hp. though 1½ hp is considered adequate for most home workshops. Belt drives are generally preferable to direct drives. Shop-made jigs can greatly extend the tablesaw's capabilities, increase its convenience, or reduce setup time. Weights can vary from a low of 40 lbs. on up to 550 lbs. Prices can range from a low of $200 for lightweight benchtop models to $1,700 or more for top-of-the-line models, such as the Delta Unisaw.

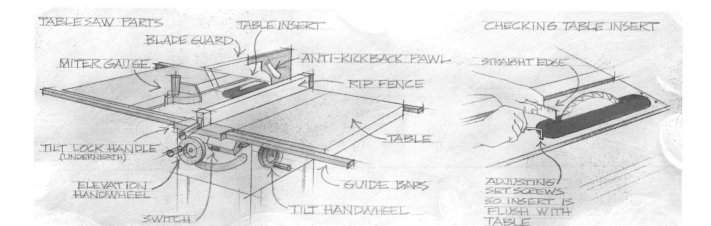

TABLESAW PARTS

TABLE INSERT

BLADE GUARD

MITER GAUGE

ANTI-KICKBACK PAWL

RIP FENCE

TABLE

TILT LOCK HANDLE
(UNDERNEATH)

ELEVATION HANDWHEEL

GUIDE BARS

SWITCH

TILT HANDWHEEL

CHECKING TABLE INSERT

STRAIGHT EDGE

ADJUSTING SET SCREWS SO INSERT IS FLUSH WITH TABLE

2. RADIAL-ARM SAW

The radial-arm saw can be an alternative, or a supplement, to the basic tablesaw. Like its counterpart, it is extremely versatile. It performs all normal cutting operations like crosscutting, ripping, mitering, and beveling. Experienced woodworkers like it best for crosscutting; many believe ripping is more safely done on a tablesaw. Its circular blade can be replaced with dado or molding heads, or it can be equipped to sand, buff, polish, grind, shape, rout, even do some drilling operations.

Radial-arm saws are categorized by cutting-blade diameter, which can range from 8″ to a 16″ contractor's saw. The 10″ is the most popular for the home workshop. The basic unit consists of a table with a back fence, an upright column at the back of the table that supports a radial-arm track, and a saw and motor assembly suspended beneath the radial-arm track. Some models have a single arm; others have a double arm. For crosscutting, work is placed on the table and the saw's blade is pulled across it. Various adjustments on the radial arm control the direction and depth of the cut. Other adjustments on the saw and motor assembly allow cutting different angles. Combining these adjustments lets you swing, tilt, raise, or lower the blade.

For ripping, the work must be pushed past the stationary rotating blade. Because of this, the tool is best located against a wall, with enough clearance at the sides to permit ripping long stock. When buying, check motor type and horsepower; depth of cut for 90° and 45° miters and 45° bevels; ripping, crosscut, and dado capacities; location of controls; table size; type of roller head bearings, and materials used for the track and column support. See if the saw allows complete adjustment and alignment of moving parts to maintain accuracy and if it has bevel and miter stops, as well as a second accessory shaft and an automatic blade brake. Prices of radial-arm saws can start around $250 and range upward to more than $1,000.

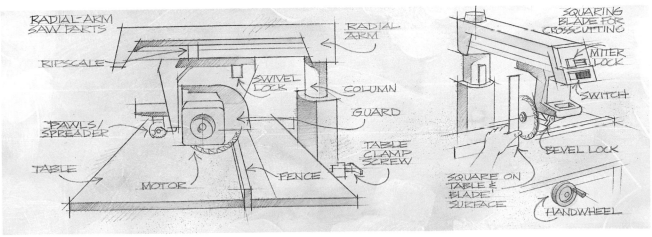

RADIAL-ARM SAW PARTS

RIPSCALE

RADIAL ARM

SWIVEL LOCK

COLUMN

GUARD

PAWLS/SPREADER

TABLE CLAMP SCREW

TABLE

MOTOR

FENCE

SQUARING BLADE FOR CROSSCUTTING

MITER LOCK

SWITCH

BEVEL LOCK

SQUARE ON TABLE & BLADE SURFACE

HANDWHEEL

3. BANDSAW

The bandsaw is the tool of choice for making curved or irregular cuts in wood or other materials. It is ideal for cutting blanks to be turned on a lathe, for mass-producing identical shapes using a stack of material, or for re-sawing stock to a thinner thickness. With a special blade and speed reducer, it can be used to cut metal or other materials.

The bandsaw has a frame supporting the upper and lower wheels, a work-support table, a drive mechanism and motor, and a continuous saw blade that travels over the rims of two, or sometimes three, wheels. One of the wheels is adjustable to control the tension of the blade. Bandsaws are sized by the clearance between the blade and the rear column. Generally, the larger the bandsaw, the greater the distance from the back of the throat to the cutting blade, and the greater the depth of cut. Throat depths for bandsaws used in home workshops fall in the range of 10″, 12″, 14″, or 16″. Depth of cut can vary from as little as 3″ to as much as 8″ or more.

Better bandsaws will have a table that tilts up to 45° to allow bevel and compound cutting, and also will have a table with a miter-gauge groove and provisions for mounting a rip fence. The tightness of the curves possible on the bandsaw depends on the width of the blade used. For example, ¼″-radius cuts are possible for intricate curve cutting when ⅛″-wide blades are used. Generally, however, the widest possible blade should be used because it will be less likely to break. Small bandsaws will accommodate blades as wide as ⅜″, while larger saws will accept blades as wide as ½″ or ¾″.

Features to check when buying a bandsaw include cutting capacities, motor type and horsepower, drive speeds, table material, blade support and blade guide block adjustments, whether doors are hinged, the mechanism for tensioning the blade, and designs to allow easier blade changing.

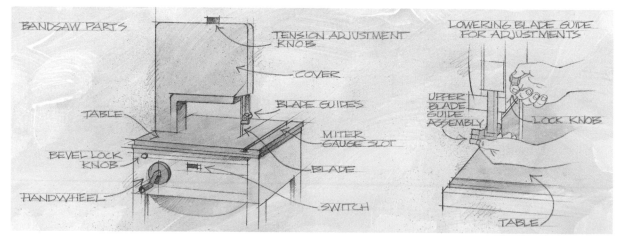

BANDSAW PARTS

TENSION ADJUSTMENT KNOB

COVER

BLADE GUIDES

TABLE

MITER GAUGE SLOT

BEVEL LOCK KNOB

BLADE

HANDWHEEL

SWITCH

LOWERING BLADE GUIDE FOR ADJUSTMENTS

UPPER BLADE GUIDE ASSEMBLY

LOCK KNOB

TABLE

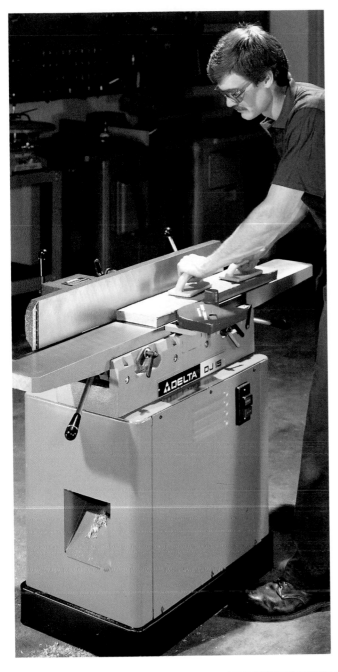

4. JOINTER

The jointer is probably the most underrated tool in the home workshop. Truing up stock with a jointer before beginning a project is a key to doing fine work. A jointer's main use is to straighten and flatten cupped and bowed boards. It can size or smooth lumber in width (edge) or thickness (surface). A jointer can also be used for beveling and tapering, and for making rabbets and tenons. The jointer is also sometimes called a jointer/planer or planer/molder, and can be confused with the surface planer (see page 140).

The jointer has a heavy metal bed, usually cast iron, with an adjustable infeed table to vary the depth of cut. The length of bed can range from about 21″ to more than 76″. An adjustable fence guides the workpiece over a revolving cutterhead and generally can be tilted up to 45° right or left for angle cuts. Wood is removed with three, sometimes four, cutting knives in a cylindrical head that revolves between 3,500 and 4,500 rpm. Fences will most often be of cast iron, but may also be steel plate, extruded aluminum, or cast aluminum. Fence heights can range from 2⅝″ to 5″; the higher the better. A spring-loaded guard provides protection from the cutterhead.

Jointers are sized by the length of cutting knives. Though knife lengths can vary from 4″ to 8″, 6″-wide knives are most popular. When buying, check the cuts made per minute; generally the more cuts, the smoother the cut. Other important features to check include maximum cutting depth, power source options (120 volt, 240 volt, or both), and motor size and type. Motors can range from ½ to 2 hp; universal motors are louder and require more maintenance than induction motors. Also check to see what adjustments are possible for knife height, fence, and infeed and outfeed tables, and whether a stand is included. Jointers can range in price from a low of under $200 on up to more than $1,500.

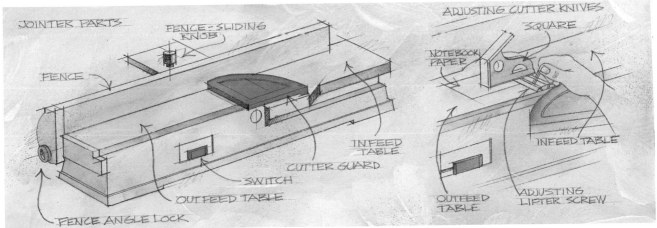

5. Wood Lathe

The wood lathe is a perennial favorite of woodworkers with an artistic bent; it is a power sculpturing tool that can provide hours of pleasure. Used mostly for producing round forms in wood, it can also be used for drilling and boring, filing, sanding, and even light metal work.

The lathe is made up of a stationary headstock and an adjustable tailstock, and the work is positioned between the two. If a lathe has enough clearance to turn a piece 12″ in diameter, it is considered a 12″ lathe. (Many lathe beds have an indentation, called a gap, in the bed near the headstock to accommodate larger work.) The distance between centers over the bed typically varies from 36″ to 39″; work that is turned between centers is called spindle turning. An adjustable tool rest supports tools used.

Faceplate attachments of varying sizes are used for outboard turning, on work that can't be mounted between centers, such as wooden bowls. With screw-on arbors, the lathe can be used for sanding, wire-brushing, grinding, buffing, and polishing. Turning speed most often is controlled at the headstock by step pulleys and can vary from about 300 to 3,500 rpm. Slow speeds are used for roughing blocks of wood and larger items, while faster speeds are used for finishing. Better lathes offer several different speed ranges. The use of a chuck can allow the lathe to be used for horizontal drilling and reaming.

When buying a lathe, compare the swing over the bed, the swing over the tool-rest base, the outboard swing, the distance between centers, the bed material (usually cast iron) and weight, the headstock and tailstock controls, and whether the headstock pivots 90° for outboard turning. Better lathes have a ball-bearing headstock. Also check motor type and horsepower; whether a stand is included; and for special features, such as indexing mechanisms for reeding and fluting, and hollow tailstocks that permit long-hole boring for lamp cords using a lamp auger. Prices can vary from about $150 to $400 or more.

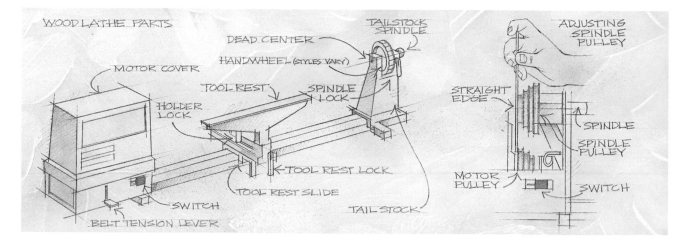

6. DRILL PRESS

The obvious purpose of the drill press is to drill holes, either at right angles to the workpiece or at various angles to it. With accessories, however, it can be adapted occasionally to sand, shape, polish, plane, rout, or bore square holes with a mortising bit and chisel housing. The tool consists of a base and a round column that supports the drill-press head. The length of the column determines whether it is a benchtop or floor model.

The size of a drill press is determined by the distance from the center of the chuck to the column. If, for example, this distance is 7″, the tool is considered a 14″ drill press because it will drill to the center of a 14″ board. The assembly at the top of the column includes the motor, step pulleys to regulate speed, and the quill. The quill housing holds the spindle and drill chuck. A feed lever attached to the quill housing moves the spindle and drill chuck.

When buying, check the maximum distance between the chuck and the table, and the maximum depth possible with a single stroke of the feed lever. The table of the drill press is raised or lowered on the column to adjust the distance between the work and the chuck; the maximum distance may fall in a range between 7″ and 39½″. The quill travel distance (how far the chuck and bit can be lowered) can range from 2″ to 5″, though for a typical 14″ drill press it will often be between 3″ and 4″. Deeper holes, however, are possible by drilling and then resetting the table.

Other specs to consider include the weight, which can range from under 50 lbs. to over 300 lbs., and chuck capacity, which can range from ¼″ to ⅝″. Also check motor horsepower and rpm ranges. While speeds on various drill presses may vary from 150 to 4,910 rpm, the range of most will fall between about 250 to 3,100. Forstner bits, circle cutters, and brad-point bits over ¾″ can require speeds as slow as 250 rpm, while small twist bits work best at around 3,000 rpm. Benchtop drill presses cost roughly from $150 to $350, while floor models will run from about $200 to $450.

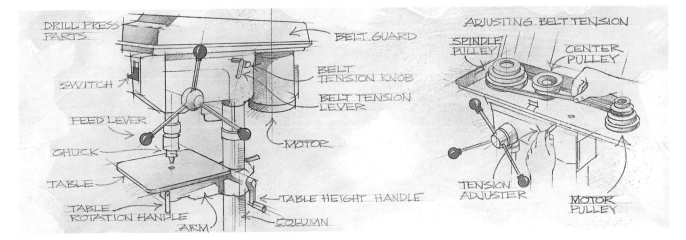

7. SURFACE PLANER

The surface planer, also called a thickness planer, is a relative of the jointer, jointer/planer, and planer/molder, but is used almost exclusively to smooth or reduce the thickness of wide boards. It allows you to square up rough lumber, reduce board size, and smooth surfaces.

Thickness planers are sized according to cutterhead knife length, which determines the width of board accepted; one accepting a 10″-wide board will be called a 10″ planer. Larger stationary planers will accept boards in a range from 13″ to 20″ wide, while smaller portable planers will take boards 10″ or 12″ wide. Machines with wider capacities allow you to thin wider boards, and sometimes let you feed two or three boards simultaneously through the machine, side by side. The other critical capacity is the thickness of boards worked, which can vary from 4″ to 8″. A thickness capacity of 4″ is considered adequate for most home workshops.

Thickness planer motors are usually either induction-type motors, which can vary from 1¾ to 5 hp, or universal motors, which are typically rated by amperage draw in a range from 13 to 16 amps. The drive train can be a combination of belt, chain, or gear mechanisms, or can consist of belt and chain only, or belt only. Single, dual, or variable speeds may be available. Thickness planers will usually have two or three knives on the cutterhead, and the maximum cut capacity can vary from about ⅛″ to 5⁄16″. Cutterhead feed rates can vary from 11 feet per minute (fpm) with single-speed drives to as much as 33 feet per minute. The number of cuts per inch can vary from about 30 to 1,000. Accessory heads can be purchased for many planers to mass-produce moldings.

When buying, check on the type of knives, and how cutter knives are installed and adjusted. Also check how high the knives protrude above the cutterhead; this height can affect kickback potential and noise. Also pay attention to weight, especially if you will be storing the planer under a bench, or taking it to the job site. Prices of thickness planers can range from under $400 on up to $1,700 or more.

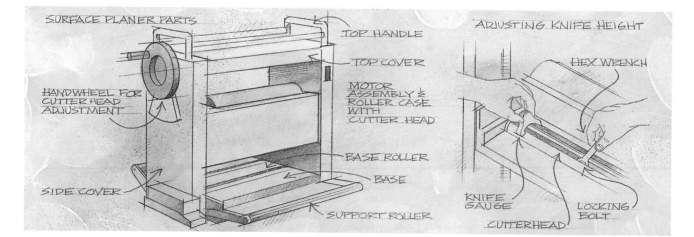

8. WOOD SHAPER

The wood shaper lets you cut moldings with complicated patterns and to decorate wood surfaces with intricate shapes. Scalloping, rabbeting, contouring, and molding are easily accomplished by this machine, which has a vertically mounted motor and spindle. The spindle can be fitted with an incredible variety of cutter blades and can be adjusted to position blades at varying heights. For most work the infeed side of the double fence is adjusted for depth of cut, while the outfeed fence supports the work that has passed the cutter.

As with any power tool with spinning blades, safety should be a top priority when becoming familiar with this type of machine. Wood shapers start at about $400 and increase to price levels of about $650 and $850, though high-end production wood shapers will generally cost over $1,000. A low-cost alternative to the wood shaper is the router/shaper, a half-step between the router table and the wood shaper, which can use both router and shaper cutters and may cost as little as $200 to $300.

Smoothness of cut depends on bits used and spindle speed. Most shapers will have speeds of about 9,000 rpm, though router/shapers may rev as high as 12,500 rpm. Mid-range shapers will usually have either 1 or 1½ hp, while production shapers may have as high as 3 hp. Better shapers will offer dual spindle speeds to match cutter diameter, reversible spindle rotation, larger table work surfaces, double-ended spindles to permit using both ½″ and ¾″ cutters, or interchangeable spindles that also allow the use of ¼″ cutters. Height adjustment of the spindle commonly is ⅞″. Other features to check on wood shapers include total weight, table material (usually cast iron or die-cast aluminum), spindle height adjustment controls, fence adjustability, guards provided, and provisions for chip removal.

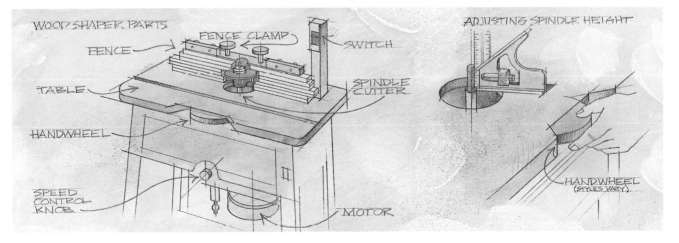

INVESTING IN HAND TOOLS

There's little that could be more important to your enjoyment, accomplishment, and satisfaction of working on shop projects than your attitude toward your tools. How you think of the tools you use, and how you select and care for them, will eventually show up in every project you work on.

For example, think of a woodturner who spends hours sharpening his chisels, polishing them to a fine edge, and studying the wood to be turned. The turner realizes that working wood requires a good deal of preparation, yet as he listens to the sounds of the stone against the chisel, his mind envisions the lumber whirring on the lathe and the edge of the chisel against the wood.

In contrast, think of someone just learning to build a house, who views both tools and materials as things to be dominated and subdued. He may try to keep his mind off what he is doing with a blaring radio. He may manhandle boards, saw, and hammer, leaving a trail of debris as he tries to force the project to completion.

Which person do you think will turn out better work? Which will suffer more lost time because of accidents, work that needs to be redone, or searches for misplaced items? Which one will enjoy the work, the finished results, or life more?

Your attitude impacts your work with power tools but even more so with hand tools, according to Garretson Wade Chinn, principal owner of the famed Garrett Wade fine-woodworking tool supply house. There are many variables that determine which hand tools you will need in your shop. Often it's just a matter of taste, budget, and function. But one thing is absolutely certain: If you have the proper tool for each job and use it properly, you will find yourself getting much better results. Here are major groups of hand tools and some general advice on how to buy and use them:

Seasoned hand tools, opposite, recall generations of projects. The combination square, above, is a versatile measuring tool, allowing fast marking for rip cuts or for 45° or 90° angles.

MARKING-OUT TOOLS. Woodturners can, of course, make use of special marking-out tools. However, for most workshops, consider the following to start: a graduated try square, an engineer's square, a marking and/or mortise gauge, a marking awl, a measuring tape, and steel rules of several lengths.

For particularly exacting work, it is a good idea to use the same measuring tools throughout the job because, in many cases, two apparently identical rules can vary as much as 1/32″ in one foot. (This is not true of those specifically called precision rules, but it can be the case with more generally available products.) Also, switching from a rule to a tape to a square may create errors during the job that cannot, in the end, be traced.

A few more tips: Try practicing reading rules upside down; this can be a very handy skill in some situations. Also, for greatest accuracy when using a tape, tip one edge down against the stock.

HANDSAWS. The difference between an adequate saw and the best lies in the balance of the tool, the ruggedness and comfort of the handle, the quality of the steel (plus the accuracy and sharpness of the teeth), and, in general, ease of use. There are many different types (both in size and design) of excellent saws made in Europe, Japan, and the United States. As you might expect, each will perform its own special function best. For example, you can crosscut a board with a ripsaw but it will work much slower and produce a very rough finish. In contrast to a ripsaw, where the teeth are set and filed to cut with their points, crosscut saw teeth are filed to cut with their edges and shaped with no hook, which prevents snagging on wood fibers.

Choosing the right handsaw for woodworking is often as much a matter of taste and budget. However, consider the following basic assortment: ripsaw, fast-cutting crosscut saw, fine-cutting crosscut saw, stiff backsaw (tenon, dovetail, or Dozuki), a small fine-toothed detailing saw, and a hacksaw. Other saws can easily be added as you complete and fill out the range in your shop.

Western saws cut on the push stroke and Japanese saws on the pull stroke. The tooth styles of Japanese and Western saws are different on both ripsaws and crosscut saws. But both Japanese and Western tenon saws function like crosscut saws. The brass back on the Western tenon saw gives the saw weight so you don't have to press on it. The Japanese tenon saw (known as a Dozuki) relies on its special tooth pattern, rather than weight on the blade, to do the work.

Here are a few tips on preparing handsaws for more effective use: First, uneven teeth on a saw make for slow cutting, not only because fewer teeth have to do the work but also because sawdust piles up in front of the long teeth, causing the saw to "ride." Keeping teeth well filed to level position will help the teeth cut evenly and carry an equal amount of sawdust in each gullet.

It's easy to forget about your stance when sawing. Putting your feet in the right place is as important as using the correct tool. A proper stance will allow your hand, shoulder, and elbow to be in a straight line with the saw blade. With a proper stance and a sharp saw, you can make the blade cut with little effort, and the sound will tell you so. If excessive force seems to be needed (assuming the blade is reasonably sharp), or if the cut sounds bad, the culprit is most probably a bad stance.

STEEL AND WOODEN PLANES. Until about 40 years ago, a craftsman could obtain literally hundreds of types of planes. In this day of power-driven tools, we are apt to forget how important hand planes are for precision work. They are the violins of woodworking. Each plane has its own special purpose, work that it can do more easily and accurately than any other. Not only can you usually do more careful and better work with a hand plane, you can also often work faster because of the set-up time required by power tools.

Skill at hand planing is one of the most important abilities of any woodworking craftsman. A hand plane is a more forgiving tool than a power tool, and experience with a hand plane will help you better understand exactly what a power tool is doing when you use it for a particular job—an important and subtle appreciation that will help you achieve consistently good results with power tools. A good plane has the components shown in the illustration, opposite page.

When using any plane, first keep the blade as sharp as

> "Experience with a hand plane will help you better understand what a power tool is doing when you use it for a particular job."

possible; bench stones and honing guides are excellent for this purpose. Second, though there are some exceptions to this rule, generally plane with the grain. If you don't work with the grain, you run the danger of catching the grain, lifting chips of wood, and producing a rough surface. When planing end grain, push the plane one way to the middle of the board only; then repeat this process going in the other direction. This prevents splitting the board at the edge.

The variety of planes available is usually confusing to the inexperienced woodworker and sometimes even to more experienced craftsmen. All planes are divided into two groups: bench planes and specialty planes. Bench planes (whether steel or wooden, Japanese or Western) have wide blades and a large flat sole. They are used for flattening, smoothing, or leveling wide surfaces or long edges. They vary greatly in width, length, and weight. You will probably find it useful to have at least one plane of short, medium, and long length.

An example of a specialty plane is a block plane, which is shaped like a small bench plane, but is used one-handed. Its function is general trimming, made possible by its small size, or cutting end grain. It comes in several different styles, and one has a special low angle to make end-grain work more effective. Every woodworking shop should have at least one block plane.

Other specialty planes include the relatively long-sole trimming planes. Bullnose planes are among the shortest of this style, and the Record shoulder planes among the longest. They are extremely useful, and a good wood shop will have a minimum of two with different lengths and blade widths. A good shop will also have one or two smaller trimming planes, such as the palm planes and the various brass planes. The variety is extensive, and you are likely to use them often. Other planes to consider when they are needed include rabbeting planes, side rabbet planes, router planes, spokeshaves, and multi-cutter planes.

Use a modest amount of common sense and your planes will last a lifetime or more. Be careful not to drop a steel plane because the casting may crack, break, or dent. When metal is dented there will be some metal displaced from the dent and pushed outward, causing a raised ring or bump around the dent. The dent won't cause a problem, but the metal raised around it can. You can rub the surface with a fine honing stone to remove the bumps from around the dents so they don't leave small scratches in the wood surface. Once the bumps are removed, you can ignore the remaining dent.

Keep a light coating of oil on the unplated surfaces to prevent rust spots and stains from the natural acids on your hands. Try, of course, to avoid denting the soles of your wooden planes. But if you get a dent or two (almost inevitable after a number of years), just ignore them. They won't affect a wooden plane's function.

The most common fault when using bench planes is "dipping." For accurate results, it is critical to avoid this. Just pay attention to this simple rule: At the beginning of each stroke, put slightly more pressure on the front of the plane; at the end of the stroke, keep slightly more pressure on the back.

FILES AND RASPS. Filing is one of man's oldest arts. A good file or rasp used properly on wood should cut cleanly and smoothly. The teeth should not catch the wood fibers. Choosing the right file will help you do filing work better and usually faster. Files are formed by raising a continuous tooth evenly across the file. There are two basic kind of files: single-cut and double-cut. The teeth run in only one direction on single-cut files, but run in two directions on the double-cut files. Double-cut files cut quicker and more coarsely than single-cut.

Rasps differ from files in that the teeth are formed individually and are not connected to one another. Files will cut smoother than rasps, but when used on wood they work much slower and are susceptible to clogging. In order of ascending smoothness of cut, files are graded as coarse, bastard cut, second cut, and smooth cut. Rasps, in ascending order, are graded as wood rasp, cabinet rasp bastard, and cabinet rasp second cut. In general, a longer file or rasp will have somewhat coarser teeth than a shorter one.

Use file handles with your files and rasps. Hold the file or rasp at the handle end with your thumb along the top edge. Grasp the other end with the thumb and forefinger of your other hand. Hold the stock firmly in a vise or clamp. For general filing, keep the stock at about elbow height. If the work requires heavier filing, it should be lower; if it is finer, it should be near eye level.

CHISELS AND KNIVES. A good chisel will be nicely balanced, properly designed for the work it is asked to do, and will hold a keen edge for a long time. Three basic kinds are good to have: bevel-edged cabinetmaker's chisels, square-edged framing chisels, and mortise chisels.

Bevel-edged and square-edged chisels are used for all general forming work and are usually struck with a mallet. Mortise chisels are narrow chisels with thick, heavy blades and a very broad bevel angle that serves to break waste when the chisel is used to cut deep square holes (mortises). These chisels are also meant to be struck, often with considerable force. Conversely, a chisel not designed to be struck is a paring chisel. These are usually longer and more delicate and are always kept shaving-sharp, because they are moved solely by hand pressure.

With the exception of the Japanese chisels, which have the hardest edges of any, the steel in most quality chisels is substantially the same. Choose a chisel for yourself based on length, type of handle, and balance. For some craftsmen, a shorter chisel may be preferable. Others may prefer a plastic handle or a wooden one that is reinforced at the top because of its "handle-heavy" balance.

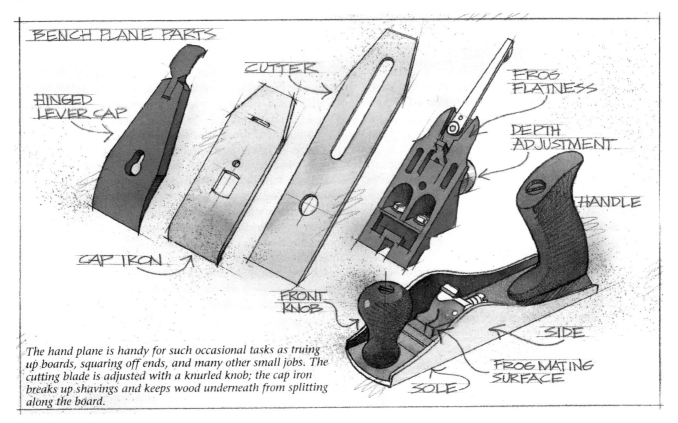

BENCH PLANE PARTS

HINGED LEVER CAP

CUTTER

FROG FLATNESS

DEPTH ADJUSTMENT

HANDLE

CAP IRON

FRONT KNOB

SIDE

FROG MATING SURFACE

SOLE

The hand plane is handy for such occasional tasks as truing up boards, squaring off ends, and many other small jobs. The cutting blade is adjusted with a knurled knob; the cap iron breaks up shavings and keeps wood underneath from splitting along the board.

TOOL DOLLARS VERSUS QUALITY

What does tool quality cost? Two price ranges are shown here for the more popular portable power tools. The first price range shown is for low-end homeowner-quality tools; the second price range is for light-duty industrial-quality tools. The prices are not exact, but merely intended to indicate general cost range. Heavy-duty industrial-quality tools can run twice the cost of their light-duty cousins.

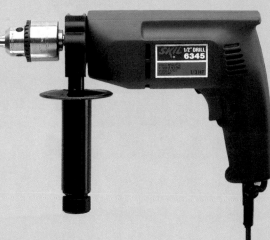

⅜″ POWER DRILL

$30 to $40: Metalwork, as well as wood; drilling in hard woods, ceramics, glass; holes up to ⅜″; light sanding.

$50 to $85: 2″ hole saws, masonry, metals, driving screws.

½″ POWER DRILL

$70 to $95: For the ardent shop owner who has a ⅜″ drill and needs more power.

$100 to $125: Holes in concrete, hard materials, large holes in wood.

the handle of clam shell configuration. A good grade of plastic has been substituted for many aluminum parts, and some manufacturers use a combination of the two.

If this method of construction is good, why did the large manufacturers develop the full clamshell tool? The reason is simple: They are cheaper to manufacture. Clamshell construction, used almost exclusively on low-priced power tools, costs less because it does not require any machining, tapping, pressing of bearings, or skilled handwork. The internal parts are dropped into one shell. When the other shell is screwed down (with self-tapping screws), the tool is finished.

A main disadvantage of the clamshell tool is that it can become somewhat less accurate than a machine-cast tool when it gets hot, particularly when overused or strained under a heavy load beyond its capacity.

To bring the price down on clamshell tools, corners are cut and the manufacturer does not use the highest-quality parts. You will not find ball bearings, precision gears, or heavy-duty wormures or fields in these tools. A bearing cannot be pressed in on a clamshell tool. The working parts inside the casting have to actually float so

moving parts will not bind. The oil-impregnated bronze bearings in clamshell tools are usually spherical in shape so they can align themselves to the shafts that go through them. The bearings, brush holders, field coils, and switches are held in place by rubber plugs inserted into grooves in the clamshell body. Because the two plastic halves are flexible, perfect alignment for the gear shafts, armature, and bearings is difficult to achieve.

Still, clamshell tools are widely used and work satisfactorily as long as they are not overused to the point where they become overheated. Many tool users are surprised to learn that the life expectancy of many low-priced portable tools can be only about 8 hours. Some shop owners may have a bargain-priced drill that is still working well after 10 years. This may be true, but the tool still may not have been used for more than 8 hours over that 10-year period, or ever been abused. That same drill used to drill ⅜″ holes in a 2x4 without interruption would likely burn out completely in a half hour or less.

From the low-priced homeowner tool, the next step up in quality is the light-duty industrial tool that has precision-machined body castings. You will find it has

CIRCULAR SAW

$50 to $75: (7¼″ blade) building outdoor furniture, finishing basements, building a small garage, cutting tile or brick.

$80 to $125: Cutting out and building a dormer, fence building, boat building, fast rough cuts in wood.

ROUTER

$55 to $80: Edging wood, machining wood joints, leveling slabs, trimming plastic, making signs, hanging doors.

$90 to $125: 1½ and 1¾ hp, general cabinetwork.

SABERSAW

$35 to $50: Do-it-yourselfer use, making children's toys, small signs, fretwork, wall paneling, cutting ¼″ plywood.

$60 to $95: 2x4s, thick plywood, curves in wood.

a better armature (more power, heavier weight, more segments on the commutator, and more windings), a heavier field coil, better bearings, harder gears, and a better cord and switch. In the case of a drill, the light-duty industrial tool will have a better chuck with hardened jaws. A circular saw of this type will have a better blade, a thicker shoe, and a better guard. Oscillating sanders will have heavier weight, paper grippers for better sanding, speeds of 10,000 rpm, which conceal scratches under stain, and better bearings. Some light-duty industrial tools use all oil-impregnated sleeve bearings. Some use a combination of sleeve and ball bearings, with the ball bearings used in areas that take the most abuse.

A light-duty industrial tool is worth considering for two reasons. First, you can use it for larger do-it-yourself jobs, such as building a small boat, cabinetwork, storage space, closets, partitions, or finishing the interior of an attic or basement, and the like. Second, you can afford this better tool, even if you are just a do-it-yourselfer, because it will last longer, require fewer repairs, and give you more satisfaction as a craftsman.

The next step up in quality is to the heavy-duty industrial tool. These tools are always manufactured with all ball bearings, machined castings, and heavy-duty motors, brushes, gears, cords, and switches. Generally these tools will weigh much more than light-duty industrial and homeowner tools, and it often takes a professional to appreciate their quality. But if you are the kind of shop owner who likes to buy expensive, professional equipment, these are for you.

An industrial-quality tool will likely last as much as 20 times longer than a lower-priced homeowner tool. This being the case, a lower-priced clamshell tool will cost you more in the long run than a more expensive industrial-quality tool. If you own an industrial tool and it needs a part, it pays to have it repaired. If you own a clamshell tool and you need a part (especially an armature), it will cost more to fix it than you paid for it. For occasional shopwork, a clamshell tool is fine. For the serious woodworker, a light-duty industrial tool is better. For a contractor, a heavy-duty industrial tool is a must.

You don't have to be a watch repairman to service a clamshell tool, but it helps. Some clamshell tools are easier to service than others. It all depends on whether they have subassemblies that make it easier to take apart and put back together. In a sabersaw, for example, this

BELT SANDER

$50 to $85: Removing stock, sanding wood, stripping paint, smoothing floors, removing rust.

$90 to $125: Heavier duty for professional work, production shops.

FINISHING SANDER

$30 to $40: Do-it-yourself use, refinishing, smoothing wood, spackling.

$50 to $95: Smoothing wood for staining and paint; sanding varnish, lacquer, shellac, urethane, and other finishes.

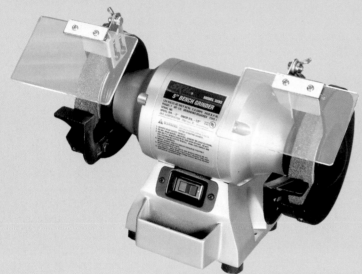

BENCH GRINDER

$50 to $75: Sharpening tools and bits; cleaning, buffing, and polishing materials.

$80 to $125: More horsepower, heavier-duty construction, more wheel-to-motor clearance.

can be the gear box and reciprocating mechanism that connects the motor to the saw blade. A clamshell-type saw may also have other features that make it easier to service. For example, the brush holders may be held in place with screws. Also, the rear bearing may be held secure with a sheetmetal fitting. In this case, the only parts that would have to be carefully laid in place are the switch, the line cord, and the connecting wires.

But most clamshell tools are not made this way. Some clamshell grinders, for example, have almost nothing secured until you put the outer half in place. The brushes are just laid in and are spring-loaded. If, before you get the upper half of the casing in place, the armature rotates even a degree or two, the brushes and the holder will pop out.

Many times, after you have a clamshell tool repaired, and try to assemble the shells, you may find that you cannot get them together snugly. This is usually because one of the wires has moved out of place and is between the ribs of the casting that normally keeps the wires where they should be. Tightening the screws on a clamshell tool that does not fit properly can cause a lot of trouble. If the case is plastic, you will bend it slightly

and the moving parts inside will not align properly. The tool may run, but it will not run efficiently. The chances are that it will heat up, and not last very long.

If you own a clamshell tool that needs repair, the question is whether it is worthwhile to fix it yourself. If the tool needs only a switch or a line cord, it may pay to do it yourself, providing that you don't figure your time as money. If the tool needs a new armature, field, or gear train, then the chances are good it won't pay you to repair it yourself unless it is an expensive tool. Also, if the tool is made of metal castings, you will need to take extra precautions when attempting repairs or you can risk electrical shocks. If you have doubts about repairing tools yourself, it is better to take them to an authorized service center.

In any case, before you throw a defunct tool away, you might open it up just to see what makes it tick. You might find the problem is something very simple; it may have a loose wire or be in need of a good cleaning. If you feel that it does not pay to have the tool fixed, save some of the parts; things like line cords, brushes, bearings, switches, and screws may come in handy for a future repair.

BUYING A ROUTER

The router is a relative newcomer to the power tool scene. It wasn't until during World War I that pattern maker R. L. Carter of Syracuse, New York, fashioned a bit from a hair clipper and attached it to an electric motor. Over the next 10 years, he sold 10,000 of what he called his "electric hand shaper." Today the router ranks number three in power tool purchases, right after electric drills and circular saws, and it is a must-buy tool if you: (1) enjoy working on shop projects, (2) have an interest in wood crafts, either as a hobby or to make money, or (3) are serious about keeping up your home.

The router is a pivotal point in buying tools, advises router expert Patrick Spielman. In fact, he says it might be the second tool you should consider buying for woodworking, after a tablesaw, especially if your projects now look like they were made by an amateur. At first, the router can appear noisy, dangerous, and complicated to use. (It is noisy, but no more dangerous to use than any other power tool, provided you learn how to use it right. It will take experimenting and time to learn how to get the most from a router.)

The router excels as a tool for making even more difficult wood joints such as through and half-blind dovetails, mortise and tenons, stopped dadoes, and grooved joints. With it, you can make wood signs, raised panels, louvered cabinet doors, or decorative panels. Plus, with some inexpensive attachments and jigs, you can use it to duplicate all types of carvings, from simple designs to intricate shapes like gun stocks. You also can make woodturnings, including router-

cut spiral turnings of table legs, lamps, bowls, and dowels. You can also use it to fit and trim plastic laminates for counters or furniture, or even cut soft metals.

For the average shop owner, the router can do the work of the more expensive (and dangerous) spindle shaper. Many woodworking joints usually done with radial-arm saws and tablesaws can be cut with a router, often faster and better. Besides using a router in the normal (vertical) position, you can use it sideways (horizontally) or mount its base upside down. You can take off the base and use it for freehand carving. You can use it as a stationary tool, taking the work to the router, or as a portable tool, taking the router to your work.

Accessories. Buying a good book specifically on using routers will help you get an idea of the accessories you need, give you a good overview of the various operations, and show you router jigs and fixtures you can make yourself. (The *Router Handbook* by Patrick Spielman has sold more than a million copies and is worthwhile buying.)

Some essential accessories include an assortment of bits, some type of router table, a template guide, and eye and ear protection gear. If you don't have one, consider a shop vacuum to clean up dust and chips the router creates.

Once you get familiar with the router, you will find a world of accessories to experiment with. They range from lettering kits and pantographs for making signs to hinge templates and special jigs to make table legs or decorative posts. You can even buy devices that let you duplicate figures in three dimensions, make bowls, or sharpen your own bits.

Professional-quality plunge routers are being eyed by more shop owners today. New models will offer both ¼" and ½" collet capacity and soft-start variable speed control. Other features on this Skil model include (1) all ball bearing construction, (2) powerful 1¾-hp motor, (3) switch with ON indicator, (4) cast aluminum base with non-mar base plate, (5) flat top with integral wrench storage, (6) bit storage module for up to three bits, (7) quick depth adjustment setting with depth scale, and (8) fine depth stop adjustment.

Router Bits. Consider buying fewer bits of high quality rather than a drawer-full of low-quality bits. Cheap bits get dull fast and getting them resharpened can cost you more than the original price of the bit. The shape of the bits you buy depends on what you plan to do. A common use of the router is to form edges. For this work, consider a round-over bit, a cove bit, an ogee bit, and a rabbeting bit. When buying edge-forming bits, consider getting the two-piece bits (integral cutter and shank) with replaceable ball-bearing pilot guide. Pilot guides can wear out or get gummed up and mess up work; it is nice to be able to change them.

If you plan to do surface work, such as carving wood signs, then a good bit arsenal would include a round-nose bit, a V-bit, and a straight (flat-bottom) bit. Later you may want to get a straight trimmer bit for working on veneer or Formica, or for doing pattern work. Tip: A good size straight bit is one ¼″ wide. You don't need various sizes unless you need them for production work. With the ¼″ straight bit, you can make several passes to widen the cut out to ⅜″ or ½″. Seasoned users also suggest considering carbide-tipped bits. They will cost double or triple what high-speed steel bits cost, but you can be reasonably sure they will be sharp and produce good work. A high-speed steel bit can dull fast, particularly if you hit a nail, or use it in plywood or particleboard.

Router Tables. Old-timers could turn out fabulous cabinets with a router table that consisted only of a piece of plywood on two sawhorses with a hole it it, with the router bit sticking through, and a piece of scrap wood nailed on for a fence. You can buy a ready-made router table or make your own with plans that are available from various sources. The fence doesn't have to be square; the only thing you have to watch is the distance from the bit to the fence. You can screw the base of the router to the bottom of the table, and consider buying another base for portable work.

Router Guides. Edge guides can be attached to the router; however, you may find that you won't use them much. Instead, for edge work it is simple to use a router table, and for joints, such as dadoes, to simply clamp a straightedge to the work and run the router against it. Edge guides have limited reach and the farther away from the edge you use the router, the less accuracy you get. A template guide, however, is a good accessory.

CHECKING OUT ROUTERS

Experienced router-user Patrick Spielman advises not to hold back when buying a router or a set of bits. If you stick to the low-end price range, you can find yourself frustrated and miss out on what the router has to offer. Be prepared to spend an extra $50 or $75 to get a quality router. Check with others to see what they like and are honestly satisfied with. See if they will let you try out their routers to see how they handle. Also consider buying a name-brand router. Even if you just drop it on the floor, you may need service and/or replacement parts. Here are some features to check:

Horsepower. Choose one with at least 1 hp, preferably 1½ hp, because you want enough power to make aggressive cuts. You'll find that as soon as you get comfortable using the router, you will want to do more and more with it. Don't be misled by high rpm; generally routers with the highest rpm will have the least horsepower.

Switches and Handles. A poorly positioned switch can be the weak link in router design. Whenever you are handling your router or changing bits, you don't want it to turn on accidentally. (It is always prudent to pull the plug before working on a router.) Double switches are preferable, one on the motor and one on the handle. That way, you need to trip both before the router starts up. A pressure switch on the handle will let you shut down fast, for example, when you bend a bit and it goes out of balance and presents a potentially dangerous situation.

Bit Changing. Check to see how easily it is to change bits on the router you plan to buy. Some require two wrenches; others only one. The easier, the better. Also check the power cord where it attaches to the router. If the cord comes out on one side, rather than at the top, you will be able to lay the router flat on its top for easier bit changing.

Depth Adjustment. Various types of depth adjustments are available, including (1) clamp systems with the motor sliding vertically in the base, (2) threaded systems with spiral grooves on the motor turning inside the base, and (3) rack-and-pinion systems. The threaded type is worth considering because the motor won't drop down accidentally and damage an expensive bit. With this system you must intentionally turn it down.

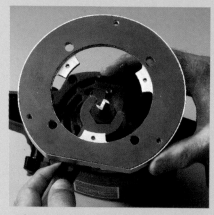

A handy feature on this router is a collet lock, which allows easier bit changing with only one wrench. Other nice-to-have features include on-board wrench and router bit storage.

BUYING A MAJOR SHOP SAW

One of the first tools to consider in setting up an adequate shop is a good stationary circular saw. Shop tool expert Howard Silken observes that, on the average, sawing will make up about 80% of your woodworking. (About 70% of sawing will be straight cuts, while curved sawing might make up about 10%.) Turning, jointing, shaping, drilling, and sanding all together might make up the remaining 20% of the woodworking in your shop. Because so much work falls to the primary shop saw, and because it will eat up a big chunk of your tool budget, selecting one deserves serious consideration.

Before laying out a major amount of cash for a shop saw, ask yourself some critical questions: What exactly do you want to do with your saw? Build things to save money? Create useful items or artistic crafts? Satisfy an urge to work with your hands? What experience have you had with power tools, especially saws? Do you study the manuals that come with tools you buy? Are you willing to buy fewer, but better-quality, tools to keep within your budget? Do you like owning fine tools, even if you use them only rarely?

Your answers will start to help you with the first decision, whether you should buy a tablesaw or a radial-arm saw. Then you need to decide whether it should be a benchtop or a stationary (floor model) saw, and then what size you need.

BUYING A TABLESAW

If you favor the tablesaw, you will be in good company; it's the traditional choice for a majority of experienced woodworkers. The tablesaw and the radial-arm saw are vastly different. On the radial-arm saw, the blade is suspended over the table. If you have used a tablesaw very much, you might find it difficult to adapt to a radial-arm saw. It may feel like it works "upside down" or "backwards." Woodworkers who have both saws usually use the

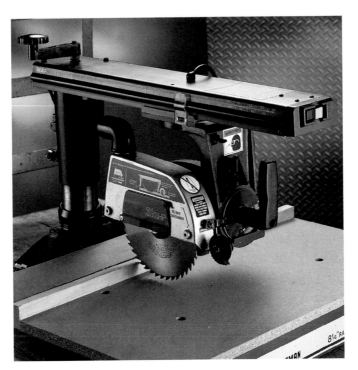

The tablesaw tops the sales charts as a first choice for woodworking shops. However, the radial-arm saw, above, and the bandsaw are also worthy considerations, depending on your projects.

radial-arm saw only for crosscutting. However, a good radial-arm saw is actually more versatile than a tablesaw. Properly equipped, it can dado, rip, shape, sand, dovetail, mortise, mold, rout (with adapter), wire-brush, grind, buff, and perform many other operations.

A quality radial-arm saw can be a beautiful, multi-purpose tool and can be a good bet if you are willing to learn as much as you can about using its full potential. (Often even experienced woodworkers will use only about 20% of a radial-arm saw's capabilities.) The radial-arm saw can be very safe to use if you follow all the rules; it can be extremely dangerous if you do not.

Many excellent professional woodworkers swear by their tablesaws. If you lean toward the tablesaw, below are some buying considerations.

Tilt Arbor. Most stationary saws on the market, including radial-arm saws, have a tilt arbor. If you want to cut (crosscut or rip) at a bevel angle, it is the blade that tilts, not the table. One tool that still uses a tilt table is the Shopsmith. The Shopsmith is a great multi-purpose machine that works best with smaller pieces of material. However, if you need capacity to cut larger pieces, you will want to make sure your saw has a tilt arbor.

Motor and Drive. One advantage of the radial-arm saw is that it is direct drive. There are a few tablesaws that are direct drive, but they are rare. Most tablesaws are belt-driven. Some tablesaws use standard V-belts, while others use rubber-molded timing belts, which are flat with teeth on the inner side. The teeth engage slots in the drive pulleys, much like a bicycle chain engages its sprockets.

Most saws using timing belts have universal motors with brushes. These motors are like those in vacuum cleaners; they rev up to speeds as high as 10,000 rpm to develop power. (All portable tools use universal motors.) To bring the rpm down to proper blade speed, the motors must be either geared down, pulleyed down, or slowed using a

Major parts of the tablesaw include: (1) elevation crank, (2) miter gauge with lock handle, (3) blade guard, (4) saw blade rising through table insert, (5) rip fence, (6) rip fence lock handle, (7) tilt crank, and (8) on-off switch. Switches with locking features help prevent unauthorized and possible hazardous use by others.

combination of both. To keep the pulley ratio about 2 to 1, the size of the drive pulley on the arbor shaft must be very small, usually less than 1˝. Timing belts are used because a V-belt pulley this size does not have much surface grip to transfer power without slipping.

If you buy a tablesaw with a standard V-belt, you can get replacements at most auto or tool supply stores. But timing belt replacements are not as easy to find. If you buy a saw with a timing belt, also buy extras so you will have a spare when the original breaks or its teeth wear away. Also be aware that you may have difficulty replacing universal motors in special castings. However, almost any 3,450-rpm motor of the right horsepower can be used with V-belt drive saws.

Saw Heft. Another main consideration when buying a tablesaw is its construction. The heavier the saw, the better. Heavy saws, for example, will have less vibration, less run-out, and usually more accurate fence and miter-gauge alignment. So if you see a low price on a 10˝ benchtop saw, pick it up to see how heavy it is. If the saw feels quite

light it's a signal to keep looking.

To keep the weight (and price) of a saw down, manufacturers like to whittle away at the tabletop. On some saws the top is made of sheetmetal. Others are, believe it or not, a plastic that looks like metal. One good whack on a corner and off it will come. The better saws have cast-iron tables. Some have solid cast-iron or cast-aluminum extensions. Either is good.

Saw Features. Also look at the saw's motor mount, the table mount, and the method used for blade tilt and elevation. You may have to turn the tool upside down to check these out. This is easy to do on cheaper saws; on better saws, you usually can make an inspection from the rear.

If the castings under the table are made of "white" metal (usually zinc), watch out. White-metal gears and drives will abrade very quickly, particularly if sawdust gets onto the teeth or threads. Sawdust from plywood, particleboard, or Masonite is very abrasive. If the mechanism underneath the table is machined cast iron, the saw will be a better tool.

Saw Blades. The saw blade that comes with the saw can tell you something about the saw's quality. It will likely be a combination (rip or crosscut) chisel-tooth blade. But if it has a painted surface, beware; chances are good it will be an untensioned blade. Always ask the salesperson if the blade is tensioned. If the answer is "I don't know," ask for another salesperson, or leave and buy your saw somewhere else.

Also be wary if the blade is chromium-coated. These blades do hold their cutting edge longer than regular blades; the chrome coating is very hard. However, the first time you have that blade sharpened, the file removes the chrome surface and you are left with a sharp, but relatively soft, metal blade. From then on, the blade will have to be sharpened often.

Saw Size. If you are convinced that the tablesaw is right for you, the next decision is whether you want a small one (8″) or a larger one (10″). To make this decision, you have to have a good idea of what you want to do with it.

Small saws are good for model making, small artistic work, framing, and small-scale woodworking, such as making toys, chairs, and small cabinets. Larger saws are better if you will be doing construction, making large furniture, using plywood sheets, or doing work that will need a 3″ depth of cut. Just remember that a 10″ saw will do everything an 8″ saw will do, but an 8″ saw will not do what a 10″ saw can do.

BUYING A RADIAL-ARM SAW

To get accuracy on a tablesaw, you must acquire a bit of skill. On the radial-arm saw, the accuracy is built into the tool and not the operator. Sounds good, but unfortunately there are two real problems to overcome before you can get the most out of a radial-arm saw. First, you have to get a good one, and, second, you have to know how to set it up correctly. Here are some additional considerations.

Saw Adjustments. Any radial-arm saw that does not hold its alignment can be frustrating, and its shortcomings can defeat the main reason you bought it in the first place. With a poor-quality radial-arm saw you may spend more time trying to get it square than using it.

There are at least seven adjustments that need to be made before you make the first cut:

(1) Eliminate any end play in the arm, (2) align the table so it is parallel to the arm, (3) adjust the roller-head bearings to a snug fit in the arm track, (4) adjust the miter locater to position the arm at a perfect 90° to the fence, (5) adjust the bevel locater so the blade is 90° to the table, (6) adjust the rear motor support to eliminate "toe" or "heel," and (7) adjust all locks so they hold any setting firmly.

All these adjustments need to be done before you use the saw. You also need to know how to set it up right for operation, as well as a certain number of alignment tricks.

Cutting Action. When comparing a radial-arm saw to a tablesaw, consider crosscutting. In crosscutting on the radial-arm saw, the lumber does not move. If the piece is long or heavy, it can be supported by any device the same height as the worktable of the saw. You can square off the end of an 8′ 2x4 with ease.

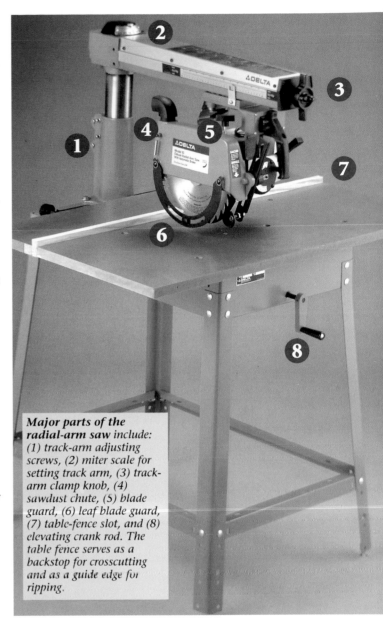

Major parts of the radial-arm saw include: (1) track-arm adjusting screws, (2) miter scale for setting track arm, (3) track-arm clamp knob, (4) sawdust chute, (5) blade guard, (6) leaf blade guard, (7) table-fence slot, and (8) elevating crank rod. The table fence serves as a backstop for crosscutting and as a guide edge for ripping.

Because the blade of a radial-arm saw engages the lumber on the top side first, you can tell exactly where the cut is going to be made before the blade strikes the wood. On a tablesaw, the blade has to cut part way into the lumber before you see the blade on the cutting line. The cutting action of the blade on the radial-arm saw pushes the lumber down and back against the fence. It can't go down because of the table, and it can't go back because of the fence. Only light hand pressure (away from the blade) is needed to hold the material in place.

If one radial-arm saw with a 10″ blade will cut 3″ deep, it does not mean that others with a 10″ blade will also cut 3″ deep. The limiting factor to depth of cut is the clearance under the motor. The ability of a blade to cut properly depends on three basic factors: (1) design and shape of the blade's teeth; (2) power and speed of the motor; and (3) material being cut. The power needed to drive the blade will depend on the hardness of the wood, sharpness of the blade, the cut you are making, clearance of the kerf,

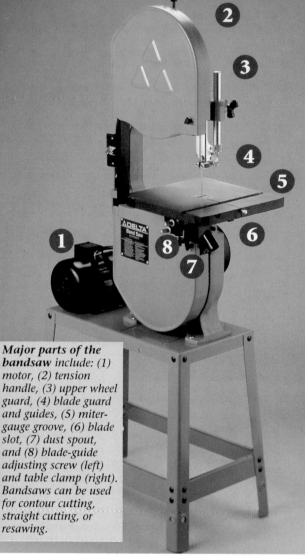

Major parts of the bandsaw include: (1) motor, (2) tension handle, (3) upper wheel guard, (4) blade guard and guides, (5) miter-gauge groove, (6) blade slot, (7) dust spout, and (8) blade-guide adjusting screw (left) and table clamp (right). Bandsaws can be used for contour cutting, straight cutting, or resawing.

type of blade, and speed of the rim of the blade (tip speed). A disadvantage of the radial-arm saw is the length of the crosscut. To cut a 4x8´ panel into two 4x4´ pieces on a radial-arm saw, you need to make multiple cuts. On a tablesaw, you can do it in one cut. But making it on a small tablesaw can be difficult, especially if the panel is a heavy ¾″ piece of plywood or particleboard. This is why shop owners who regularly need to cut full 4x8´ panels are buying and installing the increasingly popular panel saw in their shops.

Types Of Cuts. For making compound cuts (with the arm mitered and the blade tilted), the radial-arm saw has it all over the tablesaw. In truth, there is no angle at which the radial-arm saw cannot be positioned. You can even position the blade horizontally, and many attachments are used this way.

Some of the biggest complaints of the radial-arm saw relate to its ability to rip. The complaints include: (1) the work binds during the rip, (2) sawdust gets thrown into your eyes, (3) the lumber kicks back at the operator, (4) rips are tapered, and (5) the blade is 90° to the table in the crosscut position, but not in rip position. Most often such complaints are due to the operator, not the saw, or else the saw is out of alignment or the guard is not set right.

Which To Buy? Howard Silken, who has been using, selling, and developing saws and accessories for over 35 years, sums up his opinion this way: If you will take the time to learn how to use it right, go with the radial-arm saw. If not, go with the tablesaw. He suggests buying your saw (in fact, all of your tools) at a tool dealership where they know their tools, offer service, and are willing to share their knowledge.

BUYING A BANDSAW

Before you decide on a saw, however, you may want to consider whether a bandsaw may be a third alternative for you. Some woodworkers say they wished they had bought a bandsaw as their first saw. If you do decide to buy a bandsaw, either as a main saw or an auxiliary saw, try to buy a good one the first time around. It will be cheapest over the long haul. As with other saws, there are specific considerations worthy of your attention.

Construction. Howard Silken advises to stay away from plastic and/or sheetmetal, except for wheel covers. The entire base of a good bandsaw, as well as the support section that holds the upper wheel, should be made of cast iron.

One bandsaw that he personally owns, a Delta 14″, has two separate castings for the base and upper support section. They are held together with a large bolt and locating pins on matching machined surfaces. The separate castings offer an advantage. Normally the 14″ saw has a 6″ depth of cut. By inserting a 6″ riser block between the two castings, and using a longer bolt, the depth of cut can be increased to 12″. If you ever need a cut this deep, this feature is worth its weight in gold.

Table Features. The front and the rear of the table should be well supported; the front is more important than the rear because that is where you first put the material down before cutting. Also notice where the slit is in the table. Does it go from the front of the table to the center hole? Or, does it come from the right side?

Having the slit start in front seems like a good idea. To change blades, you would just remove the covers and slide the blade in the slit and up onto the wheels. However, this design allows no supports under the front half of the table. If there were supports, you couldn't get the blade back to the wheels. A slit from the right side enables the saw to have two supports, one in the front and one in the rear, without interfering with blade mounting.

With a side slit, once the blade is in the center hole, you just turn it 90° to mount it on the wheels. If a bandsaw has this design, both supports may have independent locks on them to secure the cast-iron table at the desired angle of cut.

Blade Guides. The blade guides on any bandsaw can be a weak link. The problem is having a thin, flexible piece of metal moving at a high rate of speed and being forced back and sideways as you are cutting. The guides have to keep the blade traveling straight, and keep it from wandering left or right, or front to back. If the saw is not properly constructed or adjusted, constant friction can cause the guides, as well as the blade, to wear away in a short time.

The guide system on the Delta 14″ bandsaw in Silken's shop works well. If the blade is tracked correctly and the guides are adjusted properly, cutting is easy, quiet, vibration-free, and accurate. On his Delta model, two fairly large rear bearings are used to keep the blade from being pushed off the wheels. (They are adjusted so they do not revolve except when cutting.) The sideways motion of the blade is controlled by hardened blocks of steel adjusted so they do not touch the blade except when cutting.

Wheel Crowning. What keeps the blade on a bandsaw running on the center of the wheels and tracking correctly is not the blade guides, but the crown on the center of the wheels. There are a few bandsaws on the market that do not have crowned wheels. They depend on minute adjustment of the upper wheel, as well as the guides, to keep the blade on center. Nevertheless, saws of this type constantly need repair or replacement of the blade guides.

Some manufacturers machine the crown on the wheel as the wheel is made. The crown is transferred through the rubber tire as it is stretched and glued to the wheel. Other manufacturers use tires that have the crown in the rubber. There are disadvantages to both methods.

Glued-on tires can be difficult and messy to get off. When replacing, the wheel must be extremely clean of any excess glue; a slight bump can make the blade bounce. The blade may also bounce if the tire is not stretched on evenly. Most tires are attached to the wheel with shellac or a special preparation. Once you get the tire on, it is best not to run the bandsaw for at least 24 hours. If the glue or shellac is not dry, the tire can come off and cause big problems.

Bandsaw Rubber. When replacing tires, keep in mind that shellac has a limited shelf life and if it is too old it will not dry. Check any older shellac first by applying it to a piece of scrap wood. If it doesn't dry hard by the next day, don't use it.

One major problem with tire replacement is in locating new ones. In fact, you may find it impossible to get tires for bandsaws more than five years old. Made of rubber, or some combination thereof, in time they will get hard, cracked, or glazed, and the blade will slip when cutting under a heavy load. For this reason, it's a good idea to get extras tires when you buy your new bandsaw.

TIPS ON BUYING A RADIAL-ARM SAW

Howard Silken, a Florida tool inventor who has developed his own improved version of the radial-arm saw, emphasizes that the accuracy of a radial-arm saw is built into the tool, not the operator. This is true, if (1) the saw can be aligned and will hold its alignment, (2) you know how to align it, and (3) you know how to set up the saw properly. He offers these tips when you go to buy a radial-arm saw for your own home projects:

❏ A rigid cast-iron arm with a ground-in track of precise width its entire length is best. Rollerhead bearings are adjusted to a snug fit in the track, which puts a slight drag on the saw as it is pulled forward during crosscuts. The drag should be equal and opposite to the climbing action of the blade. If the track is not parallel, bearings can be snug in one section, but loose in another. This can be dangerous, as well as inaccurate.

❏ If two rods are used for a track, those that are set into a ground-in groove in the cast-iron arm are better. The rods should be well fixed to the arm. The rods on some saws can be rotated 180° to renew accuracy; when completely worn, they can be replaced at much less cost than regrinding the arm.

❏ The arm should lock to the post so it will not move under pressure once a miter angle is selected. This is done either by squeezing the wrap-around casting of the arm that engages the post or by forcing a plug or rod against the post. The wrap-around method provides much more metal-to-metal grab.

❏ It's best if the miter-locator lever is held in place on the arm by two opposing heavy-duty adjusting screws that are threaded into cast protrusions on the arm. The slot on the post that the miter locator goes into should be hardened and tapered.

❏ When changing depth of cut, the post should move only up and down and not turn even ¹⁄₁₀th of a degree in the base. If it does, the end play in the arm will destroy precision. The best design to prevent rotation is using a key in a keyway.

❏ The large hole in the base that accepts the post should be milled in the casting, with a milled slot in the back. By slotting the back, wrap-around bolts can squeeze the base snug around the post to eliminate any end play of the arm due to either wear or misadjustment of the base to the post.

❏ The pin for the yoke locator that sets the saw for rip or crosscut should fall into a cast-iron hole. Or, if it falls into cast aluminum, the hole should have a hardened bushing. The bevel lock should be the wrap-around type, not the pinch type, and the kerf adjustment at the rear of the motor should be a three-point-suspension type.

❏ Motors should be all metal and not the clamshell type. Don't be overwhelmed by gimmicks, including electronic readouts. If the saw is not sturdy, can't be adjusted, or will not hold its adjustment, you will have wasted your money.

Buying Used Shop Tools

I f you buy used shop equipment, the first priority when evaluating machinery is to determine if it is the right size for your use. For example, don't even look at a bigger tablesaw if all you can possibly use is one with a 10″ blade. The bulk, weight, blade costs, and power requirements of an oversized machine can eat up any savings that might result from its purchase. Here are other suggestions from woodworker Jacob Schulzinger:

Examine the castings carefully. A real steal can be a bad deal if the table is cracked and needs repairing to make it serviceable. This doesn't mean that you should automatically pass up a deal when the cast-iron base is cracked, only that you should be aware of what you are getting into.

Also beware of equipment that needs machine shop work. If you are not equipped to handle the machining at home, you may find that the cost of repair is more than the cost of a new machine. Also look for broken small parts as well because replacements for these may not be readily available.

When you have made the "buy of a lifetime" and have the machine at home, it is time to get into the serious work of making it ready for use. Don't assume just because you saw the unit operate and tried it out that it is altogether safe and ready for use in your shop. Take plenty of time with this make-ready phase; there is nothing more dangerous than a machine that you aren't familiar with,

and one that isn't in top operating condition.

A good way to begin refurbishing a used piece of shop equipment is to take some photos before you start any disassembly. This may seem like an unnecessary step, but it can really reduce confusion and wasted time when you try to get it back together again. Take the photos from a number of different angles, and take close-ups of areas where you think you might have some questions later. The more complex the machine, the more photos you should consider taking. Don't overlook the use of sketches or notes, which can be especially helpful for small, complex subassemblies.

Clean the machine completely as you disassemble it. Select the cleaning agent that best meets the needs of the machinery. For accumulated sawdust and wood resins, use warm soapy water with a stiff scrub brush. If the resin is really a problem, you might try a solution of ammonia and warm water. If you do use ammonia, be sure that you let the parts soak for only a few hours because the solution will cause parts to rust if exposed to this agent for too long a time. For pieces that are covered with grease or oil, a good soaking in kerosene or a good safety solvent should do the job. If the parts are excessively dirty, consider taking them to your local coin-operated car wash. For a few quarters, you can remove tons of grime.

Carefully dry and lubricate any parts of the machine

that are to be left unfinished, and prepare for painting any pieces that should be so protected. If parts are to be painted, first wash with paint thinner to remove any traces of cleaning solution or grime, sand lightly to scuff up the surface, and then wipe lightly with a clean rag using lacquer thinner. (As with all chemicals, use adequate ventilation and observe all safety precautions listed on the labels.) The lacquer thinner will remove any traces of oil and sanding dust, and, since it evaporates quickly, the painting can be done immediately thereafter. Mask any areas that require it, and then proceed with the painting.

Save all fasteners, cleaning them as you go. Clean out threaded holes with a tap and run a die over any threaded male parts that you plan to save. Use cutting oil as you clean the threads, rinse the parts in solvent, and then coat lightly with machine oil.

Polish all shafts and remove any burrs that might be present. All keyways and keys should be carefully dressed to make assembly easier. Make sure that the bores of all pulleys and housings are smooth and clean. Dress up any rough or sharp edges, and make sure that all slots are clean. Large flat surfaces, such as tabletops, can be scrubbed with a wire brush and then polished with emery paper wrapped around a flat block to maintain surface flatness.

> "Once you have cleaned a bearing in light oil, discard the oil because any residue in it can damage the next bearing you clean."

Bearings require special care. Never soak a bearing in solvent or wash it in a water solution. Some folks have been told that soaking a bearing in solvent is the way to get the dirt out of it, but the manufacturers teach otherwise. A bearing, either ball or roller type, is a precision part made up of finely ground components. These components will rust very easily and any attempt to remove all of the lubricant in them can cause damage. A better way to service a bearing is to soak it in a very light oil, swishing it around in the solution repeatedly to get out what old lubricants there may be. Once you have cleaned a bearing in light oil, discard the oil because any residue in it can damage the next bearing you clean.

Never, under any circumstance, spin a bearing dry, or blow it out with compressed air. Instead, shake excess oil out of the bearing. Relubricate the bearing after its cleaning and wrap it in clean paper or store it in a plastic bag until you are ready to put it back in service. If you are not sure of the best way to service the bearings, don't hesitate to contact one of your local distributors for more suggestions.

Sort out all parts as you complete cleaning them. Use tags, if you feel they are necessary, to identify where the parts belong. If you think that it will help, make up small subassemblies as you go along. If you intend to put the project aside for a while, make sure that you protect the parts from rust. Clearly mark the contents of any boxes and store the photos and sketches with the parts being stored.

When reassembling the machine, substitute all rusty bolts, nuts, washers, and screws with new replacements. This is especially important if the heads are worn, or if the screw slots are rounded over. Use anti-seize compound when putting bolts and screws back in place to make them easier to remove later. Most often you won't know how old the belts are. Spend a few extra dollars to replace any drive belts; many belts that look good during a casual inspection break as soon as they are placed under load.

Check out the electronics carefully. Examine the wiring and replace any that is questionable. Check the connector ends of all wiring and replace any conductors that have been exposed to excessive heat, which can cause copper to become very brittle. Check the wire size needed for the rated motor amperage, and make sure that the cord you use is heavy enough to carry the load.

Switches and electric motors should be checked and cleaned before they are used. If the machine being refurbished was used for woodworking, make sure that you use dry compressed air to blow the sawdust out of the motor. Lubricate the motor carefully and wipe up any oil spills before placing it back on the equipment.

Check all safety devices for function and utility, and replace or upgrade any that are at all questionable. On air compressors, it is especially important that the pop-off valves and the controls that govern the upper and lower pressure limits (activating and deactivating the compressor pump) be checked and tested. If you are not sure that these parts are good, replace them. After all, it is better to spend a few dollars on safety than to have a tank explode and endanger your life.

Also don't overlook blade and belt guards. If the parts are missing or damaged, try to find original replacements if at all possible; as a last resort, fabricate something that will do the job. Before powering up the machine, check it carefully to make sure that you have properly tightened all bolts and that there is no excess movement or play in the unit. Jog the motor a few times to verify that everything moves freely, that there is no excess play, and that the motor is running in the proper direction.

Now comes the true test. Does it really work? Take as much time with this step as you need. Remember, you are using a "new" machine that you aren't really familiar with. You may have used a similar machine for years, but this one may handle differently. Try a test piece first, instead of proceeding to work on a critical part for your current project.

BUYING COMBINATION TOOLS

The scope and variety of combination tools for the workshop is virtually endless. As long as power tools have existed, marketers have experimented with combining functions as a way to reduce investment and space required, and gain more market share. Combination tools fall into various categories, such as: (1) primary tools adapted for purposes other than their main function, (2) equipment combining two or more options to accomplish a single type of task, and (3) equipment combining two or more separate types of functions.

By definition, a portable power drill equipped with one of a dozen or so accessories could be called a combination tool. Also, some of the tools you probably already have in your workshop could be called combination tools when available accessories are used for work other than the tool's primary use. For example, it is possible to equip and use a tablesaw for molding and sanding, as well as for straight cuts in wood or metal. A properly equipped radial-arm saw can be used for work as far-ranging as sanding, grinding, routing, and drilling. A drill press can likewise be used for sanding and polishing, and to a certain extent shaping, planing, or routing.

A good example of equipment described in the second category above, tools providing more than one option for accomplishing a certain type of work, is the benchtop grinder. If you check with major tool suppliers, you will find up to a half-dozen permutations of this tool whose basic, singular mission is to remove material. Starting with dual-wheel grinders in various sizes, for example, Delta also offers a grinder/finisher offering both a 5″ grinding wheel and a 3x24″ belt finisher; a belt/disc sander offering both a 4″ sanding belt and a 6″ sanding disc; a belt/disc sander with both a 1″ belt and an 8″ disc; another belt/disc sander with both a 1″ belt and a 5″ disc; plus a wet/dry grinder combining a 10″ wet grinding wheel running at 70 rpm and a 5″ dry grinder wheel turning at 3,450 rpm. In addition, any of the grinding wheels can be replaced by wire brushes, for removing rust and scale from metals, or buffing wheels for polishing and cleaning all types of materials.

Other combination tools that fit into this secondary category include those like the planer-molder-shaper combination machines sold by companies such as

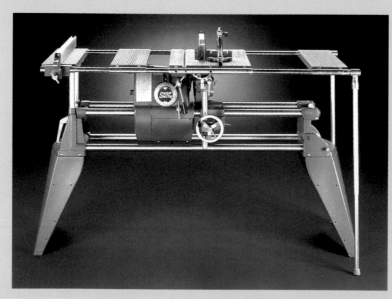

Foley-Belsaw. However, the most familiar example of what most shop owners think of when hearing "combination machines" fall within the third category above: tools combining ways to accomplish several different operations. These include the multi-purpose Shopsmith Mark V, and similar combination tools, which offer as many as five separate tool functions in one stationary unit. The Mark V, see photo, gives you a 10″ tablesaw, a 16½″ vertical drill press, a horizontal boring machine, a 34″ lathe, and a 12″ disc sander—all operating from one motor, one stand, and one single worktable. The price tag on such machines can run from $1,000 to $3,000 or more.

Such combination tools spark major controversies among shop owners. Many who buy them swear they wouldn't have anything else. Some who own them still supplement their combination machine with other major tools. Some end up relegating the combination machine to one or two main uses, such as sawing or lathe work. Others point out that the biggest trade-off is that projects must be done in sequence or else time is wasted setting up for various operations. Also, if an operation must be repeated with a multi-purpose machine, you can face the challenge of trying to duplicate precision settings previously used.

Another fact that makes some shop owners shy away from combination tools is that they are powered by a single motor. If it goes out, you are immobilized until it is replaced. However, the bottom line on combination tools of whatever nature is that they can save you money and workshop space, providing they fit your needs and working procedure, and don't duplicate tools you already have. Most tool experts agree that combination tools are worth investigating, and they will get the job done in a minimum amount of shop space.

But they caution that the decision to buy them should be made early on as you develop your tool arsenal. Buying a $2,000 multi-purpose machine will not make much sense if you already have most of the major tools it replaces already sitting in your workshop, or if your working style is going from sawing to turning to drilling to sanding on smaller individual projects completed one at a time.

A TOOL BUYER'S HISTORY

S ince most of us don't get an opportunity to do most things over, we dream with certainty about how much better things could have been. Here is an inside look at the tool history of the workshop owned by Hugh Foster, a veteran woodworker from Manitowoc, Wisconsin. Despite the fact that he is essentially satisfied with his shop, the very fact that his stationary tools are each the second of their kind suggests less than perfect satisfaction the first time around.

"Like too many woodworkers, I have bought tools the way we buy things like cars, guided by impulse, style, price, availability, or even smooth-talking salesmen. Being a good bit wiser now than when I started buying shop tools, I can make some observations about the errors I feel I made.

I have bought many tools and gadgets, but I find that I use certain ones time and again. The first tool I bought, back in about 1970, was a $99.95 radial-arm saw. I was

23, and I had bought a house that needed lots of work because it was all I could afford as a young teacher. We used the saw a lot as we remodeled. After the project was finished, I still had the saw, and its idleness generated my interest in woodworking. That may have been the best hundred bucks I ever spent on a tool.

The radial-arm saw was great for cutoff work, but it never did live up to the expectations I had for it. No doubt it could be made to do at least most of those things described in those fancy woodworking books, but not by one as impatient as myself. The best use for the radial-arm saw for me was making precisely square cutoffs. If I set up the machine to do that, and left it in place for just that purpose, I loved it. I wish I had one now, preferably one with a travel of about 25″ or so.

(What I felt was wrong with that radial-arm saw is the same thing that combination shop machines are criticized for. They are great for saving space. But most building jobs are such that we move from machine to machine, and with it comes the frustration of setup after setup. But after that observation, I must add that three of the four owners of popular combination machines I know are high school industrial arts teachers, and they all love their machines. I have often wondered whether it is because they have access to other equipment at their schools.)

In my opinion, ripping on a radial-arm saw is neither particularly safe nor particularly accurate. As a result, I bought a motorized tablesaw for a few hundred dollars. For several years it served me well for ripping and other operations. But it didn't have sufficient power to rip 2″ hard maple for whole afternoons at a time, and in the late Seventies that is what I was doing. So that saw had to go.

When the opportunity to pick up a more powerful and accurate Delta Unisaw arrived, I grabbed it. And in the process I got a real surprise. It cost well over $100 for the supplies to run 220 volts into my shop. I learned that power can be a big factor in buying tools. Over 10 years of use, the Unisaw has shown little degradation in performance. But my expectations of my own work and of my equipment have become more demanding. For instance, the plate joiner I now own has made it possible to join mitered corners very strongly. But I cannot cut the joint accurately or quickly enough on my saw to be able to plate-join it together efficiently. I cannot afford another tablesaw, so I have to try to achieve precision with the machines at hand.

My next tool was a jointer, a 6″ with a medium-length bed. I wish I still had it, though I would now want more horsepower. My local Sears store ran a special on 6″ jointers. I bought one, and it served me well for 10 years. I sold it for about $100 more than I paid for it, and I'd pay all that and another hundred to boot to have it back. A jointer is a necessity in a serious woodworking shop; in my opinion, it is probably one of the two essential stationary tools. The longer the bed, the flatter the cuts it will make.

A surface planer is another must-have machine. In the early Eighties I was doing more shopwork than ever, and I was either paying $22 an hour for planing or I had to save up all my planing until a Wednesday night so I could stand in line to use the loudest, dullest, and just plain oldest surface planer in America. (The Columbus inscription on it must have belonged to the original owner.) Complain as we did, $20 for 10 three-hour sessions in a heated shop was a bargain. But as it got harder and harder to schedule a week's work around that Wednesday night session, I started to believe I needed my own planer.

There weren't really many affordable options. The Parks planer was around. It was a fine machine, but only 12″ wide, and most panels in my work were wider than that. The Makita looked attractive; at 16″ it appeared to be a real workhorse, but its motor is roughly the same as in the Makita routers.

> **"Someone said he would rather have a good bandsaw than any other… now I know he might have been right."**

I was told it was adequately powered, but it seemed to me that a 1½-hp motor as big around as my thigh has to be more powerful than a 3-hp motor that is barely the size of my clenched fist. (I've been told that I'm wrong about this; my brain half believes it, but not my heart.) Likewise, the small motors on Hitachi planers made me look elsewhere. Discounts on the Delta machine, made in Brazil, were not that attractive at the time (but have improved since then).

I had seen the Inca 510 planer advertised, and it always looked like a toy to me. But after attending several Inca seminars and meeting countless dealers and users, I came to understand why there are so many avid Inca owners. The machines are powerful, accurately made, capable of apparently unending first-class service in exchange for moderate care. But they were expensive, even considering their high quality. I bought one, but might reconsider now that Inca has disbanded its dealer network. The only other planers I could find were in the $5,000 range or higher, and fed on larger amounts of 220 power than I have in place.

My second drill press came from a garage sale. I added hours of work to the $100 that bought it, and it is far superior to the loose-quilled original I had bought from a major manufacturer. Its main usefulness lies in the jigs I have made for it, rather than the drill itself. If your requirements are for holes more than 8″ to 10″ from the outside edge of a board, consider a radial-drill press, which, like a radial-arm saw, is probably best adjusted into a single position and then left there. (I once saw one of these very efficiently mounted from the ceiling rather than from the floor or bench.)

I read years ago where someone said he would rather have a good bandsaw than any other single saw. I read that with great skepticism. But now that I've seen some good bandsaws, I know he might have been right. Safer than the tablesaw for ripping and most other kinds of cuts, a powerful and well-tuned bandsaw can do nearly everything a tablesaw can do. I think it would be best to buy the deepest-throated, most powerful bandsaw you can afford, and learn to operate it well. I scrapped my 10″ saw for a 14″ model, and it is still neither as big nor powerful as I would like it to be.

My lathe, a decent enough machine, was purchased at a clearance sale. Underpowered and with insufficient speed variations, it has served as a trustworthy spindle-turning machine. For turning bowls, however, it leaves a great deal to be desired. I would really like to be able to afford a lathe with a useful outboard turning feature. This thought about the lathe brings to mind the major fault of most home shop equipment: It is underpowered by at least 50%. My bandsaw would likely be more satisfactory if its horsepower were roughly doubled. Had my 6″ jointer had a ¾- or 1-hp motor instead of ½ hp, it would still be in my shop. I also would still have my original motorized tablesaw had its motor been more powerful."

THOUGHTS ON HAND TOOLS

Despite the high cost of tools, it is possible to set up a shop without spending the rest of your life in debt. The trick is to plan your purchases, observes Hugh Foster, rather than make them impulsively. While the suggestions here are surely not the end-all of tool buying, they might help you avoid some mistakes as you proceed to set up a first-class home shop. Remember that making some mistakes is part of the process.

It is often easy to overlook the importance of hand tools. Here are some that have been particularly useful in Hugh's shop over the years, and some advice from him on their accumulation:

Chisels. Consider ⅛″ through 1″, by eighths, and buy good ones. A matched set would be preferable to a random assortment. I am very partial to my Stanley #60 (with the metal-capped plastic handles) for rough work like chopping dovetails, and to some old, very long, wood-handled ones I found at a garage sale for finer work.

Carver's mallet for striking chisels. Using a hammer destroys chisels; a mallet is handier as well. I bought one with a polyurethane sheath, and its no-mar feature is a wonder to behold; it doesn't mar the chisels the way a regular metal hammer would, and it has outlasted half a dozen of the regular wooden mallets.

Stanley #92 rabbet plane. Having this in the company of a Record #73 is especially nice.

Block plane #60.5 (with adjustable mouth). In a couple of hours or less, you can tune this inexpensive hardware store plane into a precision instrument. I can't imagine working wood without mine and its companion #95, which is now regrettably an ultra-expensive specialty shop item.

Marking gauge. You could get by with something much less nice than the Marples 2154, but why would you want to?

Warrington pattern 10-ounce hammer. Mine are handy beyond belief. I have two; one twice the price of the other. They are indistinguishable from each other. Buyer beware!

Oval-handled screwdrivers. I got a set of six for Christmas one year. The two biggest ones are nearly useless, and I can't even get my hand around the biggest one. Buy the smaller set; they will save your hands from blistering many times. Some makers also have 'crutch pattern' screwdrivers to

match; if you ever need a lot of torque, these are the ones for you.

Files. Regular files can come from your local hardware store, but good wood rasps have to come from a woodworker's supply house and, depending on where you live, that may mean mail-order.

Ruler. I wish I could afford good stainless-steel rules 12″, 24″, and 48″ in length. Buy as few as you figure you can live with, then add more later. A tape measure or a fold-up won't really compare.

Clamps. You can't have too many. You should have at least several of each of the following: pipe clamps with pipes 3′, 4′, and 6′ long; Jorgensen 3712 or equivalent (a dozen of these won't be enough) and 3718 or equivalent (have at least a half-dozen). Also miscellaneous C-clamps, handscrews, and cam-action clamps. Take special care to keep them clean. Remember to use pads. I once bought some pinch dogs, having read that they would save me from having to buy so many clamps. For panel making, if you can cut the panels overlength, they can be a terrific money saver. A handful of pinch dogs will replace at least an armful of clamps.

Scraper. This is not the finishing scraper, just a heavy-duty glue remover. Glue kills planer blades, so getting rid of it will save you time and money.

Sharpening system. If you can, try others' until you find the kind you like, then buy one. I use a hand-cranked set, and a Japanese flat-rotation system, and good honing stones.

Workbench. In my opinion, the only way to get a good workbench at an acceptable price is to make one. I made mine for somewhere around $200; its nearest comparable commercial bench costs around $800, and none of the commercial benches is available left-handed. Another tip: Homemade wooden bench dogs are much easier on your planes than the metal dogs that cost far more.

SECTION IV
USING THE HOME WORKSHOP

STARTING PROJECTS RIGHT

Remember that in any shopwork, if you don't start right you can't finish right. You can mess up a project in the final stages by making a wrong cut or a wrong measurement. But if you don't begin processing wood with sharp blades, or with equipment that is properly adjusted to give good, clean, square dimensions, you will be starting off on the wrong foot. From then on, you'll be haunted by problems throughout the project. It is the same thing as not getting a foundation square when you are building a house. That one error will compound itself many times over before that house is finished.

It is a fact of life that most home shop owners can't afford the most ex-

Help stack the odds in your favor by buying the best tools you can afford and keeping them properly adjusted. Visual doublechecks of cuts can alert you to tool problems that need attention.

procedures can help you doublecheck the accuracy of your shop equipment:

For example, to check the squareness of a saw blade on the tablesaw, first make sure the tablesaw insert is flat and exactly even with the top of the table. If it is either high or low, the piece being sawed can tilt one way or the other. (Two or three layers of masking tape will usually fix the problem.) Use a scrap of wood 6″ to 8″ long, 2″ wide, and ¾″ or more thick. It should be straight and flat, with parallel edges and faces. Make a longitudinal mark on one face near an end. Crosscut through this mark, using a miter gauge or a sliding table. Stop the saw and slide the pieces together so marks line

pensive, top-of-the-line equipment. Unless you have a very accurate, thousand-dollar shop saw like the professionals use, you are handicapped right from the start. With saws, for example, most professionals will use hefty 10″ or even 12″ stationary tablesaws, while you might have to work with an 8″ benchtop saw. They will use the best, most expensive blades available and will make certain those blades are kept in top condition.

The professionals may also have a leg up on you because they have planers and jointers that can be used to true up lumber to precisely square dimensions. If you don't have this equipment, find someone who does and who will dress up your lumber. Chances are that the lumber you buy at the lumberyard won't be square and true, and if you try to build a project to critical dimensions with it, you're bound to be disappointed.

To compensate for having less expensive equipment in your shop, you will need to go through extra effort in setting up. Try to buy the highest-quality blades you can afford, and spend extra time making sure you adjust equipment to be as accurate as you can get it to compensate for any built-in deficiencies. Some simple

up. They should fit tight together. If the pieces don't fit well, the blade on the saw is wobbling or the set of the teeth is uneven.

Next, flip the right-hand piece upside down and slide the pieces together. Check for a tight fit. Then put the pieces back in their original position and flip the left-hand piece upside down. Slide together again. If you have a tight fit in all positions, your blade is exactly 90° to the table surface. If you have a gap in any position, tilt the blade slightly to correct it. Which direction you move the blade (right or left) depends on which way the blade was off.

Errors can also result because the fence on the saw is not square. After you try to square up both the blade and the fence with a combination or steel square, it's a good idea to make a cut and put the pieces through the "squareness" test. You will be surprised at how much closer you will be able to get to a good, square 90° by using this test procedure and making adjustments.

The same general procedure can be used on a jointer to check for squareness. With a jointer, run an edge through the machine, then cut it in half and put the two jointed edges together two different ways. (As a constant reminder, you may want to use a permanent ink marker and write on the jointer-blade guard: Check for 90°.) A good way to check to see if your bandsaw or scrollsaw is running truly vertical to the table is simply to make a cut about ¼″ into a piece of scrap wood. Then stop the machine, turn the scrap over, and hold it directly behind the blade. Because any error will show up doubled, you will be able to get a good visual check for squareness.

There are even things you can do to increase the performance of expensive equipment. For example, you can add auxiliary wood to the blade side of the fence on a tablesaw, bolted to the original fence. Doing this can help you a couple of different ways. First, it gives you the opportunity to use shims between the original fence and the wood to make tiny adjustments so you can make sure that the wood strip is perfectly vertical. Second, you can make that new wood fence surface longer than the original fence to give you more of a guide when cutting longer pieces.

Adding auxiliary wood to the fence can be helpful in a third way. On occasion you can clamp still another strip of wood on to the fence and raise the blade into it to partially cut it out. You can do this with either a regular saw blade or a dado head. This temporary cut-out board, when clamped onto your modified fence, can allow you to move the fence surface over the blade to easily adjust for the width of the cut.

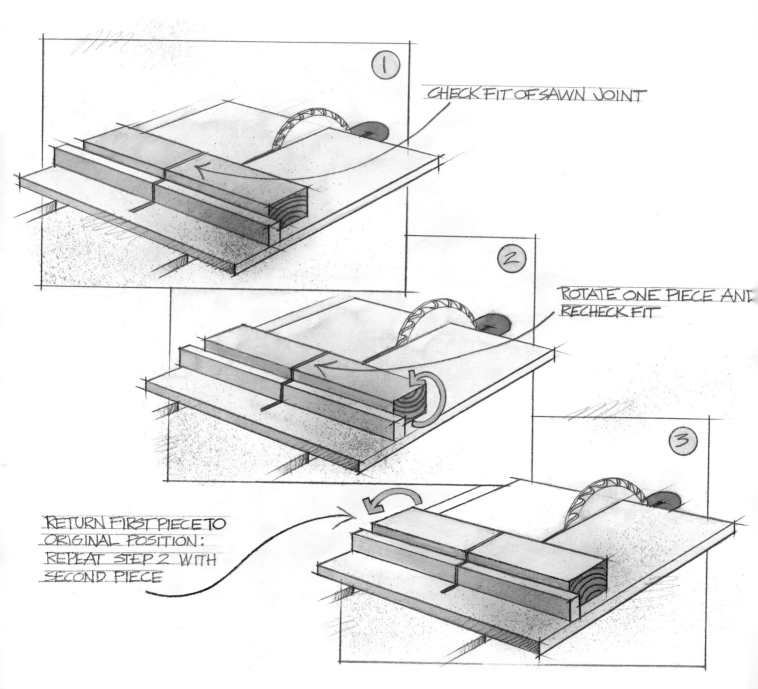

CHECK FIT OF SAWN JOINT

ROTATE ONE PIECE AND RECHECK FIT

RETURN FIRST PIECE TO ORIGINAL POSITION; REPEAT STEP 2 WITH SECOND PIECE

WORKING ON TOOLS

There are so many small tools and aids needed in any shop that it would cost a small fortune if you had to buy them all. With a little ingenuity, and a bit of labor, you can get around the potential high cost and have some fun working out new ideas, at the same time. Experienced shop owners know that modifying tools for special purposes is also a good way to learn some new skills or to polish up some old ones that would otherwise get rusty.

One tool that never seems to be available in the stores is a brass-tipped punch, which is especially handy for driving out a soft pin or for using when you want to make sure that you don't damage a part. You can make different-size soft punches by simply brazing a heavy layer of brass onto the ends of some scrap steel rods. Dressed up with a file, they become serviceable tools that will last for years. A similar approach can be taken to soften the bite of pliers. Braze a layer of brass onto the jaws of an old pair of pliers that are worn out. This gives you a pair of soft-jawed pliers to use on polished objects.

A third way to avoid damaging parts is to epoxy some scraps of leather to the jaws of a pair of pliers or an adjustable wrench. This is an effective and inexpensive way of protecting such items as chromed bolts or nuts. Scraps of leather can also be put to good use by wrapping a part in a fold of leather before clamping it up in a vise or in a pair of locking pliers. It is much less expensive to do this than to buy a set of brass jaws for your vise. An old belt or a worn-out pair of shoes is a good source for this material with no out-of-pocket cost.

Shop owners find that whatever machinery they work on, there always seems to be at least one bolt or nut that a standard wrench just will not fit. This may be because the head is rusted or was dressed up, or simply because you just don't have the right size wrench. One easy way to turn that fastener without busting up knuckles is to use a standard tap wrench in place of an adjustable wrench. You will find that you can get better results with this tool, without having to worry about the movable jaw spreading.

When working on bigger shop machinery, it seems to be a hard-and-fast rule that at least one small part will drop onto the floor only to vanish forever. A simple solution for this is to line an old cookie tin with newspaper and set it under the area where you are working. If a part drops, as it inevitably will, the newspaper softens its fall and the part will generally stay on the paper. Use this same idea when lubing tools or vehicles to help keep the floor from getting too messy. When the newspaper gets dirty, replace it.

Anyone who tinkers with mechanical work knows that many screws and bolts are installed in places where two hands can't be used. A solution is to use a piece of masking tape to keep the part on the tool to make starting it a one-handed job. For a screw, punch a hole in the tape for the screw tip and then fold the tape over and around the screwdriver shank to hold it in place. Once the screw is started, the tape will tear off, leaving the screw in place. For a bolt, lay a piece of tape in a socket with the sticky side facing the socket walls. This makes a tight fit for the bolt to be pressed into. When the bolt is installed and properly torqued, it is easy enough to take off the socket with the tape still in place.

When working with old machinery, usually there will be some special bolts that you want to salvage but you won't have the proper die to clean up the threads. An easy solution is to cut a slot in the proper-size nut, clamp the nut in a vise, and run the bolt into the nut. The slot in the nut acts like a cutter and will clean some of the accumulated goop and rust from the threads without damaging them. For more cleaning action, just tighten up the vise on the nut, thus compressing it a bit more.

Here's a tip for when you are working in an area where a washer or nut dropped into the assembly could cause a major problem: Tie one end of a long piece of dental floss to the part and the other to something solid. When the parts are finally installed, the dental floss can be cut off if it wasn't already cut by the threading action.

Also, here is a solution if you ever have brazed an egg-shaped hole in a spot where you couldn't get a drill in later to open the hole to size. Simply coat a rod that will fit into the hole with high-temperature anti-seize compound, insert it into the hole, and then braze around the rod. While it won't give a perfect job, it will hold until a replacement part can be found. The same idea can be used to make a dam when you want to braze something where the molten metal could run and ruin the part. The results usually need some prettying up, but it does work.

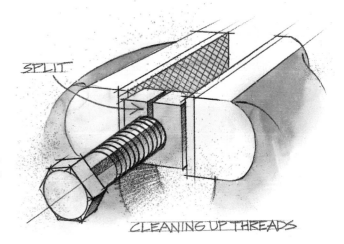

SPLIT

CLEANING UP THREADS

LEARNING TO MEASURE

If you do a sloppy job of measuring, it will affect your work, no matter what you are building. You are only as good as your measurements. The adage "Measure twice and cut once" survives today because it is good advice. If precision is important, take time with measuring and doublecheck all measurements before making cuts.

Many seasoned woodworkers don't actually measure twice, but make it a habit to read the measurement on the tape or other tool twice as a matter of course. It is also important to develop a method to allow for the saw kerf when measuring. A good way is to mark the line, then cut so the saw kerf is just on the outside of the line.

The obvious problems with sloppy measuring include wasting material, having to repeat the operation, or ending up with less-than-perfect projects. Precision measuring and marking starts with using good tools. In the home workshop, these can include a framing (or rafter) square, a try square, a combination square, straightedges, a T-bevel, a carpenter's metal tape, a measuring (or long) tape, a folding rule, dividers (or compass), and a depth gauge.

Depending on whether you are doing fine woodworking or carpentry, the level, line level, marking gauge, chalk line, and plumb bob could also be included in the category of measuring tools. But it's the straightedge, metal tape, try square, combination square, and framing square that see the most use in the home workshop. Most framing squares have one 16″ leg and one 24″ leg. For carpentry, these lengths make it easy to mark for studs either 16″ or 2′ on center. The folding rule sees little use today, but those who use it find it best to lay the folding rule on edge to make more precise measurements. This keeps the thickness of the rule from causing inaccuracies

For carpentry work, an innovation called the "speed square" is becoming popular. It is triangular and each side is about 6″ long. It is made by a number of manufacturers and is especially handy for measuring angles. Many carpenters favor the newer speed square over other tools for angle measurements, including the frame square, the folding rule, or the T-bevel, which is made especially for that purpose.

The 25′ metal tape is a must for serious shop owners, not only because of its length but also because it is 1″ wide and rigid enough to make measuring easy for one person to do without any help. The tapes have a hook on the end that moves slightly forward and back to compensate for its thickness. For example, when you are measuring the length of a board and the end is hooked over one edge, the hook slides out to the proper position for an outside measurement. If you take a measurement between two inside corners, on the other hand, the hook

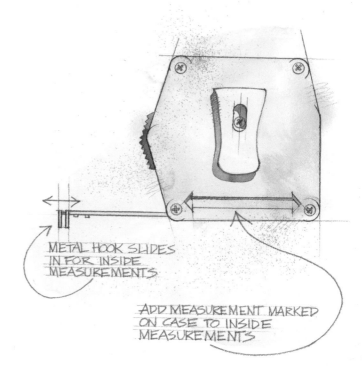

METAL HOOK SLIDES IN FOR INSIDE MEASUREMENTS

ADD MEASUREMENT MARKED ON CASE TO INSIDE MEASUREMENTS

slides inward to compensate for its own thickness.

Measuring tapes, however, eventually do wear enough to become inaccurate. Because of this, it is best to check a tape's accuracy occasionally; if it is off, simply get a replacement tape. Some carpenters and woodworkers avoid any possibility of hook error by always using the 1″ mark as the starting point, taking the measurement, then subtracting 1″ from the total. If you do this, do it consistently so that you get in the habit of subtracting the extra distance. Otherwise you may find sporadic re-cutting will be necessary.

Checking tape accuracy is especially important when two people are working on a project, for example when one person is measuring the project to find out lengths required and another person is measuring and cutting the lumber. If one tape is off by a slight amount, all lumber cut can be off. In such cases, experienced carpenters will take a minute each morning and draw all tapes being used out on a board to see that they measure the same. In other words, the tapes are synchronized, and if one is off slightly because the end hook is bent, it can be corrected or replaced.

It is difficult to make precise measurements with a metal tape beyond about 1/16th of an inch. One trick is to measure a number of pieces at once. For example, if measuring the width of a small piece, put four or eight together side by side and make a measurement. Measuring several pieces at a time will multiply any small error, making it easy to see how much a group of boards are off without having to deal with very small fractions.

If you find, for example, that the width of eight pieces is off by ⅛″, then by dividing ⅛″ by eight you know that each one should be ¹⁄₆₄″ narrower.

In some cases, especially in finish carpentry, special tools are needed to do measuring that would otherwise be nearly impossible. If you are installing a fancy piece of ceiling molding and need to cut the the end of a new piece of molding to fit exactly over it, a contour-pattern tool is handy. It consists of numerous wires that can be slid to match the contour of the existing molding to get a precise pattern to transfer.

Another way to transfer patterns quickly and easily is to use a sheet of white paper and an awl.

To duplicate the shape on the paper, simply lay the paper on top of the piece, then rub around the edges with your fingers. The outline of the piece will take form on the paper. Then, to duplicate the pattern, lay the paper with the outline on top of the wood you plan to use. Use the awl to punch small holes through the paper and into the wood. If you are working with straight lines,

holes at each end of the line are enough. For curves, punch the holes closer together. Take the pattern off, "fill in the dots," and you are ready to cut. Make the holes to the outside of the pattern line, then cut directly through the holes.

In remodeling work, many times a level or a plumb bob can help measure out vertical and horizontal lines. Though 2′-long levels are most common, serious carpenters will generally use 4′-long levels made of wood. They tend to keep a true edge longer than metal levels. Combination squares with a built-in level are handy for marking out lines parallel to the edges of material. A long straightedge, either one you make up out of lumber or one you buy, can be helpful when measuring out cutting lines on long sheets or boards. So is the chalkline. By using these you need to make only two measurements, one on each end, then either clamp the straightedge to the piece or snap a chalkline to use as a cutting guide. Snapping chalklines is a fast method when sheathing, framing up walls, or hanging wallboard.

TAKING MEASURING SHORTCUTS

Measuring is not an end in itself; it is always done so that you can do something else. In many cases the woodworker or carpenter doesn't really care what the actual measurement is, but simply needs to duplicate a specific length or width. This is where marking patterns or story poles are useful. Story poles are simply lengths of lumber, either one piece or two pieces nailed or clamped together, that allow you to quickly transfer specific distances without using numbers. For example, if a project requires five basic measurements, they can be made on a board used as a story pole, then that board can be used to transfer premeasured marks.

Story poles are really master marking patterns that eliminate the need to pull out the tape or square repeatedly. They don't have to be fancy, but they should be accurate. Carpenters often use story poles to transfer distances. A piece of lumber cut to the right length be-

tween a floor and desired ceiling height can be used, for example, to furr out a ceiling to make it level. Similarly, a story pole can be used to level out a basement floor, to mark off the sides of a house for siding, or to help frame up walls. One board can be marked with the height of horizontal members and the length of vertical members, and used throughout the project.

A version of a story pole can be used to cut studs to the same length. One stud is cut to exact length, then a scrap of plywood is nailed to the end, and this master pattern is slid over uncut 2x4s to quickly mark a cutting line. When using duplicate, repetitious cuts, it is important to avoid the "growing pattern syndrome." This happens if one stud is cut, used to mark the next stud, and that stud used to mark the next, etc. If the cut on each stud is off ¹⁄₁₆″, for example, by the time four studs are cut the last one will be off ¼″. It is best to use just one pattern for marking every cut.

For rough measuring, experienced woodworkers and carpenters learn ways of marking out "close-enough" measurements. If they need to take an inch or so off of the width of board, they may set a combination square

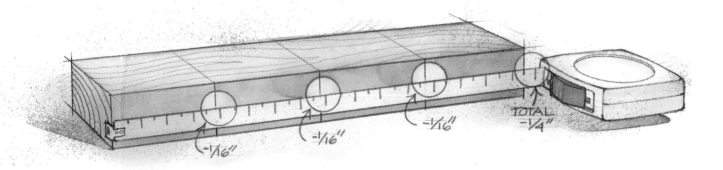

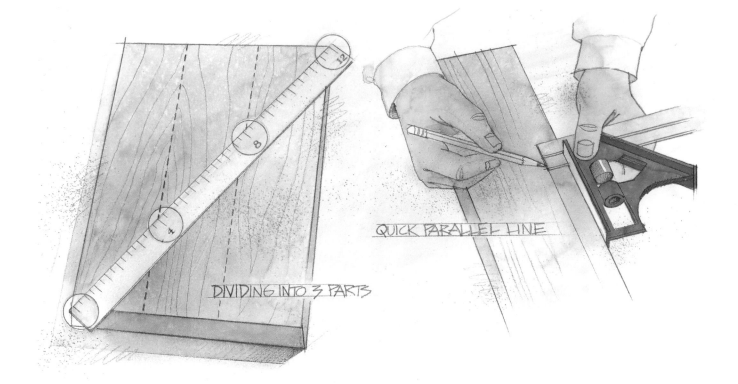

DIVIDING INTO 3 PARTS

QUICK PARALLEL LINE

to the right length, then hold their carpenter pencil at the end of the square and pull the square and pencil down the length of the board. In other cases, as when taking an inch or so off of the end of a board, they may hold the pencil between their thumb and forefinger and use their other fingers along the board edge to guide the pencil.

There are measuring shortcuts that can be used to divide up a board or a sheet of material. To divide a board exactly in half, you can use a compass, putting the pivot point at the each end and drawing an arc. The middle of the board will be where the two arcs cross. The same idea can be used with a straightedge or square by drawing an "X" diagonally from opposite corners. The middle is where the lines cross. A square can also be used to divide a board into equal parts. Lay the square on the board with the start of the scale against one edge. Then angle the rule until a number is reached that is easily divided by the number of pieces desired. For example, if you need three equal parts, angle the rule until a number easily divided by three is reached (9, 12, 21, etc.). If you select 9, then mark the board at 3″ and 6″. By making those two cuts, you will have three equal pieces.

When taking inside measurements, a metal tape can be set inside at one side and the tape drawn to the other side, the measurement taken, and then added to the length of the tape's case (usually 2″ or 3″). However, another and more accurate way is to use the metal tape in conjunction with a combination square. Position the square upside down in one corner, then draw the tape to the blade of the square and add the length of the square's blade. It is fast and precise.

Sometimes, however, no matter how careful you are in measuring you must cheat a little to get a proper fit. For example, getting a good, tight fit with trim molding can be aided by using a trick in the cutting. After the measurement is transferred, the molding to be cut is laid onto a miter saw. But before the cut is made, a carpenter's pencil is laid flat under the molding (about an inch away from the blade, on the side of the board to be used); then the cut is made. This makes what will be the front of the molding slightly wider than the back. When the two pieces are installed, the front parts of the molding will be the first to touch and gaps at the joint are avoided.

Measuring inside diameters of pipe can be tricky and is best done with calipers. When measuring the outside of pipe, you can wrap a string around it and then measure the string. But a better way is to use a metal tape, wrapping it around the pipe so that it overlaps. For example, wrap it a couple of inches beyond the tape end. This way you can keep both sections of tape flat on the pipe. Read the measurement edge to edge, then subtract the amount of the extra tape.

Sometimes it is how you do the measuring that counts. A compass can be used to mark out ceiling boxes when you are hanging wallboard or paneling. But to avoid intricate measuring for fixtures, outlets, furnace ducts, etc., you can use hard carpenter's chalk. Instead of measuring, simply rub chalk around the edge of the protrusion. Then push the sheet into position and hit it with your hands. The chalk transfers to the back of the sheet and can be used as a cutting guide.

USING SHOP SAWS

Because such a large percentage of woodworking is cutting through or removing wood, it will pay to learn as much as you can about the different kinds of blades, how to use them properly, and how to keep them sharp. Below are basic ideas that can help get you started on being a better blade manager.

BLADE ANGLE BLOCK. This block helps you adjust the table of a 1″ belt sander for touching up the teeth of saw blades. As shown, a block is cut with one 90° angle, one 105° angle to provide a 15° table setting, and one 100° angle to provide a 10° setting. To use, set the belt sander table to match the existing bevel. It will be either 10° or 15° on most common blades. Many times the face of the tooth is not beveled. The 90° angle is used on the blade's rakers, which are shorter than the other teeth and simply rake sawdust out of the cut.

The 10° setting is used for touching up the angle of the front of each saw blade tooth. The 15° setting is used to alternately touch up the top of each cutting tooth. After touching up the top of every other tooth on one side of the blade, the blade is turned over, and every other remaining tooth is touched up. The 10° setting will be used on the tops of many blades. A 15° setting used on the tops will give sharper points but these won't stay

sharp as long. Many sharpeners do not angle the face of the tooth. Always check the existing angles, then duplicate them, unless you are purposely altering a blade.

BLADE QUIT POSITION. Many shop owners find that the first piece of work run through shop equipment in the morning will end up as scrap. The reason is that at quitting time the day before, they didn't bother to return the machine to a "quit" position. The troublesome part is that if you make cuts of only 2° or 3°, at a glance you don't realize the blade is not at 90°. A good shop procedure to establish is the habit of returning saws, jointers, and other equipment to a standard 45° or 90° setting when you knock off work for the day. That way, in the morning, you will always know what the setting is. With practice, you will find it easy to return shop equipment to desired settings by keeping precise track of the number of crank turns for each setting on various machines.

BUYING BLADES. Some woodworkers who use both carbide- and high-speed steel cutters prefer high-speed steel for some uses, such as in a molding machine or shaper. Carbide gives a nice cut, but high-speed steel will also give a nice, smooth cut and is easy to keep sharp. After each use the steel cutters can be honed, which is not feasible with carbide. By holding the cutters flat on the stone, and giving each cutter the same number of strokes, the profile will not be changed. The process takes only a few minutes and the cutters are ready for the next use. High-speed steel saw blades can be touched up on a 1″ belt sander several times between sharpenings. Some knowledge of blade sharpening is needed so you don't harm, rather than help, the blade. Some professional woodworkers believe that keeping high-speed steel cutters and saw blades sharp is the key to optimum cutting at all times. The problem with carbide, they observe, is that as it gradually wears, the dullness isn't noticed until the blade cuts poorly. By then, an excessive amount of carbide must be removed to get the edge sharp again. Carbide sharpening also can be quite expensive.

RADIAL-ARM LENGTH SPACERS. Any combination of length spacers can be used in conjunction with the radial-arm stop block shown on page 118 to help minimize setup time. The spacers can be of the same length or of different lengths, depending on design, and can be added or removed between the stop block and the part being cut. If, for example, you are using a dado head to make dadoes in the sides of a bookcase for shelves, spacers of different lengths can be inserted or removed to properly space the dadoes. The nice part of using these spacers is that if a part later proves to be defective, or if a miscount was made, you can merely put the spacers back in place and cut more parts, knowing they will be precisely the same as the original parts, without need for any repositioning.

BLADE ANGLE BLOCK

105°

100°

90°

CONTROLLING WOOD MOISTURE

Many woodworkers blame project problems on bad lumber when, in fact, it is actually the reaction of wood to humidity and temperature that has caused the problems. Understanding wood and its relationship to humidity and temperature is the key to helping you to control its movement.

Water in wood is referred to as its moisture content (MC), measured as the ratio of the weight of water while in the wood to the weight of the wood when it is completely dry. Whether it is kiln-dried or air-dried from its green stage, wood will slowly start to lose moisture and will reach a condition called its fiber saturation point (FSP), which is about 30% MC. At this point, the cell cavities are emptied of free water, but the cell walls still hold bound water. Only when the cell walls lose water will the wood begin to shrink and increase in strength. Wood continues to react with moisture in the air, measured as relative humidity. When dried wood no longer absorbs or desorbs that humidity, it has reached its equilibrium moisture content, or what is called EMC.

The EMC chart shown is one every woodworker or wood finisher should have in the shop. It can tell you that at a given humidity and a given temperature, wood will remain stabilized. It also helps explain why construction-grade lumber at 19% MC, which is brought into an environment of 70° F. and 50% humidity, will often take on a new shape. When wood gains or loses moisture, wood cells do not always change dimensions evenly. This leads to conditions such as warping, kinking, bowing, cupping, twisting, and diamonding. Uneven shrinkage can cause stress and separation of cells enough to crack the wood, and leave checks or honeycombing.

Kiln-dried wood is capable of reaching its fiber saturation point or, if allowed, completely drying out. Wood seeks to establish a balance with its surrounding environment. A finish will help slow down the moisture exchange that causes wood movement. What, how, where, and when you apply a finish can affect moisture exchange. For example, one coat of varnish will reduce moisture exchange up to 8%, while two coats will reduce moisture exchange up to 78%. Here are more tips on ways to avoid lumber moisture problems:

1. Buy lumber from sources who are aware of the moisture content of the wood they sell.

2. Construction-grade lumber is dried to between 15% and 19%. If you use it for projects, be aware that moisture exchange will take place and anticipate it.

3. After buying lumber, store it in the shop where you will be working with it.

4. Store project lumber with small, uniform pieces of wood between the boards so that air can circulate around all the boards.

5. Since moisture exchange is more rapid at the end of the board, plug the end grain with wax while storing it so the moisture is forced out through the faces and sides of the boards.

6. Monitor your shop's environment for temperature and humidity so you are aware of what is taking place within wood in the shop.

7. Plan out the steps of operation for your project to minimize exposure of wood to high moisture conditions.

8. Learn more about finishes and the situations that will allow them to function the way they were designed to work.

9. If you strip a piece of furniture of its finish, anticipate the possible ups and downs of moisture exchange and work with them.

10. When you finish or refinish a piece of furniture, give the undersurfaces the same attention you give the top surfaces to achieve equal moisture exchange throughout the entire piece.

MAKING A HYGROMETER. To get a better idea of humidity levels in your workshop, you can make up your own hygrometer and use it in conjunction with the EMC chart shown. The parts you need are two inexpensive thermometers, a plastic medicine bottle, and about 6″ of wicking available at a drugstore. Mount the thermometers side by side on a board, with the medicine bottle in the center, below the thermometers. Cut a hole in the cap of the medicine bottle and run wicking from the bottom of the bottle out the cap and to one of the thermometers. Slip the wicking over the base of the glass and fill the bottle with water.

This arrangement will allow you to make your own "wet bulb" readings. To take a reading, make a paddle to fan the thermometers. After a minute of fanning, the thermometer with the wick will read less than the other because of the evaporation. By using the readings on both thermometers, in conjunction with the conversion chart, you can determine the relative humidity and also the percent moisture equilibrium (the moisture content you can expect in the wood over time at current conditions). Good target conditions for your workshop, for example, might be 68° F. and 42% relative humidity, which results in roughly a 9% equilibrium moisture content.

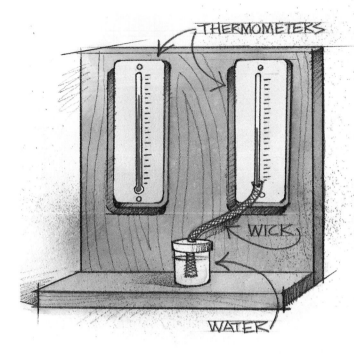

Figuring Equilibrium Moisture Content

To Use Chart: 1) Read dry-bulb temperature and find on chart. 2) Find wet-bulb temperature, and subtract from dry-bulb temperature. 3) Move up from dry-bulb temperature on chart to the line which indicates the difference. 4) Use a rule and follow from that point to the left side of the chart to find the Equivalent Moisture Content (EMC). For example, if the dry-bulb temperature is 70 and the wet-bulb temperature is 53 move up from 70 at the bottom of the chart to the curved line marked 17 (the difference). Follow this point to the left side of the chart. The EMC is 6, and the relative humidity is roughly 27%. The target range for storing wood in most cases should be from 6½% to 10% EMC.

■ Dry Bulb ■ Wet-Bulb Difference
■ Relative Humidity ■ EMC %

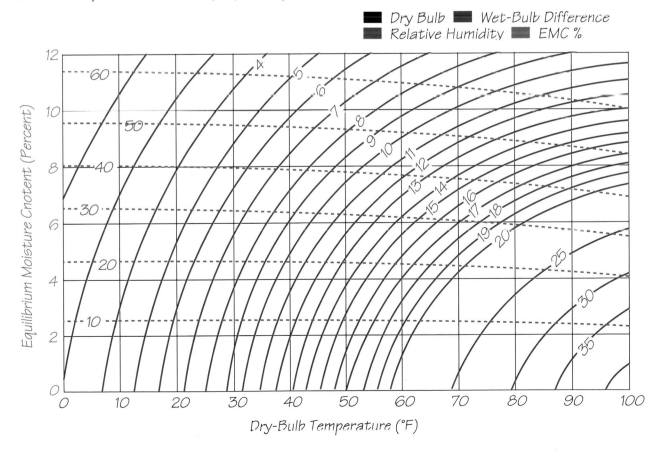

CHEMICALLY CURING WOOD

If the cost of seasoned wood keeps you from completing more projects, you might want to check into chemically seasoning green wood. A relatively inexpensive process has been developed that uses the chemical called polyethylene glycol 1000, referred to as PEG, to cut the cost of project wood and create other advantages as well.

Green lumber is normally seasoned or cured by some form of air-drying or kiln-drying. These conventional methods are relatively successful for curing boards 1″ to 2″ thick. However, they are very time-consuming and expensive for seasoning stock greater than 1″ thick. Seasoning wood with PEG is very practical for curing green wood in the form of slabs or chunks greater than 1″ thick, and avoids the shrinkage and subsequent cracking and checking common with conventional methods. PEG can be fast, economical, and relatively easy to use in the home workshop.

PEG has large molecules that displace the water in the microscopic, lattice-like structure of wood cell-fiber walls. This permanently restrains green wood from shrinking, swelling, warping, or cracking, regardless of atmospheric conditions. PEG comes as a solid chemical. But when it is dissolved in water at 104 degrees F. or higher, and when mixed in a solution of 30% or 50% water by weight, it diffuses into the fine structure of wood. When the PEG chemical is heated in special containers with heating elements, the diffusion process is accelerated. The end result is stabilized, chemically cured wood with a greatly reduced tendency to shrink.

Green PEG-treated wood is ideally suited for making pieces such as salad bowls, lamps, clocks, slab tables, and similar projects that generally require thick material. In making projects of this type, the wood is worked green and treated later. In fact, the greener the wood, the better the treatment. The project is preshaped to a rough dimension (about ¼x½″ oversize) before being treated in a container. It is not practical to treat a large, whole log for working it to shape later. With light treatments, the chemical penetrates about ½″ to 1″ into the surface, which is sufficient for most projects. After preshaping and proper treatment, the project can be force-dried in a kitchen oven for several hours. Otherwise, treated stock can be air-dried for a period of several days to several weeks. Once the outer shell is dry, the project can be worked to final shape and size, sanded, and finished.

The primary advantage of using PEG is an economic one. The raw material is natural, green wood, which is readily available. Green wood is usually free in the form of tree branches, cuttings for firewood, and waste from tree removal, logging, pruning, and sawmills. PEG is nontoxic, completely safe, won't evaporate, odorless, and nonexplosive. The PEG treatment doesn't require a pressure chamber, but it shouldn't be used in vats of ferrous metal, otherwise it will form compounds that discolor the wood. (The best containers are made of tough plastic, fitted with stainless-steel heating elements.)

Commercial sources can provide you with PEG, special containers called Thermo Vats, and the instructions needed. One is Spielman's Wood Works, 3771 Gibraltar Rd., Fish Creek, WI 54212. The directions include mixing charts and time schedules for various woods, based on research and testing by the Forest Products Laboratory of the U.S. Dept. of Agriculture. The process is not difficult to master, though some experimenting is the best way to learn. Here is some additional background:

Don't confuse PEG with antifreeze (ethylene glycol). PEG, which comes in a semi-solid state that looks somewhat like paraffin, has a different molecule. To begin with, avoid high-density woods like oak, birch, ash, maple, hickory, cherry, or apple. Instead, try low-density woods like butternut, popple, or cottonwood. With these woods you can treat a small project like a bowl overnight. Also, stick with the recommendations to start. For example, if the recommendations are to treat with PEG for a week, don't think that more will be better and leave the wood in it for a couple of weeks. Start by following the guidelines; later you may want to monitor your treatments and eventually conduct some of your own experiments.

When selecting wood, remember that greener is better. Walnut, a medium-density wood, is good to use as a guide in experiments. When making up test pieces of wood, take them all from the same branch; for example, take about ½″ apiece and treat for one, two, or three days. Mark them and put them in a household oven at 160° to 180° F. for 4 to 6 hours. By checking for test pieces that have not cracked, you will have a good idea of how long the treatment should be. PEG doesn't evaporate and is reusable indefinitely. It costs from $2 to $4 a pound, depending on how much you buy at a time. Thermo Vats with heaters are available in 10-, 15-, 30-, or 50-gallon sizes and cost from about $300 to $445 with a heater.

PEG SOLUTION

STOCK

HEATING ELEMENT

Assembling Project Kits

The biggest problem of assembling a project kit is choosing the best one for the money. When selecting a project kit, whether a butler's table, a grandfather clock, or a cedar-strip canoe, the first priority is to get one that you will be proud of once it is completed. For most people, building a fine cabinet or clock may be a once-in-a-lifetime project; you want the experience to be enjoyable and memorable, but you also want to be able to take pride in the results. Here are some tips to help stack the odds in your favor:

If possible, try to get recommendations from others who have put similar kits together. Decide what is important to you, saving a few dollars or getting a real lasting value for your investment of time and money. Look for both quality and service; you want to have a good working relationship with the company that supplies the project kit. Whenever you write or call the company, you want a helpful attitude.

If you are choosing among different suppliers, take a very close look at the catalogs and literature. They should describe the workmanship. Look at how easy it is to figure out the available choices, and how easy it is to order what you want. Also, if possible, tour the firm's plant to see how the parts are made. Some firms do not make their kits on the premises, and some won't let you in the work area for safety reasons. Still, you can learn a lot by visiting and just asking questions. Good project kit suppliers will give freely of their time and answers. Also make sure to ask about their service and repair department.

When considering a project kit, try to figure out what is done ahead of time for you, and ask to see a copy of the instructions. (Both may mean the difference between a frustrating or a pleasurable project.) If the kit is a piece of furniture, check to see if all the wood in a single kit is book-matched, a mark of fine workmanship. Book-matching takes advantage of the grain pattern to enhance the overall beauty. A single board is cut so that the pattern appears to repeat or match itself on major showing parts.

Also take a close look at the jointing. If the project has doors, check to see that there are mortises for the hinges. Also check to see that all corners are doweled instead of joined with a less sophisticated, straight-cut kitchen cabinet method. The corners of the cabinet should be precisely mitered so that you get a perfect fit. This can be critical if you haven't made miters before, or if you don't have a good miter box or miter saw. Check to see if the large pieces of the project are made up from edge-glued boards (good) or from narrow strips that look like a breadboard (not as good). Also check to see how major parts are constructed. For

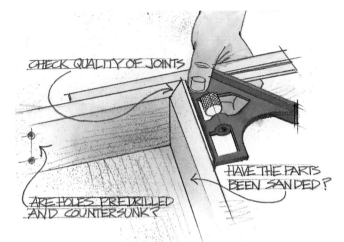

example, are they made of solid hardwood or are they just frames with hardwood panels inserted?

Remember that predrilled and countersunk holes can save you time in assembly, and will reduce the chance of errors. If holes aren't predrilled, you can count on considerably more time and worry in assembling a kit project. Also make sure that any glass for the project is included and not an extra. Check is to see whether the main parts are sub-assembled (the more, the better). Dimensions should be precise so you won't have to do any recutting, the parts should be clearly numbered, and the instructions should be easy to follow. Also check on the quality of accessories available. If, for example, you are buying a clock kit, find out what movements are available for the cabinet you want. Keep in mind that clock movements and dials are not universal, and some are easier to install than others. The best are mounted on a wood base that will easily slide into place on brackets inside the cabinet.

Also try to make sure that the project kit you choose comes in the wood you want and that the wood is hand-selected for color. Usual selections will include walnut, cherry, and oak. Walnut is a favorite; walnut trees grow slowly, creating very interesting patterns in a closed grain. Walnut is also the easiest wood to finish to a rich, dark color by adding only oil, without any stain. Cherry wood has a delicate, open grain with streaks of light and red in the same board. Its color is often evened out by staining to a fruitwood or nutmeg color. Oak is a readily available light wood with a definite open grain that can be stained either dark or light to emphasize the pattern.

A good supplier will give you some options if you want to do more of the work in your shop and save some money. Better suppliers will offer: (1) a complete ready-to-assemble kit, (2) "build from scratch" plans, which include step-by-step instructions, specifications, dimensions, material list, and full-sized patterns, or (3) plans along with a trim kit, which can include difficult-to-machine parts as well as any glass or hardware. A full-service supplier will also offer their kit projects fully assembled and finished.

Learning To Use Glue

Theories abound on the best way to glue up wood, and most professionals develop their own system. These systems can vary, but the important thing is that they work. Gluing wood can be deceiving because on the surface it appears to be so simple. But if you have had projects that didn't hold together, or held together but looked sloppy because of glue runs left on the wood, the problem can lie in the methods you use.

To help get better results, try to start with perfectly straight boards. Take any bow out of the boards you are using by face-jointing and then planing them. Starting with straight boards will help you avoid needing to use tricky clamping setups, and you won't have to force the boards in one direction or another. Also keep wood components slightly oversize; as long as you need to machine the wood anyway, you might as well do it after the gluing process, rather than before. Gluing oversize also means that you don't have to worry about using clamp pads or waste time trying to protect a piece that's cut to size.

First glue the wood pieces up to rough size. Yellow aliphatic glue sets up a little faster than white polyvinyl glues to reduce "slippage," and it also doesn't clog up sandpaper as much as the white glue. (White glue, however, is the one to use if you need a longer time before the glue sets.) Then, after gluing, joint one edge and cut the other edge with a carbide saw blade.

Try to scrape excess glue off within about 45 minutes after the glue was applied. If you wait longer on some woods, like cherry, you'll find that the scraper will take off more than the usual very thin layer of wood fibers along with the hardened glue. This timing is not quite as critical with woods like oak or walnut. Though excess glue should be scraped off in less than an hour, don't do any machining on that wood until a day later. The reason for waiting at least 24 hours is that the glue will swell the fibers slightly at the joints. If you machine that wood too soon, before the swelling goes down, you will take off some of these swelled fibers (see Troubleshooting Glue Problems, page 182). Then, when the wood later returns to normal, depressions at the glue joints can result.

Gluing tools don't need to cost much. Besides yellow carpenter's glue, poured into small squeeze bottles, you can use a pair of inexpensive brushes. One of these can be a throw-away, nylon-bristle brush about 1½″ wide, and the other can be a smaller ½″-wide brush that is sold for putting flux on metal when soldering, called an "acid brush." Before putting the larger brush into service, clip off a little more than half its bristles. The remaining bristles will be relatively stiff and won't slop glue around when used on either the edges of boards or mitered joints. Use this brush edgewise when spreading glue.

Use the acid brush to spread glue on narrow, thin pieces. To keep gluing brushes workable between projects, immerse them in plain water in a small container recycled from plastic household products, such as room air fresheners. You'll find that glue brushes will last a long time if you keep them in water. In fact, the only

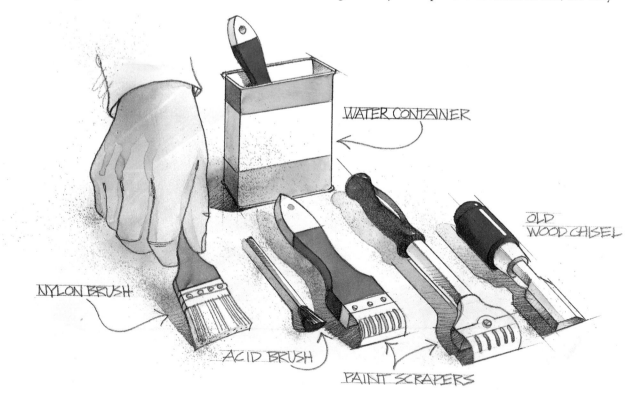

NYLON BRUSH

ACID BRUSH

WATER CONTAINER

PAINT SCRAPERS

OLD WOOD CHISEL

reason to throw them away will be because the metal part holding the bristles will start to rust after a few months.

A couple of very sharp paint scrapers and a ½″-wide sharp wood chisel can be very helpful in removing excess glue from the wood. It is best not to try to use a wet rag on unfinished wood; it dilutes the glue, which can seal the wood and make it tough to get a good finish.

Here is an example of a good gluing procedure. If you want to edge-glue some boards, first run a bead of glue about ⅛″ wide across the edges of the boards to be joined. Next, use the throw-away nylon brushes to smooth the glue out and spread it evenly across both edges. Once this is done, press the edges of the two boards together. While they are pressed together, rub the two back and forth a few inches a couple of times. This spreads the glue evenly so both edges will be covered with a thin film. The next step is to clamp the boards and let the glue dry for a half hour or 45 minutes.

After the glue has dried slightly, use a scraper or a chisel to remove the slight amount of squeeze-out along the edges. Use the chisel to scrape the glue off inside corners, or next to molding. Make sure the scraper is very sharp; press it firmly square to the surface, and in a couple of swipes you will be able to get rid of any excess glue. By using a sharp scraper you will make sure that the glue is removed because the scraper will also take off a very thin layer of wood. To make sure the scraper is sharp, touch it up often with a fine file, and occasionally when it is quite dull, on a 1″ belt grinder. You can use the shank of a screwdriver to burnish the edge of the scraper, rolling it over a little to get more of a "hook" on it.

USING HOT-MELT GLUE

The hot-melt glue gun, which first emerged in crude form in the Fifties, has evolved as a valuable workshop tool with solid-state electronics, trigger-feeding, and im-proved-comfort handles. It is as easy to work as a pair of pliers, and in the home workshop it can be used to fasten just about anything to anything, from small mending jobs to complete projects.

The glue used is odorless, waterproof, and nontoxic. Because it sets up to within 90% of its total strength within 60 seconds, you can complete multi-step projects without clamping, and you can use what you have made minutes after gluing. To use, plug the gun in, let it warm up for about three minutes, insert a round stick of glue into the back of the gun, and push it through with either the trigger (if the gun has one) or your thumb. The heated glue comes out of the nozzle in a creamy form.

Hot-melt glue sticks are sold in various lengths in both amber and clear formulations, as well as a white caulk/sealer for waterproof sealing. The glue is designed for use with porous, clean, and dry surfaces. It can be used for building projects and also to temporarily secure router jigs, fix tiles and linoleum, refasten Formica, make leather crafts, repair shoes, seal sinks, caulk win-dows and doors, repair vinyl and upholstery seats, bond cloth to cloth, join carpet seams, attach wall hangings, and wrap and seal packages. It is best to test before us-ing on stained or painted surfaces since some finished surfaces have petroleum distillates that dissolve the glue.

You don't need to spread the glue; just apply and posi-tion the two surfaces together, squeezing slightly. If pos-sible, work with the hot-melt glue at room temperature. Extreme cold will quicken the time it takes the glue to set. You can extend the "open time," the time it takes the glue to set, by slightly prewarming the surfaces to be joined with a hand-held hair dryer. Hardened glue can be removed by carefully scraping with a sharp knife or chisel. Excess glue around a joint can also be remelted to form a filet with the tip of the gun.

To keep glue from slopping onto projects, use the glue gun's wire stand or make your own stand, and set the stand over a piece of throw-away material. Wear gloves and be careful not to touch the nozzle (it reaches nearly 400° F.); keep fingers away from the hot glue until it has cooled. Dry cleaning will remove hot-melt glue from most fabrics.

HAIR DRYER

TROUBLESHOOTING GLUE PROBLEMS

Gluing problems are always expensive. Any piece of furniture or other project becomes high-priced junk if the glue joints fail, regardless of fancy design or finishing. Whenever encountering glue failure, many woodworkers venture offhand guesses as to what went wrong. Most of the time they blame the glue: wrong kind of glue, glue defective, glue too old. But when a wood glue fails, the source of the problem can be a good dozen or more reasons besides the glue itself.

Gluing success boils down to using the right glue properly. Most home workshop projects are done with ready-to-use adhesives, which include the liquid hide glues, aliphatic resins, and polyvinyl acetates. However, the latter two are the most commonly used: aliphatic resins are the yellow glues such as Franklin Titebond and Elmer's Professional Carpenter's Wood Glue; polyvinyl acetates are the white glues such as Franklin Evertite and Elmer's Glue-All. The yellow aliphatic resins are water-resistant and stronger than the white glues. Both glues set in about an hour and cure to full strength in about 24 hours. One advantage of the yellow glues is that they tend to clog sandpaper less.

Various adhesives work either by drying, cooling, chemical reaction, or a combination of these methods. The yellow and white glues work by drying, that is, by losing water from the glue line. After the glue is spread, parts are pressed together until the glue sets. During this time, the glue-and-water mix penetrates the pores of the wood surface. As the water goes through the pores, glue is retained on the wood fiber walls. The glue gains strength as the water leaves this adhesive film.

A first step in troubleshooting glue problems is to first make sure you are following the directions of the glue manufacturer closely. A good rule of thumb for any gluing is that a thin glue line or a tight joint will give you a stronger and less noticeable joint. See that the moisture content of the wood is close to what it will be in use later. Also make sure the joint has been made with sharp tools for a clean fit.

Following is a sampling of the more common gluing problems, along with some suggestions on how you can avoid them.

LOW GLUING TEMPERATURES. Low temperatures slow setting time. For example, clamp times in cold shops during winter may need to be twice those used during summer. Below certain critical points, low temperatures can cause a loss of joint strength because the glue can't form a continuous film as it dries. For the white polyvinyl acetates, this point is about 55° F. For the yellow aliphatics, the minimum use temperature is about 40° F.

WEAK DOWEL JOINTS: Some woodworkers put glue in the bottom of a dowel hole and hope that when the dowel reaches the bottom of the hole, glue will be forced up around the dowel. For a good dowel joint, the dowel must fit loosely enough to allow the glue to come up around it, the dowel must go to the bottom of the hole, and adequate glue must be used. The best procedure is to apply glue to both the sides of the hole and the dowel. Grooved dowels allow the glue to come up in the grooves, but don't guarantee that glue will be outside the grooves. A good fit is one where you can put the dowel in easily by hand, but not so loose that it wobbles in the hole.

STARVED END GRAIN JOINTS. Glues can soak more into the end grain, resulting in a starved joint. To help prevent this, you can "size" the end grain with a mixture of glue diluted with water. Dilute just enough so that when it's applied, glue drops don't form at lower edges of the wood. Another method, somewhat less effective, is to coat the end grain with full-strength glue, allow to dry 5 to 10 minutes, then recoat with glue and assemble.

SUNKEN GLUE JOINTS. If the glue joints in your finished work are sunken below the wood surface, chances are good this was caused by working the wood too soon after gluing-up. This happens because as wood absorbs moisture from the glue, it swells along the glue line. If the wood is planed before the moisture has left, more wood is removed near the glue line than elsewhere. Though the surface will appear smooth, a shallow channel results along the glue line after drying. Let the glue (and the wood) dry completely before finishing. A minimum of three days at room temperature is needed for complete drying of glued-up work.

IRREGULAR SURFACES. This problem is a cousin to the one above. If you are edge-gluing lumber, try to make sure each of the boards has relatively the same moisture content. If, for example, one board has 10% moisture while the boards next to it are at 4%, you are asking for an irregular surface. If you glue and plane boards with unequal moisture content, the boards with higher original moisture content will shrink more than the others. This will leave an irregular surface at the juncture or glue line.

BLACK GLUE LINES. Glues with a pH of less than 7 will absorb iron from a steel container, and this dissolved iron will then react with certain woods, such as oak, walnut, mahogany, cherry, and other colored woods, and form a black glue line. This is less likely to happen with the yellow glues than the white glues. Coffee cans are a common source of iron contamination. It's a good idea to use plastic or glass containers to prevent these iron stain problems.

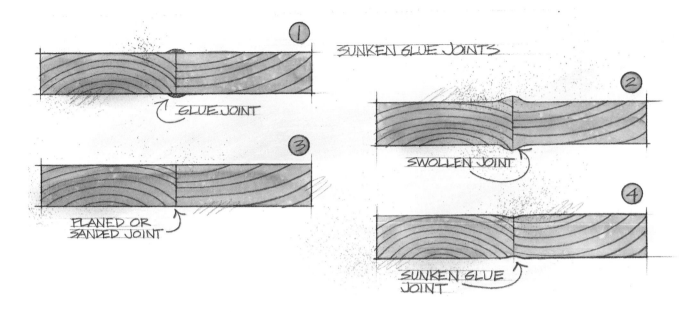

STAINS CAUSED BY GLUE. This kind of stain results when spots of glue on the wood surface fill the wood pores. This prevents stain or finish from being absorbed by the wood and leaves light-colored spots. Some glue squeeze-out is necessary; no squeeze-out can mean not enough glue and a starved joint. The key is to remove excess glue properly. One way is to remove it with a damp sponge or rag immediately after it oozes out. If you do this, be sure the sponge or rag is moist enough that you can avoid applying a lot of pressure, which can drive glue into the wood. A better method is to wait a half hour or so, until the glue dries to the consistency of cottage cheese, then use a sharp scraper or chisel to remove it.

GLUE SOFTENING. Sometimes applying a finish to glued lumber can cause a small ridge at the glue line, or even weaken or open the glue joint. Wash-off solvents may also soften the glue and cause joint failure. The trouble can be corrected by changing to a solvent-resistant glue, or by changing the finish or solvent. Liquid hide glues resist most solvents (except water), followed closely by the aliphatic resins. Polyvinyl acetates are affected by a number of active organic solvents, such as acetone or methyl ethyl ketone.

DULL WOODWORKING TOOLS. If dull cutting tools such as saws, bits, or blades are used, they can loosen but not remove a layer of fibers on the surface of edges to be joined. When this happens, the glue may not penetrate through this debris to solid wood. You can usually tell that this is causing weak joints if the glue line of a ruptured joint is coated with wood fibers. Sharpening your cutting tools will often help increase the strength of these glued joints.

IMPROPER CLAMPING. The purpose of clamping is to bring boards being glued into close enough contact to produce a thin, uniform glue line and hold them until the glue is strong enough to hold the assembly together. If boards fitted together perfectly, you wouldn't even need clamps, but since machining of wood is never perfect, a certain amount of clamp pressure must be used. Usually 100 to 150 psi of pressure is needed, but applying pressure uniformly is actually more important than the amount. When gluing veneers, it is best to use only enough pressure to get good contact so you can avoid "show-through" or "telegraphing" of imperfections from the lumber beneath.

POOR GLUE PENETRATION. This problem is common when repairing previously finished projects. It is difficult, if not impossible, to reglue dirty joints or those filled with old glue. With the exception of some antiques, first dismantle and clean the joints. Remove old paint, wax, dust, oil, grease, and glue, etc. Warm vinegar will generally soften the most stubborn glue. Dipping parts to be glued in warm water and letting them dry completely will help open the wood pores and allow glue to enter more freely. Warming the parts on top of a radiator or in the sun also helps open up wood pores.

IMPOSSIBLE APPLICATIONS. While it is a good idea to dismantle furniture to be repaired with glue, some really old antiques, such as rung-type chairs and furniture held together with wooden pins or wedges, shouldn't be taken apart. To repair loose joints in these pieces, you can try to use a toothpick to work the glue into the joint. Or you can drill a 1/16″ hole at an angle to, or alongside, the joint and force glue into it with a small oilcan, plastic squeeze bottle, or syringe.

MAKING A HAND SANDER

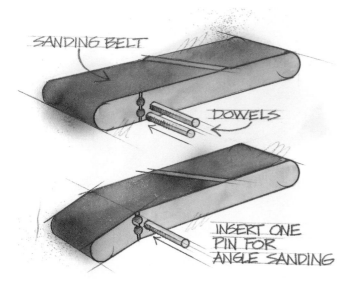

SANDING BELT

DOWELS

INSERT ONE PIN FOR ANGLE SANDING

This device not only works well for both flat and curved surfaces but also lets you recycle sanding belts that fly apart because they are old or odd-size belts that don't fit your belt sander. As the illustrations show, start with a ¾″ solid board (not plywood) of appropriate length, and round both ends. A 3x18″ sanding belt will require a ¾″ board 3″ wide and about 8½″ long, for example, while a 3x24″ belt will need a board about 11⅝″ long. Drill a ¼″ hole through the side of the board, then cut the board in two through the center of the dowel hole. The hole can be located anywhere from the middle to within about 1½″ from one end.

Place the two pieces inside the sanding belt and tap in a ¼″ dowel. If the board sections with the dowel are too long and too tight inside the belt, sand a little off one end. If it is too short, use a dowel with a slightly larger diameter. This sanding belt device can be used flat or angled as shown. If it is angled, it will stay in that position until it is changed. The rounded ends work well for curved surfaces. To change belts, knock out the dowel, put the board sections inside the new sandpaper belt, and tap the dowel back in place. If you prefer that the belt always stay flat, use double dowels as shown.

LEARNING TO FINISH WOOD

Assembling a project can be enjoyable, but the most fun can be in the finishing. Applying the final finish can be a challenge. The goal is to give that project the look of a professional finish without having the procedure take days on end.

Many woodworkers have great success using an oil finish over quality woods. When using an oil finish, a preliminary decision to be made is whether you first want to put stain on the wood. Some woods don't need stain. Cherry and oak are both very light woods, and you will most likely want to stain these. Take a piece of scrap from your project to your local stain supplier. Have several different commercial stains applied to the wood so you can see how they look. If you have a hard time making up your mind, go to a store that has a good reputation for mixing custom stains. You should be able to achieve just about any color you want; just make sure that the stain you buy is compatible with an oil finish.

If you are working with walnut, you may not want to use a stain. Walnut turns to a rich dark color the instant you apply oil to it. Within a single piece of wood, there will be natural variations in color, according to the way the wood grew in the tree. The contrast is part of its natural beauty, and there isn't anything artificial about how it looks. It all blends together.

When finishing, keep in mind that with any project everything goes more smoothly if you put a little effort into preparation. First get set up right. Work in an area that is well ventilated and well lit. Gather up all the materials you need before you start. Include plenty of sandpaper, a good supply of paper towels, and a couple of new paintbrushes. If you are working on a larger project, it is best to put it on sawhorses, or some type of horizontal surface, with plenty of newspaper underneath. Though you can mask any hardware on the project with tape, you may find it better to completely remove it. Number the pieces and keep notes so you can put the hardware back on quickly. Also, don't install any glass until after the finish has been applied to the wood. This makes it easier to reach different parts of the project and avoids unnecessary cleanup.

Woodworkers use a wide variety of finishing procedures, and you can experiment on your own when you can afford to take chances. Here is one procedure you may want to try: Following rough sanding, proceed to sand with 220-grit paper until the surface is quite smooth. (The big secret of finishing wood is in the sanding; if you spend more time at sanding the rewards will show up later.) For the flat surfaces, consider using a 4″-square vibrating sander to save time and elbow grease. Insert two pieces of sandpaper into the sander at the same time. Then, when the top layer is worn, you can simply tear it off and you are ready to go with the next layer in place.

Sand with the grain and hand-sand in grooves such as

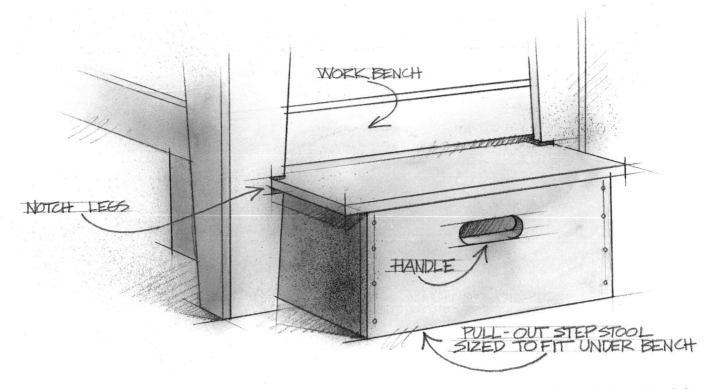

WORK BENCH

NOTCH LEGS

HANDLE

PULL-OUT STEP STOOL SIZED TO FIT UNDER BENCH

those in shaped moldings. For fluted columns and other tight areas, fold the sandpaper in half and use the edge in the creases.

Check for any glue that might have seeped out of a joint. Run across it with a sharp paint scraper. If you're pulling one out of your own tool chest, be sure it is well-sharpened. Then vacuum the wood, or use a tack cloth to pick up sawdust created by the sanding or scraping.

If you are working on a tall project, like a clock case, stand it up vertically when applying either stain or oil. That way, when it is drying, the seepage will collect where it is easier to see and remove. Don't forget about finishing the inside of your project as well as the outside, to prevent stress due to uneven moisture exchange. It is easiest to begin on the interior of any project and work to the outside. You won't have to sand the inside as much as the outside. Many woodworkers remember to finish the inside, but forget that it is also important to put the same number of coats of oil, stain, or wax on the inside as on the outside.

If you plan to use a stain, apply it with a new paint brush or a clean rag. Experiment on a practice piece before you begin so you know how long to allow the stain to sit on the wood for the right shade before wiping it off. Wipe the stain off with paper towels or rags, and allow the stain to dry overnight. After that, you can apply the first coat of oil. If you're working with walnut, you'll see the raw wood transformed to a new state of beauty as the oil enhances the depth and pattern of the grain. Allow the oil to soak in about 20 minutes and then wipe off the excess. Use a good grade of paper toweling, and take care in wiping off areas like fluted columns. The oil

will tend to pool so you'll need to go back and check for drips. The oil will also have a tendency to ooze where molding pieces meet in opposite directions. So check those areas for drips also.

Allow the project to dry overnight, or longer if you are working during summer or periods of high humidity. Now you can put on the second coat of oil. Work on a smaller portion of the wood, and apply the oil with a brush. Use 400-grit wet/dry sandpaper to rub the oil into the wood. For flat surfaces, you can use a small vibrating sander. Allow the oil to set from 5 to 10 minutes. Use paper toweling first to wipe off the excess oil across the grain, then to wipe the surface with the grain. The trick of the process is that the paper toweling picks up tiny pieces of wood and deposits them in the pores of the wood as you wipe across the grain. This creates an ultra-smooth finish.

The last step is a third coat of oil. Use 600-grit here, whether you're working with stained or unstained wood. Again, sand with the grain and wipe off the excess oil across the grain. The finish will be satiny smooth. Allow the project to dry for a couple of weeks. Then add a thin coat of paste wax to seal the finish, followed by buffing with a soft cloth. You don't have to buff the paste wax by hand; you can use a sheepskin buffer available at hardware or car parts stores. Buy a sheepskin bonnet, chuck it into your power drill, and buff away.

Again, don't wad up any oil-soaked rags or any paper towels. Spontaneous combustion is always a possibility. Instead, soak them in water, toss them into a plastic bag, and put them directly into the trash.

MODIFYING SHOP TOOLS

The attitude you have toward your tools will influence not only what tools you buy but also what you do with them after they are put into service. While some shop owners would rather buy a new tool than make any modification to one they have, others don't think twice about altering a tool to make it easier to use, perform better on a project, or more convenient to store. Here are some examples of modifications you can consider making in your own shop:

HAMMERS AND AXES. These tools always seem to be in a pile and finding the right one from the pile can waste time. To make larger striking tools like sledge hammers easier to store, you can drill holes in the handles to hang them in a spot in the shop that is out of the way, yet convenient. Drill the hole crosswise, an inch or so from the end of the handle, so the head will hang flat against the wall. Because the hole is near the end, it won't weaken the handle.

If you buy a new sledge or axe, one of the first things you can do is slip a 4″ to 6″ section of pipe over the handle up to the head, then weld it on to protect the handle right behind the head. Everybody misses the target once in a while, and the most vulnerable part of the handle is right behind the head. This way, if you miss, chances are good the pipe guard will keep the handle intact. Pipe works best on tools where you use both ends of the head, such as a double-bit axe. If only one side is used, you can get by using angle iron with the outside corner pointing down.

When adding pipe or angle iron, watch that you don't ruin the temper of the tool's head. Keep an edge of the head in a pan of water when welding; if it gets too hot, be sure to re-temper it. (Most professional welders can do the job for you without ruining the temper.) Another way to provide "hazard insurance" is to wrap the handle behind the head with ¼″ welded wire mesh and then apply epoxy cement over it.

Smaller tools like hammers don't need this kind of doctoring. But one alteration some carpenters make to wooden-handled hammers is to bore a hole into the end a couple of inches deep, a little larger than a 16d nail. Then they fill the hole with beeswax. If they begin to have trouble driving nails or splitting boards, the nails can be stuck into the beeswax reservoir. Usually the wax coating will solve the problem. (The beeswax can also be used for screws that are hard to drive.)

Smooth and polished hammers look nice. But when the striking face of a new or used hammer is too smooth or slippery, it can slip off nail heads and cause excessive bending of nails. When this happens, use a piece of emery cloth to roughen up the face, or just rub it against a concrete floor or cement block. Another thing to check on a new hammer, especially a cheaper one, is the inside edges of the V-slot of the claws. If they are not sharp, you can use a file to touch them up so they will get a better grip on nails you want to pull out.

DRILLING EQUIPMENT. One hassle for just about everybody who uses a power drill is keeping the chuck key close at hand. Often new drills come with some kind of device to attach the key to the power cord. But the problem with many of these is that the device allows the key to slide down to the end of the cord, just out of arm's reach. You waste time by having to retrieve the cord to get the key. The solution is either to buy a chuck-key holder that stays in one place, or to fashion your own improved version.

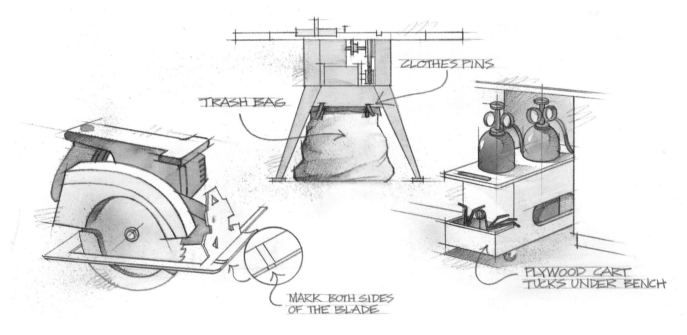

CLOTHES PINS

TRASH BAG

MARK BOTH SIDES OF THE BLADE

PLYWOOD CART TUCKS UNDER BENCH

One method is to simply tape the key directly onto the cord, a couple of feet down the cord from the drill. You can also use scrap electrical wire to attach the key; with either method, take care not to damage the cord. You can make a chuck-key holder by welding the key to a washer with a hole just large enough to fit over the cord. Cut the washer so you can bend it open to put it on the cord, then bend it back to the normal position.

Another alteration you can make on a drill is to add a small, stick-on level vial to the top of the drill to help keep a horizontal hole straight when drilling into a vertical piece of lumber. Watching the level is easier than holding up a square as a guide. One thing no one should do without is a drill-bit index box. The index box can save time wasted searching for the right bit and trying to read sizes marked on the shank. If you have more than a half-dozen bits, buying an index box will pay for itself many times over in time saved.

SAWS AND CUTTING TOOLS. Before putting a bandsaw, tablesaw, or miter saw into service, apply a good coating of paste floor wax to the top of the saw table. This not only protects it from rust but also helps keep lumber from sticking and binding. Add another coat every few months, and years from now the saw table will look like new. (You can also use the wax on your handsaws.)

For a portable circular saw, you can make alignment markings that will help you every time you use them. Scribe lines onto the top of the base, straight out in front of both sides of the blade. To do this, put a square flat up against the blade and scribe the mark with a sharp awl. Do this on both sides and from then on you always know where the saw kerf will be.

On a sabersaw, it is helpful to make sure the allen wrench used for changing blades is somewhere on your saw at all times. Newer sabersaws come with a clip to hold the little wrench. If your sabersaw doesn't have this clip, you can weld on a metal clip of the kind used to hold screens and storm windows. Or, you can fashion some other holding device; at the very least, tape the wrench to the cord to make sure it is always there if you need it.

Sawdust is a natural by-product of sawing. If you don't have a larger dust collector or a dust-collection system, you can fasten ordinary plastic trash bags under stationary saws with snap-type clothespins. What doesn't fall in the bags, you can just scoop up and throw in. This is a good clean-up alternative, especially if you can't stand the noise of your shop vacuum.

Whether your shop is small or large, outfitting stationary tools with casters will let you move them around easily. If you can't afford casters, you can drill holes to slip a steel rod through two legs on the same side to use as an axle for small wheels. Position the axle so the wheels nearly touch the floor. Then to move the tool, simply lift the side opposite the wheels. Small carts are handy for tools like a small gas welding outfit and attachments. If you put casters under such carts, you can just slide them under a workbench or out of the way when they are not being used. A small, two-wheel utility cart is also handy to have around the shop; you can even strap a shop vac onto the cart when you need to move it over rough terrain around the shop or yard.

If you have an older shop vacuum, you will notice that when you pull on the hose, the casters tend to catch on the cord on the floor and tip it over. One solution is simply to tie a length of elastic cord around one of the caster legs, up to the hose, about a foot from where it connects to the vac. Now when you pull the vac by the hose, the elastic will pull the bottom so it hops over any cord in the way.

SCREWDRIVERS AND WRENCHES. Old screwdrivers come in handy if you need a special type of tool that is not in your tool drawer. If you have just a few special types of screws to remove, you can fashion a tool that will work from an old screwdriver. You can make tack pullers by heating up the end, bending it over about 35°, then filing a V-slot in the blade. You can also make your own brake tools from an old screwdrivers.

The challenge with wrenches is to keep them organized, accessible, and not lost. For some small tools you keep losing, one solution is to paint them a bright color. Another solution is to add bright-colored tape or stickers. Marked tools, as well as good fences, make good neighbors. Mark all your tools, either with paint, tape, or an inexpensive vibrating engraver. If someone borrows the tool, the mark will help remind them to bring it back.

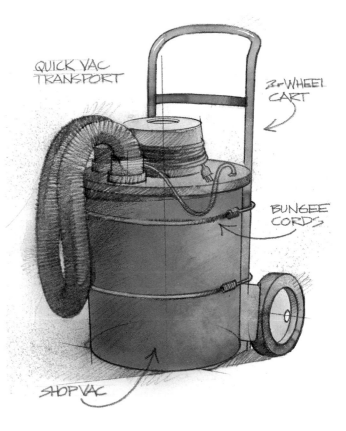

QUICK VAC TRANSPORT

2-WHEEL CART

BUNGEE CORDS

SHOP VAC

Many toolboxes sold for sockets seem like they are designed to keep sockets mixed up and lying all over. If your box is this way, there's probably too much space above the sockets when the lid is closed. You can fix this with a little foam rubber. With an electric knife, cut a section to fit inside the lid, thick enough to keep the sockets tight in position when the box is closed. If your sockets are in a pile in a toolbox, take a look at some of the newer plastic fishing tackle boxes. Some can work well as a see-through socket box.

One tool that usually needs help is the file or rasp. Though wood handles are available, most files you see have a bare tang instead of a handle. Bare tangs are not only dangerous, they make it difficult for you to use the tool. If you don't want to buy file handles, you can drill out sections of wood dowel to slip over the tangs. You can also use metal doorknobs, or even larger electrical wire nuts to get rid of that sharp point. It's worth the bother.

LADDERS AND BENCHES. Because of the possibility of injury, toss out any ladder that isn't solidly constructed and 100% stable. Buy heavy-duty ladders, even if they take a little muscle to move around. It can be helpful to put a mark at the center balance point on the sides of both legs of a ladder. This way you can simply grab the ladder near the mark and it will always be in balance when you carry it. Another worthwhile idea is to pad the end of the legs of an extension ladder with foam rubber, old socks, or towels to protect your house inside and out.

Sawhorses get cut into and nicked up. No matter what kind you have, you can fashion another 2x4 across the top to protect the sawhorse from abuse. You can nail small wooden cleats on the 2x4s to hold them in place.

Over time, workshop owners make a number of modifications around the workbench. If you have a small shop, one addition that will pay off is to install one or more ceiling outlets. They will allow you to cluster stationary tools and plug them in without extension cords running through the work area. You can use ordinary screen door springs over your workbench to keep power cords of portable tools out of the way. When using extension cords, always tie the two ends into half of an overhand knot before plugging them together. This saves a lot of running and replugging.

WORK CLOTHES AND GEAR. If you use the common cloth nail aprons that stores sell for a dollar or two, you can insert small metal or plastic containers into the pockets so you can keep various nails, screws, or small tools separated. Good work clothes have lots of pockets to carry things in. The right footwear is important, too. While using a ladder, wear good work boots that have a good separate heel. The boots protect your arches much more than athletic shoes, and the heels will help catch the rung in case of a slip.

WORKSHOP SOURCES

ASSOCIATIONS

American Plywood Assoc.
P.O. Box 11700
Tacoma, WA 98411

California Redwood Assoc.
405 Infrente Dr., Suite 200
Novato, CA 94949

Hand Tools Institute
25 N. Broadway
Tarrytown, NY 10591

Hardwood Plywood Mfgs. Assoc.
1825 Michael Faraday Dr.
P.O. Box 2789
Reston, VA 22090

National Paint & Coating Assoc.
1500 Rhode Island Ave.
Washington, DC 20005

Portland Cement Assoc.
5420 Old Orchard Rd.
Skokie, IL 60077

Power Tool Institute, Inc.
605 E. Algonquin Rd.
Arlington Heights, IL 60005

Southern Forest Products Assoc.
Box 52468
New Orleans, LA 70152

Western Wood Products Assoc.
Yeon Building
522 S.W. Fifth Ave.
Portland, OR 97204

PUBLICATIONS

American Woodworker
33 E. Minor St.
Emmaus, PA 19098

Fine Woodworking
63 S. Main St.
P.O. Box 5506
Newtown, CT 06470-5506

Popular Mechanics
224 W. 57th St.
New York, NY 10019

Popular Woodworking
3300 Walnut Ave.
P.O. Box 58279
Boulder, CO 80323

WOOD Magazine
1912 Grand Ave.
Des Moines, IA 50309

Woodsmith
2200 Grand Ave.
Des Moines, IA 50312

Woodwork
42 Digital Dr., Suite 5
Novato, CA 94949

Workbench
700 W. 47th St., Suite 310
Kansas City, MO 64112

MANUFACTURERS

AEG
Chicago Pneumatic Tool Co.
2220 Bleecker St.
Utica, NY 13501
(800) 243-0870
(315) 792-2939

American Machine & Tool (AMT)
Fourth Ave. and Spring St.
Royersford, PA 19468
(215) 948-0400

Atlas Copco Electric Tools
Chicago Pneumatic Tool Co.
(see AEG listing)

Belsaw
4111 Central Ave. N.E.
Minneapolis, MN 55421
(612) 781-2345

Black & Decker
701 East Joppa Rd.
Towson, MD 21286
(800) 762-6672
(410) 716-3900

(Bosch) S-B Power Tool Co.
100 Bosch Blvd.
New Bern, NC 28562-6997
(800) 334-5730
(919) 636-4200

Bridgewood
(Distributed by Wilke Machinery)
3230 Susquehanna Trail
York, PA 17402
(717) 764-5000

Delta
246 Alpha Dr.
Pittsburgh, PA 15238
(800) 438-2486
(412) 963-2400

DeWalt
626 Hanover Pike
P.O. Box 158
Hampstead, MD 21074
(800) 433-9258

Dremel
4915 21st St.
Racine, WI 53406-9989
(414) 554-1390

Elu
(see Black & Decker listing)

Freud
218 Feld Ave.
High Point, NC 27264
(919) 434-8300

Grizzly Imports
(east of Mississippi River)
2406 Reach Rd.
Williamsport, PA 17701
(800) 523-4777
(west of Mississippi River)
P.O. Box 2069
Bellingham, WA 98227
(800) 541-5537

Hegner
(Distributed by
Advanced Machinery Imports)
P.O. Box 312
New Castle, DE 19720
(800) 648-4264

Hitachi Power Tools USA Ltd.
3950 Steve Reynolds Blvd.
Norcross, GA 30093
(404) 925-1774

Jet Equipment Ind. Tools Inc.
P.O. Box 1477
Tacoma, WA 98401
(206) 572-5000

Lobo
9031 East Slauson Ave.
Pico Rivera, CA 90660
(310) 949-3747

Makita USA Inc.
14930 Northam St.
La Mirada, CA 90638-5753
(714) 522-8088

Milwaukee Electric Tool
13135 W. Lisbon Rd.
Brookfield, WI 53005
(414) 783-8311

Performax Products
12211 Woodlake Dr.
Burnsville, MN 55337
(612) 895-9922

Penn State Industries
2850 Comly Rd.
Philadelphia, PA 19154
(800) 288-7297

Porter Cable
4825 Highway 45 N.
Jackson, TN 38302-2468
(901) 668-8600

Powermatic
Morrison Rd.
McMinnville, TN 37110
(615) 473-5551

RB Industries (RBI)
1801 Vine St.
P.O. Box 369
Harrisonville, MO 64701
(800) 487-2623
(816) 884-3534

Ryobi America Corp.
5201 Pearman Dairy Rd.
Anderson, SC 29622-1207
(800) 323-4615
(803) 226-6511

Sakura
(Distributed by Amana Tool Corp.)
120 Carolyn Blvd.
Farmingdale, NY 11735
(800) 445-0077
(516) 752-1300

Sears Merchandise Group
Craftsman Power Tools
D3 181A, 3333 Beverly Rd.
Hoffman Estates, IL 60179
(or contact local stores)

Shopsmith
3931 Image Dr.
Dayton, OH 45414
(800) 762-7555

(Skil) S-B Power Tool Co.
Marketing Communications
4300 W. Peterson
Chicago, IL 60646
(312) 286-7330

Williams & Hussey
P.O. Box 1149
Wilton, NH 03086
(800) 258-1380
(603) 654-6828

Wirsbo
5925 148th St. W.
Apple Valley, MN 55124
(612) 891-2000

Woodmaster
1431 N. Topping
Kansas City, MO 64120
(800) 821-6651
(816) 483-0078

INDEX

CREDITS

Produced by North Coast Productions, with assistance from the following. All photos indicated as from Sears are from Sears, Roebuck and Co., and Affinity Marketing Inc., Chicago, IL. All illustrations, except where noted, are by Brian Jensen, RKB Studios, Minneapolis, MN.

Section I photo spread: photo, Sears. A Place Of Your Own: photos, Richard Howard and WGBH, Boston; illustration pages 12 and 13 adapted by Brian Jensen from original illustration by Nina Coles. 20 Ideas For Setting Up A Workshop; photo, Delta. Tool-Buying Strategies: text source, Howard Silken; photo page 17, Delta; illustrations pages 18 and 19, Marlyn Rodi; photo page 21, Sears. Devising A Tool-Buying Plan: photo, Delta. Shop Tool Buying Menu, Shop Accessory and Supply Menu, Suggested Space Allotments, and Workshop Tool Inventory: design, Barbara Bowen. Pursuing A Dream Workshop: photos pages 35, 36, and 37, Mark Duginske and Gregory Foye. Shop Plan Idea Starters: concepts, Russ Barnard; illustrations, Barbara Bowen. Mapping Out A Workshop: tool outlines and plan worksheet, Barbara Bowen. Searching Out Shop Space: text source, Russ Barnard. Shop Climate Control: illustration source, Walbro. Finishing The Workshop: illustration source, Homestyles Plan Service Inc. Controlling Shop Sawdust: text sources, Delta, Murphy-Rodgers, and Sears; photo, Sears. Shop Planning Checklist: photo, Sears. Section II photo spread: photo, Sears. The Start-Up Workshop: photo page 63, Sears. Starter Floor Plans: concepts, Russ Barnard; illustrations, Barbara Bowen. Stage I Workshop Tool Close-Ups: photos, Sears. Making Personal Shop Gear: text sources, Russ Barnard and Marlyn Rodi. The Homeowner Workshop: photo page 75, Sears. Starter Floor Plans: concepts, Russ Barnard; illustration, Barbara Bowen. Stage II Workshop Tool Close-Ups: photos, Sears. Shop Sawhorses: text source, Ted McDonough. Making A Vise Portable: text source, Marlyn Rodi. Board Touch-Up Tool: text source, Russ Barnard. Shop Air Movers: text source, Robert Tupper. Setting Up For Thin Work and Finger Boards: text source, Russ Barnard. Shop Pushsticks: text source, Russ Barnard. Dowel Tenoning Jig: text source, Don Taylor. The Woodworker Workshop: photo page 87, Sears. Starter Floor Plan: concept, Russ Barnard; illustration, Barbara Bowen. Stage III Workshop Tool Close-Ups: photos, Sears. Plywood Bench: text source, Russ Barnard. T-Square Jig: text source, Don Taylor. Storing Tools Book-Style: text source, M.E. Walberg. Veneer Press: text source, Hugh Foster. Board-Straightening Jig, Surfacing Jig, and Radial-Arm Angle Jig: text source, Russ Barnard. Shop Forge: text source, Marlyn Rodi. The Craftsman Workshop: photo page 101, Sears. Portable Lumber Storage: text source, Robert Tupper. Adapting Shop Vises: text source, Russ Barnard. Starter Floor Plan: concept: Russ Barnard, illustration; Barbara Bowen. Stage IV Workshop Tool Close-Ups: arc welder photo, Century; other photos, Sears. Reversible Table: text source, Hugh Williamson. Improving Shop Tools: text source, Russ Barnard. Clamp Improvements: text source, Robert Tupper. Dowel Maker: text source, Russ Barnard. Dowel-Cutting Jig: text source, Robert Tupper. Folding Bench: text and illustration source, Shopsmith. Laminating Jig: text source, Don Taylor. Grinder Tool Support: text source, Russ Barnard. The Professional Workshop: photo page 115, Sears. Workhorse Workbench: text source, Robert Tupper. Radial-Arm Stop Block: text source, Russ Barnard. Starter Floor Plan: concept, Russ Barnard; illustration, Barbara Bowen. Stage V Workshop Tool Close-Ups: surface sander photo, Performax Products; wire-feed welder photo, Century; other photos, Sears. Sliding Saw Tables, Tablesaw Inserts, and Bandsaw Helpers: text source, Russ Barnard. Screw Clamps: text source, Hugh Foster. Grinder-Polisher: text source, Marlyn Rodi. Radial Blade Support: text source, Russ Barnard. Shaving Horse: text source, Jack Gilbertson. Square-Stock Tenoning Jig: text source, Russ Barnard. Section III photo spread: photo, Sears. Shop Tool Buying Options: photos, page 131 and 132, Sears. The Workshop Big Eight: photos, pages 133 through 141, Delta. Investing In Hand Tools: text source, Garretson Wade Chinn; photo page 143, Stanley Tools. Buying Portable Power Tools: text source, Howard Silken and Terry Treacy; photos pages 147 through 154, S-B Power Tool Co. Buying A Major Shop Saw: text source, Howard Silken; photos, pages 155 through 159, Delta. Buying Used Shop Tools: text source, Jacob Schulzinger; photo, page 160, Sears. Buying Combination Tools: text source, Russ Barnard; photo, page 162, Shopsmith. A Tool-Buyer's History: text source, Hugh Foster; photo, page 163, Sears. Thoughts on Hand Tools: text source, Hugh Foster; photo, page 165, Sears. Section IV photo spread: photo, Sears. Starting Projects Right: text source, Russ Barnard; photo, page 169, Sears. Working On Tools: text source, Jacob Schulzinger. Learning To Measure and Taking Measuring Shortcuts: text source, Kim Rasmussen. Using Shop Saws and Controlling Wood Moisture: text source, Russ Barnard; photo, page 176, Delta; chart, page 177, Barbara Bowen. Chemically Curing Wood: text source, Patrick Spielman. Assembling Project Kits and Learning To Use Glue: text source, Russ Barnard. Troubleshooting Glue Problems: text source, Dr. Robert Snider. Making A Hand Sander and Learning To Finish Wood: text source, Russ Barnard. Modifying Shop Tools: text source, Marlyn Rodi.

In **The Home Workshop Planner** you'll find...

■ Refining a home workshop is a worthwhile lifetime
pursuit. A shop can become your own personal place,
where life's worries fade and peace of mind prevails.

■ It is not great tools that turn out professional work,
but what you do with the tools you have.

■ With a little ingenuity, and a bit of labor, you can get
around the potential high cost (of tools) and have some
fun working out new ideas.

■ The goal is to invest in your shop as wisely as you can
and do as much as you can to keep costs down.

■ Buying the best tools you can afford and keeping them
properly adjusted will help stack the odds in your favor
when building any project.

■ The best advice is to start now, plan out as much as you
can in advance, and keep the plan as flexible as possible.

EAN

UPC

ISBN 0-696-20335-9

$14.95
Price higher
in Canada